BUSINESS IN AFRICA
CORPORATE INSIGHTS

Compiled by DIANNA GAMES

PORTFOLIO
PENGUIN

First published by Penguin Books (South Africa) (Pty) Ltd, 2012
This edition by Portfolio Penguin, an imprint of Penguin Books,
a Penguin Random House company

Registered Offices: Block D, Rosebank Office Park, 181 Jan Smuts Avenue, Parktown North, Johannesburg 2193, South Africa

www.penguinbooks.co.za

Copyright © Dianna Games 2013

All rights reserved
The moral rights of the authors have been asserted

First edition 2012
This edition 2013

ISBN 978-0-14-353849-3

Cover by publicide
Maps by Ian Games
Printed and bound by CTP Printers, Cape Town

Except in the United States of America, this book is sold subject to the condition that it shall not, by way of trade or otherwise, be lent, resold, hired out or otherwise circulated without the publisher's prior consent in any form of binding other than that in which it is published and without a similar condition including this condition being imposed on the subsequent purchaser.

CONTENTS

Preface — xii
Dianna Games

Introduction — xiii
Nick Binedell (*Dean, Gordon Institute of Business Science, University of Pretoria*)

Foreword — xv
Professor Mthuli Ncube (*Chief Economist and Vice President, African Development Bank*)

PART 1: AFRICA'S BUSINESS LANDSCAPE

The State of Play — 1
Dianna Games (*CEO, Africa @ Work*)

20 Tips on Doing Business in Africa — 13

PART 2: THE ECONOMIC LANDSCAPE

Africa's Economic Evolution — 17
Dr Duncan Clarke (*Chairman and CEO, Global Pacific & Partners*)

Africa's Growth Story — 29
Acha Leke and Mutsa Chironga, (*Partner and Principal Associate, McKinsey & Associates*)

Africa: The West and the Rest — 41
Dr Lyal White (*Director: Centre for Dynamic Markets, Gordon Institute of Business Science*)

Understanding Africa's Competitiveness Challenge — 53
Dr Greg Mills (*Director, Brenthurst Foundation*)

Building African Entrepreneurs — 61
Tony Elumelu, (*CEO, Heirs Group; Chairman, Transcorp*)

Making a Noise: Africa's Women in Business — 69
Khanyi Dhlomo (*MD, Ndalo Media*)

The Making of the African Brand — 77
Doug de Villiers (*CEO, Interbrand Sampson de Villiers*)

PART 3: CORPORATE INSIGHTS

Private Equity | ACTIS — 85
Simon Harford (*Partner, Actis*)

Mining | ANGLOGOLD ASHANTI — 95
Richard Duffy (*Chief Financial Officer, AngloGold Ashanti*)

Hospitality | CARLSON REZIDOR HOTEL GROUP — 107
Andrew McLachlan (*Vice President Business Development, Africa & Indian Ocean Islands, Carlson Rezidor Hotel Group*)

Retail and Services | COCA-COLA COMPANY, THE — 117
William Asiko (*Director, Public Affairs and Communications; President, The Coca-Cola Africa Foundation*)

Science and Technology | DUPONT — 123
Carlman Moyo (*Regional Director, Sub-Saharan Africa, DuPont*)

Diversified Industrial and Financial Services | GENERAL ELECTRIC — 131
Lazarus Angbazo (*President and CEO, East, Central and West Africa, GE*)

Logistics and Supply Chain | IMPERIAL LOGISTICS — 141
George de Beer (*Financial Director, Imperial Logistics Africa*)

Property | LIBERTY PROPERTIES — 151
Samuel Ogbu (*Group Executive: West Africa Business Development, Liberty Holdings; Former CEO, Liberty Properties*)

Telecommunications and Entertainment | MULTICHOICE — 161
Nico Meyer (*CEO, MultiChoice Africa*)
Collins Khumalo (*CEO, MultiChoice South Africa*)

Franchising and Retail | NANDO'S — 171
Robert Brozin (*Co-Founder, Nando's*)

Telecommunications | MTN — 181
Sifiso Dabengwa (*President and CEO, MTN Group*)

Oil and Gas | SACOIL HOLDINGS — 191
Robin Vela (*Former CEO, SacOil Holdings*)

Agriculture | SEED CO — 199
Morgan Nzwere (*Group Chief Executive, Seed Co Ltd*)

Advertising | M&C SAATCHI AFRICA 207
Rick de Kock *(Managing Director, M&C Saatchi)*

Financial Services | UNITED BANK FOR AFRICA 213
Phillips Oduoza *(Group MD and CEO, UBA Group)*

Legal Services | AFRICA LEGAL NETWORK 221
Roddy McKean *(Anjarwalla & Khanna, Founding Member of Africa Legal Network)*

Tourism and Environment | WILDERNESS HOLDINGS 235
Andy Payne *(Former CEO, Wilderness Holdings Ltd)*

Index 244

AFRICAN COUNTRIES

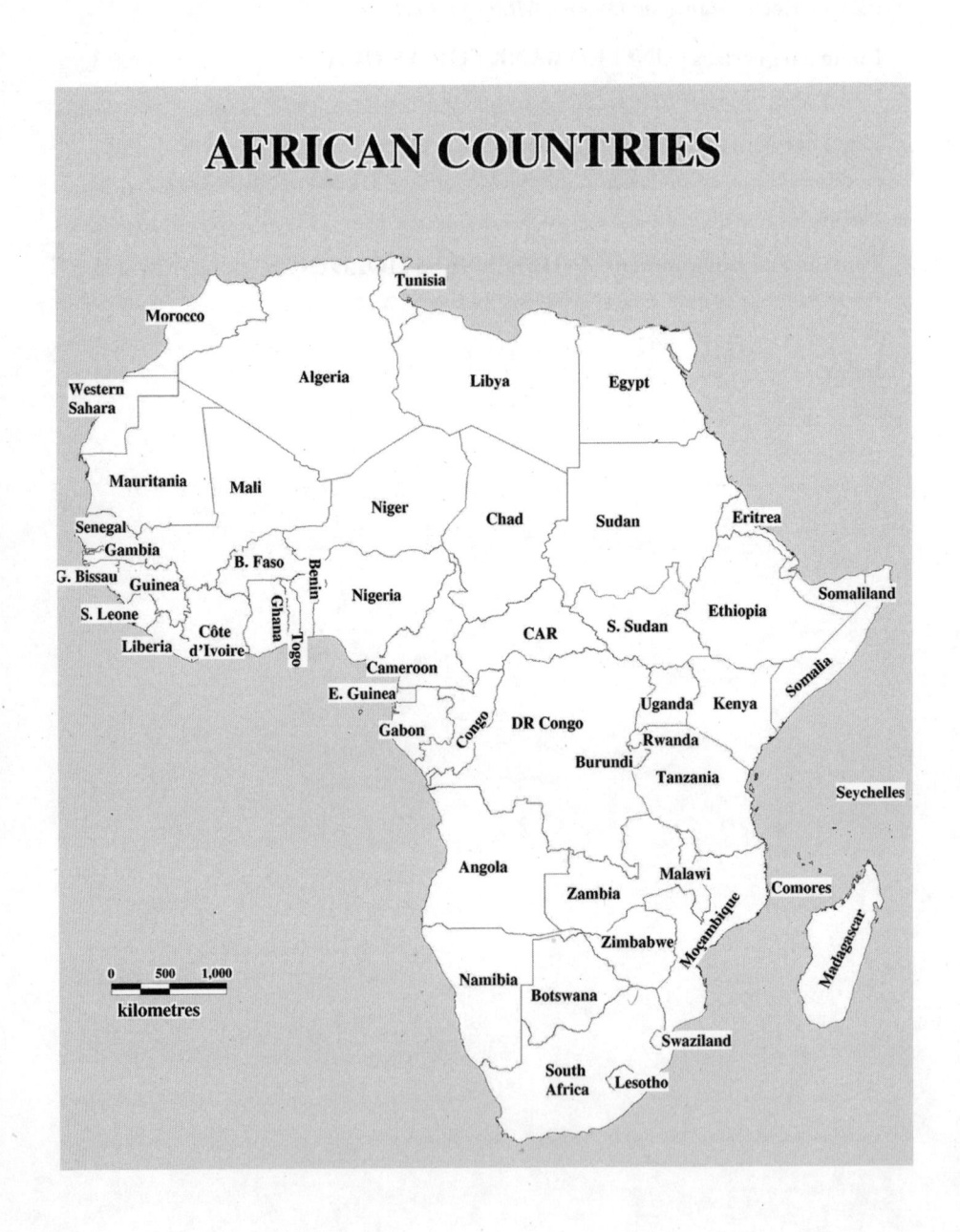

AFRICAN CITIES

PREFACE

When I became the editor of a pan-African magazine in the 1990s, based in Johannesburg, the rest of Africa was in a state of economic and political transition and it was regarded as a far-off 'country' by most people in the world, including many in South Africa.

Travelling around the continent was extremely difficult. There were few flight connections; it was difficult to find a decent hotel and running water was often a luxury; cash was king and currency exchanges were generally done in back alleys; working telephones were in short supply; basic goods were sometimes hard to find, and many countries were either in the grip of autocratic and military rulers or just emerging from calamitous socialist experiments. There were a number of positive exceptions. Zimbabwe was one of them, as it is now one of the exceptions to the progress made by African countries since then.

It was also a time of structural adjustment programmes, policy experimentation with liberalisation and economic reform, privatisation and the influence of the Bretton Woods Institutions.

It was a major learning curve for everyone – investors, African businesses, the governments that were liberalising their economies and the citizens who were being exposed to an array of goods and services they had not seen or experienced before.

Just over ten years later, the continent is a different place. The improvements in economic performance, ease of doing business, flights and accommodation options, communications and technology, provision of financial services and other aspects are a world away from what they were even a decade ago.

Africa is seeing the tangible benefits of a decade of positive economic growth and a changing global order that has seen the rise of strong emerging market economies, even as those in the developed world decline. A continent that has been shunned or ignored by all but the hardiest of global investors until recently is now being viewed as an exciting frontier economy.

Analysts who, even a few years ago, could not tell you how many Congos or Guineas there were in Africa, or even name a single African-owned company outside South Africa, are now 'experts' who charge hefty fees to advise multinational clients across the globe on developing their Africa strategies. They sit behind desks in Johannesburg, London, Paris and New York and make liberal use of the internet to draw up reports on African economies, business and investment trends and opportunities.

But to succeed in Africa is to properly understand its markets. There is no substitute for first-hand experience on a continent where local conditions can upset even the most sophisticated business plan conceived in an air-conditioned office in a far-off city.

This view informed the decision to compile a dossier of opinions and personal experiences of senior executives who are at the coalface of doing business in Africa. It is their insights gleaned from first-hand experience of sectors, countries, governments, business partners and different business environments that are captured in the series of interviews and articles in this book. The focus is on countries outside South Africa, because the target readership includes South African companies looking at other African markets and because the South African business environment is more familiar to international investors than are those of other countries on the continent.

The publication is designed to give the reader a glimpse of the opportunities the continent offers – but also the challenges. It is tempting to focus on only the good news and there is plenty of it, but many challenges remain and these are as much a part of the African business story as the evident opportunities.

One section of the book consists of articles by experts on different aspects of economic history, performance and prospects – setting the scene and providing a solid background to understanding Africa.

Another is a series of interviews with senior executives, covering their company's activities in Africa and airing their opinions, insights and predictions about where Africa might be heading. The enthusiastic response from some of the world's and Africa's biggest multinationals to the invitation to participate in this book was amazing. Many more executives and companies could not be included due to time, space and other constraints.

In just over six months from its official launch in South Africa, the book had sold out, highlighting a gap in the market for such information. When we updated it for the paperback version, it emerged that several of the interviewees had either changed positions within their companies or had left for greener pastures. We have kept the interviews in this version to ensure continuity with the first book but these changes have been reflected.

I would like to thank all the people who helped with the project in terms of writing or giving of their time for interviews. Thanks also to Michael Moon for helping with the concept of the book and editing it and to other friends for their enthusiastic support.

Dianna Games
Johannesburg 2013
diannagames@mweb.co.za

INTRODUCTION

As Africa enters a new era of investment and business opportunities, the global community has begun to pay attention to the extraordinary potential, in terms of both human capacity and resources, in the continent of Africa.

There are an increasing number of home-grown companies and multinationals that are positioning themselves to take advantage of the continent's reforming business climate, improved governance and, importantly, new opportunities presented by a wealth of global investor interest not seen on the continent before.

They are evolving to become part of the competitive global business culture. But this new generation of corporate leaders and executives faces challenging times. In order to prosper, they will need to become agile and innovative and adapt to the fast-changing business environment and new trends, including a demand for quality goods and services on an unprecedented scale.

They are also going to need entrepreneurs and managers adequately equipped to deal with the road ahead.

As one of Africa's premier business schools, the Gordon Institute of Business Science (GIBS) has played, and will continue to play, a role in this process of change.

It is common cause, as many emerging countries have shown, that the effective management of institutions and the quality of organisational leadership is at least as important as, if not more important than, natural resources.

Institutions need people who can manage and lead them effectively, changing and developing as they go along.

The African Association of Business Schools (AABS) has 23 members who are actively working to improve business education and management effectiveness in Africa.

There is also a new commitment to growing executive education and we are increasingly having 'strategic conversations' about the future with our colleagues from across the continent. There is a long and exciting journey ahead to ensure that the continent's full potential is met.

There is no better way to learn about the exciting, albeit complex, markets of Africa than from executives who are already there. *Business in Africa: Corporate Insights* is a valuable tool to this end. It not only reflects the way that doing business is changing in terms of attitudes, practices and engagement, it also tells us a little about the corporate journey of some of the continent's – and the world's – biggest companies.

These insights are now part of the collective body of work that is capturing on a dynamic and changing Africa. These insights will help us to deal with the exciting future that lies ahead.

Professor Nick Binedell
Dean, Gordon Institute of Business Science
University of Pretoria, South Africa

FOREWORD

The private sector is undoubtedly a driver of change in Africa and improving governance is laying the groundwork for countries to leverage increased investment and partnerships for inclusive, sustainable growth – the kind of growth Africa really needs.

The stage is already set. Since the beginning of the new millennium Africa's economic growth has gained momentum and, between 2000 and 2010, the continent was the third fastest growing region globally. This has been accompanied by high levels of foreign direct investment. Infrastructure, too, is finally receiving the attention it deserves as a catalyst for improving not just the business environment but also people's lives.

Growth in Africa continues to be diversified. In addition to significant expansion of the resources industry, there is growth in many other sectors such as consumer goods, technology, property development and agriculture. The middle of the pyramid is growing rapidly, with 30 per cent of the population now earning between US$2 and US$20 a day.

As the private sector expands, companies are becoming more regionally focused, seeking new markets. We are seeing more partnerships with foreign investors, including those from new emerging markets – countries that have embraced the opportunities Africa offers. Investors are increasingly putting down roots in the continent with local partners and making significant investments in communities, which is helping to counter the scourge of poverty.

There is no doubt that Africa is changing and that it will continue along a positive growth trajectory, notwithstanding upsets both on the continent and in some of its markets. Conditions for investment are also improving.

The African Development Bank (AfDB) is currently putting as much as 70 per cent of its investment into infrastructure to address the significant deficits that are contributing to lost productivity on a massive scale and shaving several percentage points off otherwise impressive continental growth.

The AfDB is helping to build not just African economies, but also the indigenous private sector through its increasing participation in private equity initiatives. The Bank Group is also starting to pay more attention to key interventions, such as in higher education, in an effort to improve the employment outlook. We are also encouraging African governments to support anti-poverty interventions that have worked well in other regions of the developing world.

We, as Africans, have to accept that a lot needs to be done to make the continent a far more competitive region and one in which doing business will be a lot cheaper and easier than it is now, to enable not only good returns for investors, but also to enable companies themselves to be more competitive.

The continent needs private sector involvement to sustain and augment existing development levels and counter a trend of mostly jobless growth that is not adequately addressing poverty alleviation – despite the growth of a middle class that is attracting new investment.

Africa needs new partnerships to enable it to realise its full potential. To ensure Africa is one of the chosen frontier markets in this new global era, we need a new honesty about what is required to make the continent work.

Business in Africa: Corporate Insights is a valuable contribution to the debate as it offers not only information on business opportunities on the continent, but also details some of the risks and challenges from those who are at the forefront of operating in Africa. Their insights will be valuable to policy makers as they forge a new future for our continent.

Professor Mthuli Ncube
Chief Economist and Vice President, African Development Bank

THE STATE OF PLAY

DIANNA GAMES

THE RECENT PAST

On my first visit to Nigeria in 1995, I had to fly through Ghana as there were no direct flights from South Africa. After an overnight stop in Accra, I took a taxi to the airport as dawn broke. The driver asked where I was going. Lagos, I replied. 'You should turn around now', he said, slowing the car, 'it's a very rough place'. And it was. The scars of decades of mostly military rule – infrastructural decay, uncontrolled urbanisation and a lack of municipal services – characterised the massive, sprawling city.

The situation in many other post-colonial African states was little different in the 1980s and early 1990s. African cities that are today thriving, such as Dar es Salaam, Lusaka, Kinshasa and Maputo, had barely any power or running water, buildings were neglected and shops had scant goods for sale. Many currencies were in freefall against the United States dollar and other hard currencies and economies stood as symbols of poor economic choices and development experiments. It was an era of autocratic dictators, military *juntas* and increasing poverty. The rapid spread of HIV/AIDS hit the headlines as it threatened to decimate African populations.

The heavy hand of government suppressed economic activity and entrepreneurialism. Local companies survived behind high tariff walls.

When African countries began to liberalise their economies, local businesses struggled to compete with well-resourced companies from developed countries that benefited from economies of scale, greater efficiencies, quality products and sophisticated supply chains. From 1994, South African companies across a range of sectors began their northward expansion, armed with post-apartheid war chests and well-tuned business plans, ready to find new opportunities after several decades of existing in a pariah state on their own continent.

Structural adjustment programmes and privatisation were the buzzwords of the 1990s. There were many successes but also many failures as governments found out the hard way that they could not successfully run factories and banks. Foreign aid from Western countries provided a lifeline to slowly reforming economies, and the continent was flooded with well-intentioned donors providing yet more aid, building a philanthropic system that later proved wanting as a catalyst for economic growth.

A look into the past is crucial to understanding African countries and the challenges of operating in them today. The evolution of their economies resulted in structural dysfunction that has become part of business culture in many countries, even as governments move to put in place new systems and reform processes to address old and new challenges.

Despite the opportunities sparked by improved economic growth, it has taken a while for Africa, as a continent, to register as more than a blip on the global investment radar. It has generally been regarded as high-risk, poor, inefficient and politically unstable. Until recently, the multinationals operating in Africa comprised mostly European and British companies with long histories in the former colonies, Western oil companies and South African companies eager to find new markets in their hinterland.

Even wealthy Africans regarded the continent as a high-risk place and stashed billions of dollars in overseas bank accounts. A lack of transparency in government allowed corruption to mushroom and even metamorphose, in time, into a business culture with its own dynamics. Many young Africans took their talents to international markets, seeking the job opportunities and quality education they could not find at home.

It was a time when not many companies had the foresight or the courage to invest in Africa, despite the often high returns on offer.

However, two decades later, Africa is much changed. The risk for many businesses now is *not* being in Africa. It is now not only logical to invest in the continent, but often an imperative.

CONTEMPORARY AFRICA

Nigeria, Zambia, Ghana, Ethiopia, Tanzania, Uganda and Mozambique, once among Africa's poorest and most politically challenged states, are now among the best performers on the continent, with some of the highest growth rates and measures of gross domestic product (GDP) in the world.

This sea change in Africa's fortunes has seen growing interest in the continent's bounty from resource-hungry emerging markets – China and India key among them – for more than a decade. Analysts predict that China's investment could rise by 70 per cent from its 2009 figure to $50 billion by 2015 and that the volume of bilateral trade between China and Africa might rise to $300 billion over the same period.

China has been a key driver of the global commodities 'super cycle' that has been turning since the dawn of the new century. The heightened demand for Africa's oil and minerals, due in part to China's resource-intensive growth over the past decade, has been a trigger not just for growth, but for large investments in infrastructure as part of offset agreements for acquisition of those resources. New emerging market interest in Africa has also provided a catalyst for global investors to pay attention to what Africa has to offer. Executives who have been sitting on the fence are taking a closer look at the investment opportunities.

Since 2008, emerging market performance has stood in sharp relief to the relative decline of developed world economies following the global financial crisis that pushed investors to look for frontier markets with better potential. Africa, which has experienced average growth of about five per cent for a decade, seems to fit the bill.

One clear signal of the way the world has changed is reflected in the appeal in 2011 by a former colonial master, Portugal, to its former colony, Angola, for investment to boost the eurozone country's ailing economy. Angola has been one of the fastest growing economies in the world, with double-digit growth between 2004 and 2008, touching nearly 20 per cent in 2005. Angolan companies have already made significant investments into Portugal in the banking sector, telecommunications and energy and this appears set to rise as Portugal faces further GDP contraction.

Africa's high population growth, of major concern to development experts a decade ago, is now regarded by some as a key driver of growth and new investment. It is seen as a 'demographic dividend' on the back of sustained economic growth across the continent – rather than as a crisis waiting to happen. The African Development Bank in 2011 stated that the size of Africa's middle class, which it measures as being people of higher than the average income among Africans, but with a lower average than elsewhere, has tripled over the last 30 years to 313 million people, or about 30 per cent of the continent's population.

Analysts estimate that more than half of Africa's population will be living in urban areas by 2030 and 60 per cent by 2050 when the population is expected to be two billion. This trend will have particular significance in already heavily populated countries such as Nigeria, where the cities are likely to have 140 million more people living in them by 2050, and South Africa and Angola, which could see up to 80 per cent of their people living in cities.

Urbanisation, too, was viewed as a major threat to Africa's progress a decade ago but is now seen as an inevitable part of growth, providing opportunities in a range of sectors because of economies of scale and easy access to infrastructure – which are now considered to be tools in the advancement of socio-economic well-being. Urban poverty rates in Africa are about 35 per cent, compared to 52 per cent for rural areas.

Underpinning this new economic order is greater relative political stability. Peaceful governing transitions through elections have become the norm in many countries. Although sub-Saharan Africa experienced two *coups d'etat* in 2012, in Mali and Guinea Bissau, the continent has generally become more adept at taking action against blatantly undemocratic actions – even though it has failed to act effectively on the subversion of democracy through rigged elections and human rights abuses in countries such as Zimbabwe. Nonetheless, several 'liberation era' leaders, many with dubious political records, are moving on and the door is opening to younger leaders more in tune with the growing numbers of young people that make up Africa's population of one billion.

New technology has played a positive role. The impact of mobile phones has been significant, driving economic growth by enabling business activity at a new level. By 2012 there were more than 700 million mobile phone users in Africa and it is predicted that by 2015 the continent will have the highest mobile subscription rate in the world. This phenomenon has unleashed a range of new opportunities for Africa's inhabitants in trade, banking, information flows, consumer messaging and other areas. New sea cables connecting Africa to the world have pushed up the availability of bandwidth by more than 60 per cent since 2010, albeit off a low base. The highest increase was in sub-Saharan Africa – 82 per cent to reach 368 Gbps – and in North Africa, which increased by 45 per cent to reach 433 Gbps.

Global brands are jostling for centre stage in an increasingly crowded marketplace as the African consumer becomes a target for international companies, particularly from developed countries, but also from emerging markets and Africa itself. Marketing executives say the message to African consumers needs to expand outwards from traditional media to social networks and mobile phones as people on the continent become increasingly sophisticated.

Multinationals from developed countries are positioning themselves for increased competition from emerging markets. Standard Chartered Bank, brewer Diageo and manufacturers Unilever and Nestlé are among the firms that are ramping up their investments. Nestlé has invested $446 million in Nigeria alone since 2003 and planned to invest a further $635 million over the next decade to triple sales to $2.2 billion by 2023. Standard Chartered, which makes ten per cent of its profit from African operations, plans to invest $100 million in Africa to double the size of its business within five years. Brewing giant Diageo has invested more than $1 billion on acquisitions in Africa since 2007. The continent already accounts for 14 per cent of total group sales and the company has enjoyed annual sales growth of 15 per cent over the six years to 2013.

African companies, too, are growing and expanding. Corporate entities from South Africa, which has been a serious investor on the continent for almost two decades, retain a strong foothold in most sectors and a new wave of top executives from Africa's biggest economy is rolling across the continent. In other large markets, the number of multinationals is growing as companies in Nigeria, Kenya and other places increasingly take a regional view and are setting up shop, both in their immediate hinterland and further afield.

These companies are mostly in a few sectors – financial services, agriculture and consumer goods. But there is also growth in oil and gas where, out of about 800 companies operating in the sector, more than 100 are African players – in addition to several dozen African state-owned oil companies.

Increasing amounts of private equity are chasing acquisitions and funds are seeing new interest from emerging markets as they exit thriving African companies. The growth of the African private sector has been one of the key changes over the past decade, with West and East African firms in banking, retail and manufacturing increasingly focusing on regional expansion.

Many governments have improved the operating environment for private investors. The World Bank's *Doing Business Index* shows that African countries are among the fastest reformers in recent times, with 28 out of 46 countries measured between June 2011 and June 2012 having implemented reforms in at least one of the areas measured by this report. In the six years up to 2011, 43 sub-Saharan countries had made the regulatory environment more business friendly while steps had been taken to harmonise regional business regulation, for example with the 16 Francophone countries that are members of the Organisation for the Harmonisation of Business Law in Africa (OHADA).

African entrepreneurs have a new-found confidence, not least due to the 'leap frog' new technologies and media that have given them effective new business tools. Skilled Africans are returning to the continent to take up opportunities with both international and African companies, opportunities that are proliferating in an era of increasing pressure for local hire.

THE REALITY CHECK

It is easy, with all the optimism and hype about Africa in consultants' reports, newspaper articles and the mushrooming number of conferences on the topic, to think that all is well. But the continent is still a place of many harsh realities, which might yet dent the ambitious growth prognoses.

In 2010, GDP per capita in Africa finally reached levels last seen in the 1970s, which means there were almost 40 years of lost growth and investment. This decline had its roots in politics and political risk is still a significant issue in many African economies. A prime example is Zimbabwe, once a thriving economy that experienced a decade of lost growth and is yet to recover despite some economic stabilisation and political accommodation. Côte d'Ivoire is another example. The biggest economy in Francophone Africa buckled under a civil war that drove many investors, including the African Development Bank, to safer havens. Lingering political problems following recent uprisings in Egypt, Libya and Tunisia will dampen the future outlook for the continent.

Another danger is the lack of diversification of Africa's economies, a factor that leaves them vulnerable to exogenous shocks from trading partners. As stellar as Angola's growth was in the mid-2000s, it was one of the worst affected by the global financial crisis and, in 2009, experienced negative growth.

High growth rates used to highlight opportunity in Africa are often in undiversified, resource-rich economies and, despite the significant opportunity resources these offer for sustainable and broad-based growth and development, few of Africa's governments have played this scenario well.

Dazzled by the apparent profits being made by mining companies, governments and communities expect a lot, ignoring high and rising production costs and the long-term nature of an industry that has to consider all the commodity cycles, not just the boom times. The focus is usually on how to extract more of those profits rather than how they could best benefit future economic development. The problem is made worse by a lack of transparency in revenues and spending priorities.

The trend towards greater national participation in resources is well accepted, but there are question marks over whether governments are doing it in the best way to keep international investors interested and not violating contracts and investor agreements signed on entry. For example, in Guinea the government's mining code introduced in 2011 arbitrarily changed the government's stake in resource companies there from 15 per cent to allow it a 35 per cent stake. Resources companies often need to put large infrastructure projects into their capital expenditure budgets in order to secure contracts as competition for lucrative licences increases.

Governments are better at putting pressure on resources companies to extract more revenue for the fiscus than they are at ensuring that the money is used for the good of the communities living in areas where the resources are extracted, or for the country's overall development. Mining companies are now focusing on how they can be a catalyst for growth rather than the sole source of opportunity. They are also seeking new models that will enable them to add more value to their non-mining investments and reduce dependence on the mines.

Multinational companies often come in for criticism by African governments for failing to contribute sufficiently to local economies despite huge profits. However, this overlooks the broader benefits of foreign investment that, apart from direct revenues into the national fiscus, include employment, skills training and technology transfer.

Even as governments put pressure on mines to beneficiate, often they cannot supply sufficient power for the mine, let alone a smelter or refinery. Local content and procurement demands are not accompanied by supply-side measures to address the lack of capacity and skills that forced companies to source from outside the country in the first place.

Africa's policy makers have testing times ahead. The hype about investment opportunities tends to obscure the fact that African countries mostly have modest experience of huge capital inflows, and an inability to absorb them may create dysfunction in small local economies with small, illiquid markets with little financial infrastructure.

The pressure to develop greener economies is another looming challenge for countries that have not yet found a way out of persistent energy crises. In coming years, African governments will have to deal with a growing network of international bureaucrats, consultants, non-governmental organisations and other stakeholders, all giving advice on how to refocus their economies in the quest to address global climate change.

This may have the unintended consequence of diverting policy makers from reforming the costly and dysfunctional operating environments that exist in many states and add considerably to the costs and difficulties of investment and doing business.

Healthcare is another looming issue. Although the issue hardly makes the headlines anymore, more than 60 per cent of people living with HIV are in Africa and they are swamping the already inadequate capacity of health facilities. African governments are not spending sufficiently or efficiently on either health or education – the key building blocks of many successful economies around the world.

According to the World Health Organisation, by 2011 only two African countries had met the Abuja Declaration pledge, signed by 53 countries in 2001, to dedicate 15 per cent of the national budget to improving healthcare, while seven decreased spending. However, private healthcare investment is set to increase as a growing African middle class and rising expatriate numbers make private healthcare more viable.

Despite the opportunities urbanisation represents, many of Africa's largest cities have become sprawling entities with large areas of squalor barely touched by municipal services and infrastructure. Many of the towns that will be at the forefront of urbanisation are not the capital cities and urban sprawl of Lagos, Nairobi, Kampala and Accra but smaller places that are poorly resourced and less able to absorb the numbers productively.

South African cities such as Johannesburg and Durban, which are much better organised and resourced than other African cities, are experiencing many new urbanisation challenges, so their counterparts with far fewer resources are going to struggle. South Africa has 40 per cent of the continent's installed power capacity and even this country has had to spend billions on meeting increased power demand.

The issue of food production must be noted here. African agriculture is modestly commercialised and continues to rely on smallholder farmers, many without decent inputs, technology, storage facilities, funding or infrastructure to connect them to local, regional and international markets. With people moving into the cities, there needs to be a concerted effort to promote smarter farming and commercial enterprise, otherwise food costs are going to push up inflation and costs for urban dwellers, building conditions for potential conflict.

Related to food production is the continued existence of trade barriers, which compound the infrastructural and other issues that suppress the growth of intra-African trade. This trade is a very low 11–12 per cent of Africa's total trade and compares very poorly to Europe's 60 per cent. The barriers to regional integration are a concern for many investors looking at pan-African strategies rather than just localised investments.

The continent is slowly moving towards large trading blocs with negotiations under way for the creation of a free trade area stretching from Cape to Cairo. Plans to harmonise three regional economic communities – Southern African Development Community (SADC), East African Community (EAC) and Common Market for Eastern and Southern Africa (Comesa) – were given impetus at a heads of state gathering in Johannesburg in mid-2011 although little detail on progress in this initiative has emerged since then.

A larger regional market will be more attractive to funders of infrastructure projects and will enable greater co-operation in areas such as agricultural development and the formulation of common regional positions and strategies in multilateral and international trade forums. There are other potential benefits such as the development of national and even regional industrial policies, which are currently absent, to allow the development of comparative advantage and value addition in an environment of increased competition and reduced protection.

The de-industrialisation of most African countries has created an undue dependence on trade taxes – more than 30 per cent of state revenue in most cases – and countries will now be pushed to search for new ways to boost revenue. For politicians, putting a signature to a deal is the easy part. African states have a poor track record of implementing the many agreements they sign up to and building regional infrastructure is already facing problems of political will.

Africa's manufacturing industry has declined since the early 1990s due to a number of factors, including power shortages, uncompetitive operating environments, lack of policy support for exports and competition for international markets coupled with small regional markets. Manufacturing's share of Africa's total GDP fell to below ten per cent in 2010 from a high of 15 per cent in 1990, in stark contrast to Asia where the continent's share of manufacturing increased by a third over the same period.

The success of the Asian manufacturing sector is founded on increased production of high-technology goods, for which there is increasing demand, and export-led growth – both areas in which Africa is weak. Africa exports just 20 per cent of its total amount of manufactured goods, while Asia exports 70 per cent, and more than half of Africa's regional industrial output is from one economy – South Africa. A great many consumer goods in Africa are produced cheaply in Asia and sold at lower prices than locally made products.

Most exports from Africa continue to be raw materials. A number of governments have tried to address the issue of beneficiation, both with incentives and punitive measures. But beneficiation has been slow to take root and is undermined by policy and infrastructure constraints. Africa's labour advantage has also been eroded by poor education levels and inadequate skills development.

THE FUTURE

Although there will be more bumps in the road, investor interest in the continent is likely to continue and companies and funds wanting to get on the bandwagon should do so sooner rather than later.

The price of assets is rising and the number of bargains available is diminishing rapidly. An investor who walks away from a deal might return later to find the price has increased, as MTN did with its purchase of Investcom (see MTN chapter), or that the opportunity has gone to someone happy not to quibble about the price tag.

Although risk is still a factor in African countries, most investors will say that perception is not matched by the reality. Levels of risk are indeed far lower than they used to be on the back of improved governance, economic reform and increased public-private engagement. But new risks come with changes in the business and political environment and it is important to keep abreast of these. Changes to protocols and requirements that are being put in place in Western economies also present new risks and costs for companies operating in other regions. This means that tracking risks has become more nuanced and it is more difficult to keep up and to find ways to manage them than it was a decade ago.

Many of the old problems and risks linger. They include corruption, trade barriers, weak legal systems, excessive and inefficient bureaucracy, infrastructure deficits, a surfeit of politics, a lack of technocrats in government, poor national health and education systems and a lack of political will to implement regional projects as politicians continue to focus on quick wins designed to woo voters.

The continent is still vulnerable to externally driven shocks and slow growth in major trading partners in the West and in emerging markets. Although increased trade from Asia has helped to offset declines among Africa's traditional trading partners – European countries and the US – Africa has arguably become too dependent on the growth of its non-African trading partners, such as China.

But Africa as a whole seems to be going in the right direction, notwithstanding political problems in certain countries. Its biggest challenge is to develop areas of specific competitiveness and sustainable economies on the back of its resources and people.

20 TIPS ON DOING BUSINESS IN AFRICA

1. Always follow due process when entering or working in a new market and be patient about the extra time it might take. If you take short cuts, you may be in trouble if the government changes, or even if a minister or bureaucrat you have allowed to smooth the way for you loses his or her job. This can stall a project, make agreed protocols unenforceable or even result in a deal being reversed. Patience is important when operating in Africa. Build longer time-frames into doing deals and expecting profits than you would in other regions. Allow your team time to adapt to the new business environment.
2. Always have country strategies that underpin regional strategies, as every market has different local challenges, even though there may be similarities in the broad challenges across countries.
3. Find local partners. They provide local knowledge, ease entry into a market and, ideally, have influence.
4. Build strong relationships with Africans in the markets in which you operate. They underpin deals in Africa. If you do not get the relationship right, the deal might suffer.
5. If possible, work with a local company in a mutually beneficial relationship before you take the plunge into an equity-based partnership.
6. Do deep due diligence, not only on the operations of local partners, but also on directors and board members. Given the turbulent political history of many African countries, you may find skeletons in the closet later that could affect your company's reputation.
7. Understand the cultural nuances of local management and ensure there is a good fit with your company. In the case of mergers and acquisitions it is important to make sure you know early on who you should keep and who needs to go. It will get harder to get rid of local senior managers later and, depending on their influence in a market, this may have negative repercussions for your business.
8. Be aware of trademark issues. You do not want to look at a new market only to find a local company is trading off your brand – and doing so legally as you have not registered your trademark as a precautionary measure.

9. Understand and respect local protocols and make sure you are fully conversant with local rules and regulations, as well as any recent changes in legislation. It is good to get to know the relevant local authorities that may have an impact on your business, such as a council or the chief of police in an outlying area where you operate. Being friendly with a government minister might not help you when your truck full of goods is impounded at a roadblock far from the city limits.
10. Put in place strong governance and control structures that are implemented across African operations. This closes the gap for any breaches of corporate governance.
11. Make sure you leave enough time to plan properly at the beginning of the project and do not be pressured by local partners to act prematurely. Spending extra time upfront can mean the difference between success and failure.
12. Give proper support to local partners and do not treat them as window dressing. They are an important component in the success or failure of your business.
13. Do not assume that, because incomes are generally low in Africa, consumers want cheap products. African consumers are highly aspirational and seek value for money.
14. In many African countries, it is normal to work and have meetings late into the night and at weekends. If a local business partner or contact invites you to their home, accept. It is an important part of business bonding and building trust – and hearing the local gossip.
15. Be aware that in many countries cash is still king. Credit cards are not in widespread use and the service is often only available at top hotels and restaurants in capital cities and, even then, not all types of credit cards are accepted.
16. Be aware of the ethnic breakdown of countries and take this into account in hiring practices and in the composition of company boards.
17. The cost of African assets is rising as competition increases. If you are inclined to walk away because a price seems too high, assess how badly you want to be in that market. If the asset is of sufficient quality for you to want it in the first place, the price will only go up. If you hesitate it might be snapped up by a less price-sensitive competitor.
18. Be wary of doing large deals close to election time, particularly if there

is a chance that the political incumbent might not win. If you must conclude a deal, clarify the political links to the deal and try to ensure that there is little chance of it being reversed if a new government comes into power or there are significant changes among the relevant ministers, state or provincial governments.
19. Once you have agreed on a deal, move quickly to conclude it. Do not believe that having memoranda of understanding and heads of agreement in place are sufficient to prevent the deal being scuppered at the last minute by an offer from someone else.
20. When your interface with an African company is at the level of CEO or managing director, do not engage the company at middle management level. You need to show you are taking them seriously.

Johannesburg-based Dr Duncan Clarke is Chairman & CEO of Global Pacific & Partners, a private advisory firm, and author of *Africa's Future: Darkness to Destiny* (Profile Books, 2012), and *Crude Continent: The Struggle for Africa's Oil Prize* (Profile, 2010, now a CNBC Africa TV/Film Documentary), among a number of other books and published works.

AFRICA'S ECONOMIC EVOLUTION

DUNCAN CLARKE

Africa's unique economic evolution configured the continent's current economies and will shape its future.

Many pathways, some of them dead ends, weaved Africa's economic story – a story of investment, unlocked natural capital, complex adaptive process and competitive struggle for survival, with modest accumulation. What we are left with is today's mix of medieval-with-modern economic modes.

Underperformance is the *leitmotif* of contemporary state-dominated economies. Nonetheless, Africa has grown, illustrating the power of multiple economic entities over the political regimes that impede them. This relationship is the root cause for optimism about future growth.

Most interpretations presume that Africa is poor. This is not true. Africa is not really 'poor' as many portray it: it is poorly managed and yet-to-be developed. Vast potential lies in abundant natural capital and resource-based industries, the full monetisation of which could provide for enhanced long-term growth. Until this occurs, talk of an 'African Century' and proclamations of an era of strong and sustained growth are premature.

Lessons from Africa's past show that long-cycle growth is central and sustained capital accumulation essential to this process. Capitalist evolution over the long-term has been at the core of modern progress to date.

LA LONGUE DURÉE

Africa's economic future will be shaped by the continent's formative evolution, a view much neglected in contemporary projections.

GDP and income per capita data for the last 2,000 years, crafted by international scholar Angus Maddison, are our best source for past trends (the data is shown in real 1990 US dollars, updated to 2010 using official data and the methodology is found in *Africa's Future: Darkness to Destiny*, Profile Books, 2012).

Maddison estimates that when Rome commanded North Africa in 1CE (common era, previously referred to as AD or anno domini), Africa's population was 17 million. By 200CE it was 20 million, with half in the far north. It took 1 000 years to reach 32.3 million, and a further 500 years to become 46.6 million. To 1500, the average annual population growth rate was barely 0.06 per cent. Malthusian realities prevailed. At 1CE Africa's annual per capita income was $472; by 1000 it had fallen to $425. In 1500 it was even lower, at $414, showing that most of Africa went backwards for 1,500 years – a salutary lesson in the result of ultra-long cycle stagnation with chronic decline.

Overall, from 1500 to 1820 Africa's economies flatlined: in 1820 GDP per capita was $420 (population 74 million). The post-1700 continental economy concentrated in the south, around the Cape, with growth poles on northern littorals. Living standards in tropical interiors were worse. Monetisation was minimal. This was an era of unremitting stasis, begging the question: how did Africa cut the Gordian knot of material misery?

Subsequent growth came mainly from capitalist penetration into a few locales on the edges of Africa. From 1820 to 1870 Africa achieved real GDP per head growth at average annual rates of 0.58 per cent, as opposed to the 0.05 per cent of the period from 1500 to 1870. This first notable long-run cycle of growth enabled per capita income to rise to $500 by 1870. Adding just six per cent to average real income in 1CE of $472, it reflected recovery post-1500. Africa's long-run growth cycle, now marginally positive, was still chronically abysmal. Tough conditions dominated traditional Africa as population numbers (110 million by 1900) placed pressure on real income per capita.

From 1500 onwards, Africa continued on a subsistence level, except in isolated zones. Abundant land, scattered populations, slow demographic transition, weak rural economic landscapes, nomadic pastoralism and migration to more benign ecologies enabled its varied subsistence world to survive, though under austere conditions.

Eventually all this fractured and the storyline for ancient, bare-bones economies became one of disruption with relative disintegration. Yet the millennia-old, embedded subsistence economies, although ruptured by late-19th century colonialism, did not crumble entirely. Nor did early modernity herald a quantum shift in economic progress. Old and new had to cohabit Africa's economic space. This fateful inner schism formed the drama of the century to follow and remains today.

AFRICA'S OPENING

Africa's engagement with the world saw real income per head reach $637 by 1913. GDP grew 0.61 per cent annually between 1870 and 1900, but only 0.46 per cent between 1900 and 1913 as the population grew to 125 million. Compared to 1820, there had been a 50 per cent rise in income per head. Still, long-term cyclical growth was slow, at only 0.6 per cent per annum from 1870 to 1900. This was presaged by the fundamental switch from rural subsistence to more varied economic foundations as more natural capital was unlocked.

Colonisation brought major capital investment. By 1950, with 228 million inhabitants, income per head was $889, growing over the period 1913 to 1950 at 0.91 per cent annually – a significant relative shift in growth and income standards overall. But substantial shocks wracked traditional economies, etching new patterns of capital formation and income differentiation into economic landscapes. Lifestyles of the rich contrasted sharply with those of the preponderant poor. Even the middle classes attained income standards that Africa's potentates had not enjoyed.

This became Africa's first real period of solid long-run growth. Important institutions and technical advances from elsewhere were brought to Africa and transformed its economic destiny – in capital markets, companies, factories, literacy, electricity, railways, infrastructure and organisational capacities

By 1960, GDP per capita was $1,055 (population 285 million). Investment was still sizeable. Growth flowed from large foreign capital inflows, domestic investment, infrastructure spread, economic linkages built inside Africa and with the world outside, as well as from technologies to augment the scale and efficiency of the capital stock. Capital-to-output ratios had risen, while more land was made commercially viable as technical coefficients and productive efficiencies improved.

Pre-market economies became smaller in terms of GDP measurement. Land surpluses were of less significance in the wider capital asset base. Urban-industrial and skilled workforces enabled increased productivity and even exports. This amounted to a revolution across Africa. More transactions than ever were conducted in monetised form and Africa became more extensively connected to global evolution.

Whatever the rationale of this imperialist era, it induced the growth and industrialisation that reconfigured nascent and previously backward economies. Yet Africa's 'winds of change' blew again.

POST-COLONIAL AFRICA

Decolonisation brought abrupt changes in regimes and expectations across Africa. This watershed resulted in major disruption and decay in many state institutions and economies. Still, the early years of independence, coincident with a global economic boom, witnessed growth.

GDP per head rose to $1,181 in 1965, $1,335 in 1970 and $1,515 in 1980. On the long-term cycle, annual growth rates of 1.8 per cent were achieved between 1960 and 1980, although this modest outcome was dampened by demographic expansion. Employment growth rarely matched the numbers entering Africa's labour markets and structural unemployment reared its head. Informalisation proliferated in step with the weakening capacity of traditional economies to provide subsistence. After the colonial interregnum of but 70 years there emerged the struggle for survival: of the fittest, fastest, favoured and fattest.

By the time the turbulent 1980s and 1990s came around, mistakes by newly-emergent nation states in economic management, with multiple civil conflicts and wars and struggles for Cold War control, took a heavy toll on living standards. Africa went downwards: by 1990, GDP per capita slipped to $1,425 (dropping $90 a head), while the continent's population rose to 633 million.

It took a decade for recovery to transcend demographics and break above the 1990 per capita level, at $1,447 in 2000 (still below 1980's real level). In effect, Africa experienced two lost decades, with a huge cost to the long-run cycle. Annual growth per capita for the period 1980–2010 was only 0.7 per cent.

Only during 2000–10 did Africa show much mettle, witnessing its most productive period, allied to the world commodity boom. By 2010 real income per head was $1,870, with the continent's GDP at about $1.9 trillion and a population of 1.05 billion. The annual income per head growth rate was 2.36 per cent – positive, but no miracle. This left average income per capita at only $5.12 a day.

During Africa's post-colonial era (1960–2010), GDP expanded six times from $300–million, yielding annual average compound growth of 3.78 per cent. Yet per capita income only rose 1.15 per cent annually over the 50 years, a mark of demographic burden.

Looking at the past brings certain questions to mind. Was Africa's growth rate 'naturally' inhibited at some ceiling over time? Are there upper limits to future growth and over what duration? The big picture question remains: what long-cycle growth rate can Africa expect to 2050?

SHIFTING VISTAS

Africa's population will be 1.5 billion by 2030 and two billion before 2050. To retain the same per capita income in real terms as in 2010, GDP will need to be $2.86 trillion and $3.74 trillion for 2030 and 2050 respectively, or at real annual GDP growth of 2.0 per cent and 1.7 per cent for the next 20 to 40 years. These long-cycle growth rates portray the minimum required to retain average income standards while accommodating inevitable population growth. Reversals in North Africa (Libya, Egypt and Tunisia) have already partially compromised this trajectory, providing reminders of deep-seated fragilities.

Is there any 'natural growth rate' for Africa that ought to guide expectations, derived from long-term trend data, with its episodic, patchy, cyclic periods – and occasional reversals?

Over the past two decades – the best in Africa's growth history, including economic recovery in the 1990s – the average GDP growth rate was 3.8 per cent annually in real terms. For the 40 years to 2050, 1.7 per cent will be required just to stand still in income per head, so mortgaging a large amount of future net growth. Africa needs to do much better to lift its economies out of underdevelopment, let alone offset vast and growing income gaps with the rest of the world. Africa's GDP at 1CE was $7 billion (seven per cent of the world's GDP) and per capita income was higher on average, but is now only 23 per cent of world income per head.

Could Africa now be on the cusp of a decades-long boom, an era unlike those of the past that wilted under local difficulties and external market pressures?

There is widespread optimism about Africa. Bullish storylines have gained traction worldwide. A bright future is predicted by 'economic cheerleaders', from politicians, diplomats and bankers to analysts, rock stars and academics. Almost all punt Africa's inevitable future economic success. Capitalist Africa has been portrayed in an almost revolutionary mode. The Africa giant, once sleeping and bedevilled by nightmares, is stirring.

FUTUROLOGY AND ECONOMICS

In 2010 the World Bank forecast growth of 'at least five per cent' for Africa for the following five years. This would bring Africa's GDP to $2.44 trillion by 2016 (on Maddison's data), extending long-cycle growth for nearly 20 years. Justin Lin, World Bank Chief Economist, even told *African Business* magazine in July 2011 that Africa could grow at seven per cent for the next 30–40 years: 'there is no reason why … this should not happen', he asserted.

The Institute for Security Studies (ISS) in South Africa set a high-water mark in optimistic long-term projections in its study *African Futures* 2050, a collaborative report with the University of Denver (Pretoria, 2011; note – data used differs from Maddison's 1990 real dollars). The ISS put Africa's income per capita in 2010 at $900 in constant dollars, compared to $500 in 1960 (with $150 'lost' in the mid-1990s). Yet, from 1960 to date, Africa's growth rate had topped six per cent, on five-year moving averages, only once or twice. The futurists claimed that GDP would exceed $13 trillion by 2050, similar to the US and EU in 2010 (this projection at a 5.1 per cent compound annual growth rate for 2010–50), implying GDP for 2010 at $1.8 trillion. This model prognosticated income per capita in constant prices at about $6,500 in 2050, way up from $900 today. At that level, Africa would have 'arrived' and would have a radically changed destiny.

Most would love all this to happen. But is it realistic, on the basis of known past long-cycle growth trends? Here Maddison is our only real guide to valid long-term growth performance for comparison.

Africa recorded the following annual cycles of real constant price GDP growth rates: 1500–1870 at 0.15 per cent, then 1820–70 at 0.7 per cent, moving upwards to 1.3 per cent for 1870–1913, and 2.8 per cent for 1913–60. For 1960–80, growth continued at a rapid clip, around 4.5 per cent – the most promising to date. Over the next decade it was 2.3 per cent, below net natural demographic expansion. For 1990–2000 Africa's GDP notched annual rates just below 2.8 per cent, barely offsetting population growth. The golden decade of 2000–10 saw it expand at 4.8 per cent on average.

On the longest measurable cycle, 1CE to 2010, annual growth rate performance was only 0.05 per cent, the last thousand years at a roughly similar rate, the last hundred years at more than 2.2 per cent and the last 50 years at 3.8 per cent.

In annual growth of income per capita, the rate for 1500–1870 was at 0.05 per cent, for 1820–70 at 0.58 per cent, for 1870–1913 at 0.57 per cent, for 1913–50 at 0.91 per cent and for 1960–80 at 1.8 per cent. Thereafter sharp decline set in, with –6 per cent recorded in 1980–90, leaving the 30-year cycle to 2010 at only 0.7 per cent. The best result was the decade from 2000 to 2010 at 2.36 per cent. On the 50-year cycle (1960–2010), only 1.1 per cent was achieved. For the last 2,000 years, capita growth has been barely 0.07 per cent, and in the last 110 years 1.0 per cent. This is no world-class long-term performance.

High and sustained secular growth cycles have been hard to secure. Small variances in growth rates, especially in early years, have devastating 'loss' impacts on GDP and income per capita down the line. Any one tough decade does serious harm. Ups and downs have been a consistent element in Africa's track record, with no guarantee against recidivism. Annual real GDP growth rates of five per cent (let alone seven per cent) for 40 years have never been achieved.

Extrapolations from 'golden periods', even for parts of Africa, readily mislead and could court fantasy. Official Africa growth rates in 2011 were radically scaled back within six months from 5.5 per cent to 3.7 per cent due to events in North Africa. A third of growth projected had been lost. In September 2011 another downward revision was made, to 3.2 per cent – as the growth rate was cut by more than 40 per cent within 12 months.

If GDP ($1.8 trillion at 2010 constant prices) progressed at only four per cent annually, in 2050 it would be not $13 trillion but $8.6 trillion – a huge deviation. At three per cent, the size of GDP would be only $5.7 trillion. If Africa's GDP expanded at the last 50-year cycle rate (1.1 per cent annually) it would come out at just $2.8 trillion.

With income per capita in 2010 at $900, growth rates at (a) four per cent, (b) two per cent and (c) 1.1 per cent, yield respective income per capita for 2050 at: (a) $4,321, (b) $1,987 and (c) $1,394. These scenarios are way behind the $6,500 mooted for 'heroic' growth trajectories for Africa's GDP based on compound growth of 5.1 per cent uninterrupted for 40 years, illustrating the power of demographics and the sensitivity of outcomes to small downsides in long-term cyclical rates achieved. *Quo vadis* Africa?

GROWTH *IMPRIMATUR* AND *REALPOLITIK*

Despite actual growth rate erosion, the official story is one of almost unrestrained optimism. In 2010, a World Bank 'strategy' concluded that Africa was on the brink of an economic take-off, much like China was 30 years ago and India 20 years ago. The bank's '10 Year Vision' foresaw Africa's income per capita as being 60 per cent higher by 2020. This would mean average individual income growth of five per cent each year going forward, once more projecting the future beyond historic record. By 2011 this strategy had already been watered down.

The AfDB joined the party (see *African Economic Outlook 2011*). Though the AfDB estimated that 25 countries would not cross the four per cent GDP growth mark in 2011–12, it forecast that sub-Saharan Africa's GDP would grow 6.2 per cent in 2012, while North Africa (including Sudan) would recover off the floor and rack up 5.1 per cent. Such prognoses tend to be thwarted by unfolding and often unexpected events.

The World Bank and AfDB have not been alone in trumpeting Africa's economic virtues. The chorus has been joined by private companies, accounting firms, consultants and media. The 'investment case' for Africa has been touted as compelling, even irresistible.

Rating agencies have joined in. Moody's claims the pace of growth has been fundamentally altered. Funds have lined up capital commitments. The continent is seen to be at an historic turning point and the corporate giants have discovered Africa. It is the 'next big thing'. In its prognosis for sub-Saharan Africa in 2010, MasterCard Worldwide sang a similar song, suggesting new stirrings of rapid growth.

Many drivers will navigate the road ahead, they all say: urbanisation, 'demographic dividends', rising consumer incomes, economic hubs and growing markets. Optimism is infectious: why not a ten per cent growth rate for Africa?, one economist asked. Another remarked that emulation of China's success story was on the cards. The cheerleaders have taken command of the stage. Africa has arrived and there will be no turning back.

The award for bullish optimism might go to Renaissance Capital's report in mid-2011, *Africa: The bottom billion becomes the fastest billion*, signalling epic economic shifts in motion. It was easier than ever to catch up, it asserted. Others had done so, why not Africa? Nigeria would move to double-digit growth and become a trillion-dollar economy by 2027. Sub-Saharan Africa outside South Africa would account for $4.5 trillion by 2030, assuming nominal GDP growth at ten per cent per annum, on a path of six to seven per cent real growth. This might even be conservative, it intimated – despite the heroic secular growth rates deployed.

Yet significant constraints lie in Africa's future. They include its antiquated economic paradigm, restrained net capital accumulation and investment deficits in industries and infrastructure. These are central to long-term growth, especially for unlocking natural capital in mineral-energy complexes, as well as in capitalist and pre-modern agrarian development. These limitations may constrain 'maximal growth rate' potential, placing a ceiling on feasible expansion.

Real annual growth at five per cent for 40 years that is uninterrupted or averaged will be a tough task. Demographics will not assist. Labour absorption in employment will be a major problem, with more informalisation the likely outcome.

Past long-cycle growth has taken decades to reach positive territory and slowly climb upwards. Interrupted economic cycles, not uncommon, have wreaked material damage on continental trajectories. None of this can simply be discounted in future.

Inherent curses on Africa's economic house still need to be confronted: weak nation state structures, failed and failing states, low competitiveness, poor productivity in land-agrarian assets, uncertainties about foreign investment, rising resource nationalism and the challenge of sustaining high rates of long-run real growth, with net capital accumulation built on unlocked natural capital.

Africa's states have yet to address the parasitic burden of growing parastatal dominance, with economic blight derived from defective models adopted years ago. Many state entities remain as throwbacks of flawed ideologies crafted generations before.

Relapse from growth paths has been Africa's albatross before. Measured images of Africa's future should not discount the past and present in the continent's future economic evolution.

Acha Leke is a Director at McKinsey & Company and runs the Lagos, Nigeria, office. His work includes investment and growth strategies, business building, turnarounds and economic development across sub-Saharan Africa. He is also a co-founder and board member of the African Leadership Academy and a co-founder of the African Leadership Network.

Mutsa Chironga is Associate Principal in McKinsey's sub-Saharan office. He previously worked at the World Bank in Washington DC and as an economist for the United Kingdom Government.

They are co-authors of *Lions on the Move*.

AFRICA'S GROWTH STORY

ACHA LEKE & MUTSA CHIRONGA

The world now recognises that Africa has taken a big economic step forward. Real GDP growth averaged 4.7 per cent per annum between 2000 and 2010, almost double the rate of the preceding decade. This makes Africa the world's second fastest growing region – second only to Asia and growing at the same rate as the Middle East. Interested observers, including our clients, have started asking whether this uptick in growth is real and driven by fundamentals, or something transient.

To help address this question, in 2010 McKinsey & Company published a report on African economies called *Lions on the Move: The progress and potential of African economies*. Our report came to four vivid conclusions:

- Africa's increasing growth is about more than just resources
- Africa's future growth potential remains strong
- The growth opportunities and challenges vary widely across Africa's 54 countries
- Africa will present an eye-popping $2.6 trillion business opportunity by 2020 ($1 trillion more than in 2008) across four sectors – consumer-facing industries, infrastructure, agriculture and resources

Since then, many other publications and reports have agreed that things have changed in Africa, and that there is a real business opportunity on the continent. Several consultancies – for example Monitor, Boston Consulting Group and Ernst & Young – have published reports on Africa.

Harvard Business Review published an article on Africa by the authors of this article and perceptions about Africa have clearly undergone a major positive shift in recent years.

Africa's economic growth accelerated after 2000

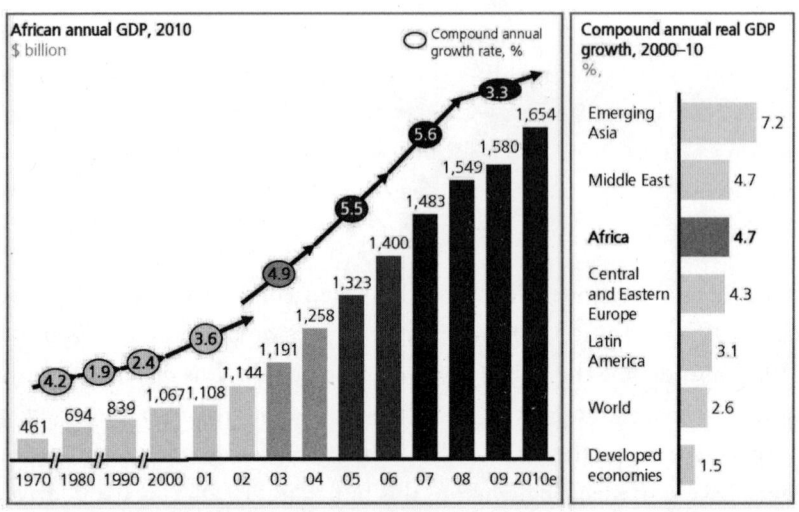

African annual GDP, 2010 ($ billion)	Compound annual growth rate, %
1970: 461	4.2
1980: 694	1.9
1990: 839	2.4
2000: 1,067	3.6
01: 1,108	4.9
02: 1,144	
03: 1,191	
04: 1,258	5.5
05: 1,323	
06: 1,400	
07: 1,483	5.6
08: 1,549	
09: 1,580	3.3
2010e: 1,654	

Compound annual real GDP growth, 2000–10 (%)

Region	%
Emerging Asia	7.2
Middle East	4.7
Africa	4.7
Central and Eastern Europe	4.3
Latin America	3.1
World	2.6
Developed economies	1.5

SOURCE: International Monetary Fund; Global Insight; McKinsey Global Institute

We will briefly revisit the main findings of *Lions on the Move*, before discussing two challenges Africa faces: the need for growth to be more inclusive, especially in creating jobs; and the risk of a global slowdown (potentially catalysed by a euro crisis) dampening Africa's growth prospects.

REVISITING *LIONS ON THE MOVE*

More than just a resources boom

Africa has benefited from the past decade's surge in commodities prices. For example, oil rose from less than $20 per barrel in 1999 to touch highs of more than $145 in 2008 and has retained its relative strength ever since.

But natural resources, and the government spending they financed, generated just 32 per cent of Africa's GDP growth from 2000 to 2008. The remaining two-thirds came from other sectors – including wholesale and retail, transportation, telecommunications and manufacturing. Indeed, economic growth accelerated across 27 of Africa's 30 largest economies, with GDP growing at similar rates in countries with significant resource exports and in those without.

Major reasons behind this growth surge included government actions to end armed conflicts, improve macroeconomic conditions and undertake microeconomic reforms to create a better business climate. The number of countries in serious conflict (defined as causing 1,000 deaths or more per annum) halved from five to 2.5 during the 2000s. African countries' average inflation rate fell from 22 per cent in the 1990s to eight per cent after 2000. And most African governments increasingly adopted policies aimed at energising markets. They privatised state-owned enterprises, increased trade openness, lowered corporate taxes, strengthened regulatory and legal systems and started putting in place critical physical and social infrastructure. Nigeria, for example, privatised more than 116 enterprises between 1999 and 2006.

Together, these structural changes helped to fuel an African productivity revolution. After declining through the 1980s and 1990s, the continent's productivity has started growing again, averaging 2.7 per cent growth since 2000 – gains that have been replicated across countries and sectors.

Continued growth, despite some lingering risks

One critical question is whether Africa's growth surge since 2000 represents a one-time event or a sustainable economic take-off. Africa's growth also picked up during the oil boom of the 1970s, but slowed sharply when oil and other commodity prices collapsed during the subsequent two decades. Today, however, while there are still short-term risks and individual countries may suffer setbacks, Africa's long-term growth prospects are strong, propelled by both external trends in the global economy and internal changes in Africa's domestic society and economy.

Private capital inflows surged during the 2000s, from $15 billion in 2000 to $90 billion in 2007. Despite a slight dip during the global financial crisis to $64 billion in 2008, there has since been a strong rebound in capital flows, reaching $84 billion in 2009 and $85 billion in 2010. Africa now provides the second highest return to foreign direct investment (FDI) among emerging markets. We believe this helps explain the marked increase in private capital flows into the continent.

What is encouraging is that the decline in private capital flows in 2008 was not caused by a slump in FDI – stable in 2007–8 at $50 billion a year – but rather by volatility in portfolio capital flows. Such flows seesawed from positive – $15 billion in 2007 – to negative – $13 billion in 2008 – back to a positive $18 billion by 2010. Swings in this 'hot money' reflect not economic fundamentals but rather a general deterioration, during the global financial crisis, of investor sentiment towards emerging markets.

Interestingly, investment into Africa increasingly comes from emerging markets. For example, India has grown its share of FDI into Africa from one per cent in 2003 to 14 per cent in 2010; the Middle East increased its share from three per cent to 12 per cent, and China grew its share from one per cent in 2004 to ten per cent in 2010. Meanwhile, North America's share has shrunk from 31 per cent of African FDI in 2003 to eight per cent in 2010; the UK's share has fallen marginally from 12 per cent to 11 per cent, and France's share has dropped from ten per cent to eight per cent. Emerging market investors are thus increasingly important, between them providing 50 per cent of Africa's FDI.

A similar trend is evident in trade: more than 50 per cent of Africa's trade is now with emerging markets.

FDI into Africa is also concentrated in relatively few recipient countries. More than 50 per cent of Africa's FDI between 2003 and 2010 went to five countries: Egypt (16 per cent), Nigeria (12 per cent), South Africa (ten per cent), Algeria (eight per cent) and Angola (seven per cent). Add just another six countries, and you get to 80 per cent of Africa's FDI: Tunisia (seven per cent), Libya (six per cent), Morocco (six per cent), Ghana (three per cent), Mozambique (two per cent) and Kenya (two per cent).

In terms of sectors, 51 per cent of Africa's FDI is in resources: 38 per cent in oil and gas and 13 per cent in mining. This is unsurprising as these sectors are highly capital intensive and Africa is an important resource supplier globally. Another capital intensive sector, infrastructure and construction, accounts for another 23 per cent of Africa's FDI. Consumer-facing sectors account for at least 17 per cent as follows: telecoms (eight per cent), consumer (four per cent), financial services (four per cent) and retail (one per cent). Other sectors attracting a slice of FDI include tourism (four per cent) and manufacturing (two per cent).

In short, Africa is attracting growing private sector investor interest from a diversifying set of countries and in a wide range of sectors.

Rising African urban consumers will further fuel growth

Many Africans are joining the ranks of the world's consumers. In 2008 about 85 million African households had an annual income of $5,000 or more[1] – the threshold above which households start spending roughly half their income on non-food items. By 2020 there will be 128 million such households. Africa already has more 'global' households (those with incomes of $20,000 a year or more) than India does. This trend has seen many consumer-facing companies experiencing fast growth in Africa across sectors such as telecommunications, consumer packaged goods, consumer electronics and financial services.

By 2020 more than half of African households will have discretionary spending power

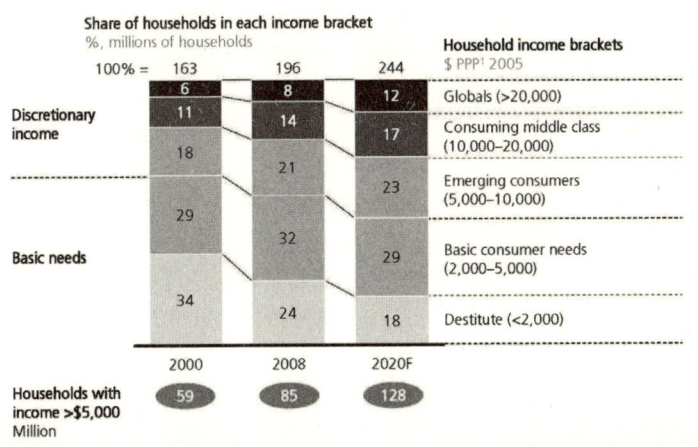

Share of households in each income bracket
%, millions of households

	2000	2008	2020F	Household income brackets $ PPP[1] 2005
100% =	163	196	244	
Discretionary income	6	8	12	Globals (>20,000)
	11	14	17	Consuming middle class (10,000–20,000)
	18	21	23	Emerging consumers (5,000–10,000)
Basic needs	29	32	29	Basic consumer needs (2,000–5,000)
	34	24	18	Destitute (<2,000)

Households with income >$5,000 Million: 59 | 85 | 128

1 Purchasing power parity adjusts for price differences in identical goods across countries to reflect differences in purchasing power in each country.

Africa's consumers are also increasingly concentrated. Urban dwellers have increased from 28 per cent of the total population in 1980 to 40 per cent today, a share comparable to China's and larger than India's. In absolute terms, between 2000 and 2010, 115 million Africans moved to cities – 26 million in Nigeria alone. Looking at a map of Africa's cities, it is clear there are large urban centres for consumer-facing companies to target.

---

[1] Measured in terms of purchasing power parity (PPP). This takes into account the relative prices of non-tradable goods in different countries.

AFRICA'S $2.6 TRILLION BUSINESS OPPORTUNITY

In *Lions on the Move*, we estimated that Africa would represent a $2.6 trillion business opportunity by 2020, $1 trillion more than today. The business opportunity is across four groups of sectors:

- *Consumer-facing.* We estimate these sectors will contain the largest opportunity in Africa, with a $1,380 billion revenue opportunity by 2020 – $520 billion more than today. The largest subsectors include food and beverages ($175 billion of the growth from 2008–20), housing ($101 billion) and non-food consumer goods ($62 billion). Some of the fastest growing subsectors are telecommunications (five per cent annual growth); and financial services (six per cent).
- *Agriculture.* Africa's agricultural potential is largely untapped. The continent has 60 per cent of the world's available arable land, but yields remain well below those in other regions. We estimate agriculture will represent a $880 billion opportunity by 2030, $600 billion more than today. This growth will be driven by better yields ($235 billion of the growth); more land under cultivation ($225 billion), and a shift from lower value crops such as cereal to higher value products such as horticulture and livestock ($140 billion). There are also adjacent opportunities in food processing ($239 billion by 2030) and inputs ($35 billion by 2030).
- *Infrastructure.* Africa's infrastructure levels are well below those of the original BRIC (Brazil, Russia, India, China) countries. For example, 39 per cent of Africans have access to power, compared to 84 per cent in those BRIC states. Infrastructure spending during the 2000s averaged $72 billion a year, compared to an estimated need of $120 billion a year. But governments are increasingly committed to infrastructure investment, supplemented by private sector participation that is growing at 13 per cent per annum. By 2020, infrastructure should be attracting $200 billion in investment per annum, $130 billion more than today.
- *Resources.* As the global race for commodities continues, we expect Africa will continue to be a big beneficiary. African countries are well placed on the global cost curves for the extraction of many commodities, including oil and gas, coal and iron ore – between them making up 85 per cent of Africa's resource production. We estimate Africa's total resources opportunity will be $540 billion by 2020, $110 billion more than today.

Four industry groups could have combined revenue of $2.6 trillion by 2020

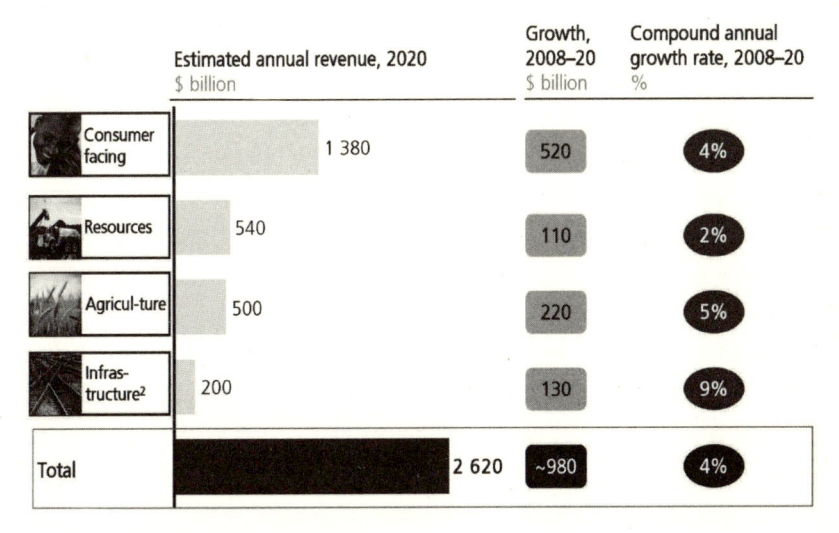

	Estimated annual revenue, 2020 $ billion	Growth, 2008–20 $ billion	Compound annual growth rate, 2008–20 %
Consumer facing	1 380	520	4%
Resources	540	110	2%
Agriculture	500	220	5%
Infrastructure[2]	200	130	9%
Total	2 620	~980	4%

1 Took 2030 value of $880 billion and calculated straight line equivalent for 2020.
2 Represents investment. Assumes need remains as same share of GDP through 2020.

These business opportunities are attracting many companies to Africa, now including 230 companies with revenues exceeding $1 billion. Many are global household names – there are 42 *Fortune* 100 companies in Africa, such as General Electric, Siemens, Proctor & Gamble, LG, Carrefour, Vodafone and Ford.

TWO CHALLENGES ON THE HORIZON

African economies have made real progress and display enormous future potential – companies and investors are realising this and showing increasing interest. But, to reach their full potential, they will have to navigate two big challenges in the next decade or two – one international and one domestic.

The risk of contagion from a slowing global economy

Africa, like all other regions, is exposed to the global economy. And the world economy is in a difficult place in light of the eurozone crisis, sluggish economic growth in the US and marginal declines in growth projections for China and India relative to the past decade.

There are three factors to consider when looking forward:

- Firstly, Africa's growth did not fall much during the global financial crisis of 2007–10. Growth was a respectable 3.3 per cent during 2008–10 and Africa was the third largest absolute source of economic growth in the world during this period, after India and China.
- Secondly, projections of Africa's growth have fallen, but not crashed. In 2010 the International Monetary Fund's World Economic Outlook projected Africa's 2011 growth would be 5.5 per cent. In 2011, it reduced this forecast to 4.7 per cent. And in 2012 it projected 4.9 per cent.
- Thirdly, Africa has diversified its trade and FDI sources – Western Europe's share of trade with Africa fell from 51 per cent to 28 per cent, while Africa's share of trade with emerging markets grew. So Africa has increased its exposure to emerging markets – those parts of the world economy projected to do relatively better over the next decade.

African governments should continue pursuing prudent fiscal and monetary policy – areas which saw marked improvement on average across the continent in the first decade of the 2000s. For example, oil exporters should continue to budget based on prudent oil price assumptions, as in Nigeria where the government budgets according to a price of $70 per barrel even while global oil prices remain well in excess of $100 per barrel.

Maintaining stability and avoiding jobless growth

Africa's second challenge is domestic. When we wrote *Lions on the Move*, we warned that Africa's growth outlook depended on continued political stability. A few months later the Arab Spring struck Tunisia, Libya and Egypt and has since spread across the region. A fundamental driver of that phenomenon has been autocratic, and in some cases, repressive regimes. Thankfully, many African countries moved to much more democratic governance in the 2000s, including Nigeria, Ghana, Tanzania, Zambia and Côte D'Ivoire. In all these countries, we have seen a change in leadership at the ballot box.

But a second underlying driver of the Arab Spring was lack of economic opportunity for young people. Mohamad Bouazizi, who sparked the Arab

Spring by setting himself alight in Tunisia, was frustrated and humiliated at losing his right to sell his goods at the market, the only livelihood he had managed to secure. This is the type of challenge millions of people in Africa face. Overall, African unemployment averages nine per cent, which is comparable with many other regions, in particular Europe and the US. But unemployment is exceedingly high in some African countries (for example in South Africa, at 25 per cent). And current demographic projections suggest Africa can expect an additional 600 million people to join its workforce by 2040.

Job growth has so far just about kept pace, but in future Africa will need to focus even more on creating economic opportunity for its young people and preparing them to be productive members of the workforce. We showed in *Lions on the Move* that there has been some progress in primary and secondary school enrolment rates, but even educated Africans cannot find employment. In a sample of African countries that included Algeria, Egypt, Ethiopia, South Africa and Senegal, unemployment among those with tertiary education was 17 per cent.

This suggests the solution will not only involve improving the availability and quality of formal education. Also required will be a combination of on-the-job up-skilling (supply side), lower wage levels (market clearing) and faster growth in job-creating sectors such as retail and wholesale and construction (demand side).

Over and above creating jobs overall, Africa also needs to reduce the share of its jobs in so-called 'vulnerable' employment – employment that is not salaried and is often informal or located in subsistence agriculture. Vulnerable jobs represent 68 per cent of all Africa's employment, compared to 28 per cent in Latin America.

At Africa's current pace of reducing the share of vulnerable employment (0.5 percentage points per year), reaching Latin American levels could take more than 70 years. But if Africa matches East Asian countries' rate of reduction in vulnerable employment, the gap with Latin America could be closed within 30 years. In this area, as in others, Africa could benefit from a careful study of policies adopted by leading emerging market economies elsewhere.

TURNING THE CORNER

Africa has turned an important corner and its prospects are bright. Even through the global economic downturn of 2008–9, Africa performed relatively well on economic growth and investor interest has now returned to pre-crisis levels. Furthermore, several domestic and international trends are adding wind to Africa's economic sails.

African governments must, however, navigate two challenges – limiting the impact of a potential long downturn in the world economy through prudent fiscal and monetary policy, and creating the enabling environment to give young Africans meaningful future employment and livelihoods.

If these challenges are adequately addressed, Africa is likely to continue its trajectory of increased opportunity for businesses and individuals – and ultimately its strong growth relative to most other regions of the world.

Article references

Charles Roxburgh, Norbert Dorr, Acha Leke, Amine Tazi-Riffi, Arend van Wamelen, Susan Lund, Mutsa Chironga, Tarik Alatovik, Charles Atkins, Nadia Terfous, Till Zeino-Mahmalat, 'Lions on the Move – the progress and potential of African economies', McKinsey Global Institute 2010

Acha Leke, Susan Lund, Arend van Wamelen, *Lions on the Move – the progress and potential of African economies*, McKinsey Quarterly 2010

Dr Lyal White is founding director of the Centre for Dynamic Markets (CDM) at Pretoria University's Gordon Institute of Business Science (GIBS) – an internationally accredited business school based in Johannesburg. It is the only business school in Africa ranked in the *Financial Times* global ranking of executive education. The CDM is the only centre of its kind in Africa. White is also a Senior Lecturer at GIBS, where he teaches in the area of political economy and strategy in Africa, Asia and Latin America.

AFRICA: THE WEST AND THE REST

LYAL WHITE

Brazilian soap operas such as *Insensato Corazao* and *Passione* are among the most popular shows on Angolan television, popularising Brazilian fashion and culture – and goods that have yet to make it to African shops, but which are snapped up by wealthy Angolans on their trips across the Atlantic.

With more than 100 Brazilian firms operating in Angola, Brazilian products and services are becoming household names and available in the supermarkets of Luanda and elsewhere in the rapidly growing petrostate.

Angolans today claim a closer cultural affinity with Brazil than with their former colonial master, Portugal. In an ironic twist, in 2011 a recession-hit Portugal turned to its former colonies for investment and financial assistance. Angola agreed to buy up Portuguese state assets and Brazil considered contributing to bail-out packages.

Brazil's relationship with Africa extends well beyond Angola, with its global companies eyeing and exploiting the many opportunities on the continent. Roger Agnelli, the former president of Brazilian mining giant, Vale, once said, 'Africa is the new frontier of natural resources ... and the future of Vale'. He insisted that the continent would be a different place in the future and Vale wanted to be part of that future.

When the Angolan government speaks of the $20 billion of infrastructure investment required to bring the country up to speed, it is likely it has Brazil and China in mind to fund and build that infrastructure. Both countries already have a significant presence in Angola and are playing important roles in rebuilding it after the devastation of decades of civil war.

Africa has become the last big opportunity for global firms to grow their market share. After the four original BRIC countries, Africa is regarded as the most exciting investment destination of the next decade for global investors. The continent is well placed to benefit from the growing economic strength of the BRIC countries themselves and other rapidly growing dynamic markets. Africa's largely untapped resources, growing consumer markets and infrastructure deficits are attractive to companies from Asia, Latin America and the Middle East, and to investment funds looking for good returns in emerging markets.

THE BRICS

Statistics tell the story of a changing global order that is symbolised by the BRICS trade grouping, which since 2011 has included South Africa. The member states make up about 18 per cent of international trade and contribute 25 per cent of global GDP. Trade among BRICS countries, which was $27 billion in 2002, was expected to reach $250 billion in 2012. BRICS was responsible for more than half of the world's growth in 2012, according to analysts.

The growth of trade between African countries and new emerging market investors has been remarkable. Trade between Africa and the four original BRIC nations increased from just one per cent of Africa's total trade in 2000 to more than 20 per cent by 2012. The BRIC bloc is now Africa's largest trade partner, with total trade reaching more than $120 billion in 2011.

While Africa's trade with India and Brazil has grown around sevenfold since 2000, each still represents just a quarter and a fifth respectively of Chinese trade with the continent.

However, it is noteworthy that China's loan portfolio to African countries far outweighs its actual investments. According to a Fitch Ratings report released in December 2011, the largest Chinese lenders to Africa are China's Export–Import Bank (EXIM) and China Development Bank (CDB). It estimates that between 2001 and 2010 China EXIM loans to sub-Saharan Africa reached $67.2 billion, overtaking World Bank lending, which was $54.7 billion to Africa for the same period.

Investment growth has followed a similar trend, drawing in companies from a diverse array of industries and geographies. Foreign direct investment in Africa from BRIC nations is expected to double in the five years to 2017. FDI is still largely focused on resource extraction. In 2010, for example, Brazil was responsible for nearly 30 per cent of mining investments in Africa, followed by China (13 per cent), Australia (ten per cent) and South Africa (nine per cent). However, there is growing diversification, particularly with investment from India.

In 2012 China's FDI in Africa stood at about $50 billion, India's at about $30 billion and Brazil's at nearly $20 billion, with each country having grown its investments at a rate of between 50 and 80 per cent per year over the previous decade.

Non-traditional investors from other countries are also looking for business and acquisition opportunities. They include the United Arab Emirates, South Korea, Turkey, Malaysia and Argentina.

THE WEST

For all the changing scenarios, Africa's historical links with developed countries in the West remain strong. European countries, particularly France, and the US have the largest share of investment in Africa. At last count, the EU accounted for as much as 40 per cent of Africa's total investment stock.

American companies are large investors in mining and oil extraction and 37 per cent of Africa's non-oil exports still go to European markets, with almost a third of Francophone African countries' trade still being with France. Many European companies are increasing investment in their African assets. But, as competition grows, traditional investors on the continent are likely to lose market share.

Research conducted by Standard Bank in 2011 calculated that, out of a total of 3,062 investment projects in Africa between 2003 and 2009, 763 were US and French projects and 287 were British projects. Although South Africa and China had only 96 and 86 projects respectively, the investment growth from these countries was more than double that from the traditional investors.

The developed countries are looking for new ways to exploit their 'soft power' in Africa through aid programmes, effective diplomacy, historical links and other measures. They are being forced to review their foreign policy priorities and initiatives in the region in order to maintain relevance.

A NEW APPROACH TO AFRICA

The new investors in Africa have a high appetite for risk, ready capital to deploy and strong political support from their governments. The continent has provided an opportunity for them to broaden their international footprint and experience.

Innovative business practices and fresh thinking are their trademark qualities, forged by their experience of challenging environments in their own back yards, which are often similar to those they find in Africa.

They are also building strong relationships at government-to-government level, using high-powered diplomacy and displaying long-term commitment to their chosen investment destinations, thus gaining the trust and confidence of African leaders. Strategic partnerships have become essential as the competition for assets and resources increases.

Business innovation has helped emerging market investors to improve competitiveness and operational effectiveness in new markets, the success of which is premised on an acute understanding of the political, social and business peculiarities of different markets. The ability to combine business, development and politics through hard investments, credit lines, development assistance and rapid expansion are qualities that have helped them to succeed in African markets.

Brazil, for example, put a stake in the ground as early as 1975 when it became the first 'Western' government to officially recognise the MPLA government in post-independent Angola. Brazilian construction multinational, Odebrecht, took advantage of the diplomatic gesture by setting up an office in Luanda in the early 1980s, paving the way for other Brazilian companies to find a preferential footing in one of Africa's fastest growing markets.

Despite such historical ties, many emerging market companies are on a steep learning curve in Africa's complex markets, which are becoming more about sustainable development than the bottom line.

Likewise, British, French and US companies have deep roots in Africa, but the business environment they forged is changing rapidly, and they too will have to change with it if they are to remain competitive.

As the dynamic market multinationals move into areas of business long dominated by companies from developed countries, new rivalries and competition emerge. There is already a debate about whether the terminology of 'developed' and 'developing markets' and 'traditional' and 'non-traditional' investors is outdated, so rapidly has the landscape changed. Even the notion of 'emerging markets' might be reaching its sell-by date since many of them are driving global economic growth.

African governments that are accustomed to aid-dominated discourse are being wooed by a range of new actors offering them not just investment, but generous credit lines, infrastructure deals and other sweeteners in exchange for their resources. Countries looking for development finance are no longer at the mercy of Western-dominated financial institutions.

This puts African countries in a favourable negotiating position. States with strong institutions and which develop a diplomatic sophistication capable of dealing with myriad actors, interests and activities will be able to derive benefits from multiple regional powers simultaneously.

THE NEW MULTINATIONALS

Which are the new companies putting down stakes in Africa? What are the names behind large infrastructure, mining, construction and other projects springing up around the continent?

One of them is Petrobras, Brazil's state-owned oil and gas company, which is exploring the entire western seaboard of Africa. Its $250 billion market capitalisation makes it the largest company in the Southern Hemisphere. It is well placed to develop deepwater oil reserves around Africa given its expertise in the Atlantic, where it is spearheading the move into offshore pre-salt oil and gas deposits.

Vale, the world's second largest mining company by market capitalisation, after BHP Billiton, is quickly becoming a household name in Africa's corporate world as it forges ahead with mega-projects in Guinea (iron ore) and Mozambique (coal). In 2012 Vale's total investments in Africa exceeded $4 billion and they continue to grow as the company seeks further opportunities. It is building a copper mine in Zambia, for example, and investigating possibilities in Democratic Republic of Congo, Gabon and other places. It plans to invest $12 billion in Africa by 2016.

Odebrecht, the construction and engineering company with interests in energy, agriculture and even retail, is the largest construction firm in Mozambique, working with Vale on its giant Moatize coal project, and one of the top four construction players in Africa. With more than 30 years' experience in Angola, Odebrecht is the largest private sector employer in that country. But its interests extend well beyond Lusophone Africa, and it has championed projects in Liberia, Libya, Djibouti and other countries. In 2011 Odebrecht opened a regional office in South Africa to gain better access to new markets in Southern and East Africa.

Chinese investors tend to fall under the umbrella of state-run oil and gas companies or financial institutions, working closely with each other on projects. Flush with capital, they have built their political leverage in Africa through historical liberation era ties and substantial financial packages for investment in infrastructure, resources, telecommunications and other sectors.

Some of the big players include China National Offshore Oil Corporation (CNOOC), EXIM bank, China Steel and the Industrial and Commercial Bank of China (ICBC), the largest bank in the world that acquired a 20 per cent stake in South Africa's Standard Bank in 2007 for $5.5 billion.

Although Chinese brands are not well known in Africa, an exception is perhaps telecommunications equipment manufacturer Huawei. Employing more than 110,000 people worldwide, Huawei has become a global company that has prioritised Africa in terms of product development, manufacturing and market access. In 2010, it invested nine per cent of its turnover in research and development in Africa, showing its commitment to a long-term presence on the continent.

Indian companies have long-standing commercial ties with Africa and also represent some of the largest investments in Africa in recent years with more projects than China, albeit mostly smaller ones. Their interests are multi-sectoral, covering services, pharmaceuticals, telecoms, mining, infrastructure and energy.

Companies such as Essar and Tata have long track records in Africa and continue to grow their footprints. But the Indian initiatives that have captured the headlines as a result of their size and scope include ONGC-Mittal Energy's $6 billion investment in Nigeria in 2005 and Bharti Airtel's acquisition of mobile phone company Zain's assets in 15 African countries for $10.7 billion in 2010. These transactions marked a new dawn for Indian corporate interests in Africa.

Just ten years ago, emerging market companies were relatively unknown outside their home countries. Today they are global players that are playing a role in shaping Africa's new economic landscape and are rapidly becoming household names.

WHERE DOES SOUTH AFRICA FIT IN?

South Africa has been a leading investor in Africa for the past two decades, with a diversified portfolio of investment, differentiating it from the resources-driven focus of both traditional and non-traditional investors. Research conducted by consulting firm Ernst & Young for its 2011 African Attractiveness Survey, titled *It's Time for Africa*, found that South Africa was still the top investor in ten of Africa's 15 most attractive economies.

These include Mozambique, Zambia, Kenya, Uganda, Ghana and Nigeria, countries in which South African companies dominate telecommunications, retail, financial services and tourism and have a presence in large-scale mining and construction projects.

While South African investment continues to grow on the continent, its companies are starting to lose market share to new rivals from dynamic markets. South African mining and construction firms, which have dominated these sectors in Africa by virtue of proximity and history, are finding it difficult to compete with firms from China, India and Brazil that are able to undercut their costs through their sheer size or through support from their governments and development banks back home.

Some of the fiercest new competition in the construction sector is coming from Chinese and Brazilian companies. China is a major price competitor for the South African companies and its builders do not face the same constraints in terms of shareholder concerns, labour laws and corporate governance principles. This allows them to come in as much as 30 per cent ower on bids for infrastructure projects.

South Africa has only recently started to look at ways to leverage its funding agencies' operations in African projects as part of a new economic strategy for the continent. It has also been slow to use diplomatic engagement to bolster its position in Africa for the benefit if its companies and parastatals, focusing instead on engagement with markets outside the continent, particularly since it became a member of the BRICS in 2011.

Its lack of an economic strategy is in contrast to the other BRICS nations, which have taken a much more aggressive diplomatic stance in Africa. For example, former Brazilian president Luis Inacio 'Lula' da Silva, who led Brazil's diplomatic *tour de force* on the continent, visited no less than 19 African countries on ten trips during his tenure and the country has doubled the number of its embassies in Africa. His dedication to economic diplomacy in Africa highlighted Brazil's long-term commitment to the continent and advanced the emerging giant's geostrategic and commercial interests.

Development banks in countries such as Brazil and China play a critical role in boosting business opportunities for their companies, linking funding of development initiatives to involvement by their companies. For example, Brazil's development banks, BNDES and Banco do Brasil, have extended credit lines to countries like Angola and Mozambique for infrastructure or agriculture development projects that involve Brazilian firms. This well illustrates the Brazilian approach to commercial expansion through development cooperation, which in turn builds trust and political leverage for Brazilian interests in Africa.

China has a similar approach, though its financial support and credit lines far outweigh those of Brazil. China's approach is also far more directly political.

Despite the lack of political support, South African companies remain a force to be reckoned with in specific sectors such as financial services, construction, ICT, hospitality and retail. However, the country will almost certainly continue to lose its competitive advantage in African markets if it does not sharpen its competitive edge. The government needs to improve its use of diplomatic leverage and develop a more coherent economic strategy that brings the state, the private sector and development banks together to promote South Africa's competitive advantage.

South Africa's future competitive advantage lies in services, and the country is well placed to provide the soft infrastructure and know-how of doing business in Africa in a cross-section of industries and sectors. Companies' experience and their footprint in Africa make them ideal acquisition targets for foreign multinationals still feeling their way on the continent. Several South African companies have formed partnerships with firms from Brazil, India, China, and elsewhere, to leverage joint opportunities on the continent. This trend is likely to grow.

South African law firms such as Webber Wentzel have a growing list of clients from Brazil, India and China. Odebrecht has worked with South African companies Murray & Roberts and Stefanutti Stocks (not to mention a number of smaller service providers, especially in Mozambique). Huawei works closely with mobile telephony operator MTN in various African markets. The most obvious example of this cooperative strategy is ICBC's stake in Standard Bank, which the state-owned Chinese bank effectively uses as its principal driver into African markets.

LOOKING AHEAD

As global growth and capital shifts from West to East, Africa will grow increasingly dependent on investment from dynamic market players in Asia, Latin America and the Middle East. With a small domestic market, Africa is reliant on foreign capital for growth and development. This may change over time, but for now the drivers of global economic growth will also be the principal drivers of investment and development in Africa.

Diversifying from Europe and the US helped Africa to emerge relatively unscathed from the downturn in 2008. But lingering debt problems in developed countries will have an impact on African markets. Both the US and Europe are important commercial partners and providers of aid to Africa. Europe is still collectively Africa's largest trade partner and a shortage of capital in Europe and the US will have a knock-on effect in African markets. A drop in demand from European countries and US consumers will make export markets in Asia and beyond that much more important for Africa.

Intra-African trade is still very thin and any slowdown in countries like China and Brazil would have a very negative affect on Africa, as will continuing debt problems in Europe.

While there are significant opportunities in resource extraction, infrastructure development and agribusiness, capital constraints in emerging markets may affect their appetite for Africa, with the potential for pressure from their governments to re-focus operations on the domestic market during difficult times. For example, Vale might have to cut back on its proposed long-term African investment of $12 billion due to political pressures at home.

Africa remains key to the rise of new economic powers. It is a principal provider of natural resources for industrialisation and development and is poised to become a critical source of food and agricultural products, not to mention a market for consumer goods from around the world. These dynamics are likely to drive ongoing investment in Africa despite the global economic slowdown.

As the new players from China, India, Brazil and other dynamic markets grow their investments and become more competitive in Africa, companies from Europe, the US and South Africa should look to engage with them. The real opportunity in Africa is through collaborative efforts.

Dr Greg Mills heads the Johannesburg-based Brenthurst Foundation, an economic think-tank focusing on strengthening Africa's economic performance. He is the author of many books including *Why Africa is Poor: And What Africans Can Do About It* and *Africa's Third Liberation: The Search for Growth and Jobs* (co-authored with Jeffrey Herbst).

UNDERSTANDING AFRICA'S COMPETITIVENESS CHALLENGE

GREG MILLS

Scarcely a week goes by without someone saying something positive about Africa.

At the end of 2011, *The Economist*'s cover story was 'Africa Rising', explaining why four of the world's fastest growing economies were from a continent only a decade earlier labelled by the same magazine as 'The Hopeless Continent'. It is not alone. At the start of 2012, the United Kingdom's *The Guardian* newspaper published an editorial entitled 'A fresh chapter is opening in Africa's history', while the *Financial Times*, hardly known for its hyperbole, followed suit with 'Why Africa is leaving Europe behind'. These stories are backed up by a welter of statistics, projections and news of fresh African business opportunities.

It is a refreshing change. Over the past five decades, African performance has been exceptionally poor. Over the 50 years from 1960, sub-Saharan African countries managed to increase their annual per capita income by little more than $200 (as measured in constant 2000 US dollars), to $636 by 2010.

The overall growth record of the continent can be broken into three periods: First, the immediate post-independence period, with a high point touching $600 in 1974. The drivers of this growth were the immediate post-independence redistribution plus high raw material prices.

African Per Capita Income, Constant (2000) US$

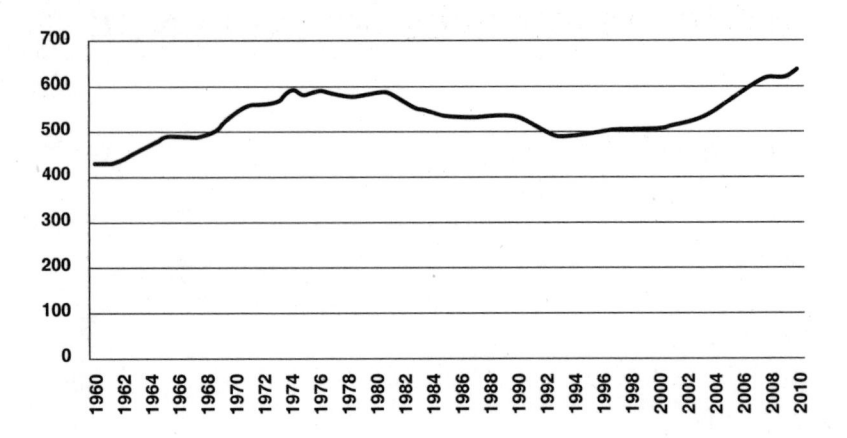

The second period was a protracted decline, the result of worsening (and increasing non-democratic) governance, military government and high oil prices. While Africa declined, other developing regions rapidly increased their incomes. This divergence was even the case among those countries, such as Indonesia and Nigeria, for example, that seemed on the face of things to share certain similarities – including ethnic diversity, colonial inheritance, war and instability, external intervention – yet had wildly differing performance records. This period of relative and absolute economic decline was especially traumatic for Africans. In contrast, the tipping point for the improving states seemed to be the moment that they decided on policies that delivered growth.

Now a third period, starting in 1994, has seen positive continental per capita economic growth, propelled by governance reforms, the end of several wars, relatively high raw material prices and, for the first time in decades, external investment. Although per capita income has increased to 1974 levels, a massive amount of time and effort has been devoted to simply playing catch-up. That the continent now seems poised for economic growth will not diminish the trauma of a generation of essentially stagnant economic performance.

The situation today proves, in part, that the richer the world gets, the harder it is to remain poor. But it also points to a change in political systems. Since the end of the Cold War, African countries have largely moved toward freer political systems, albeit at different speeds. In 1990, 70 per cent of African countries were considered to have 'unfree' political systems as classified by Freedom House. By 2010 more than two-thirds were 'free' or 'partly free'. Democracy has largely won the intellectual argument, even if the practice varies markedly from country to country. Even authoritarian countries like Robert Mugabe's Zimbabwe hold regular elections, albeit of problematic quality. Moreover, conflict is on the decline in Africa.

Overall, Africa's contemporary turnaround shows, fundamentally, that growth matters. A six per cent annual increase for a decade does make a difference, and begets stability and, in turn, further growth. Little wonder the number of African conflicts has declined threefold to just four today from the peak in the mid-1990s, though that should not obscure a new prominence by African, rather than foreign, peacemakers.

This economic upswing has little to do with charity. Remarkably, in just the mid-2000s, then British Prime Minister, Tony Blair, together with celebrity economists, including a chorus of aging pop-stars, led a campaign at the Gleneagles G8 summit to double aid to Africa as apparently the last and best hope of transforming the continent's fortunes. Yet, in an era of higher commodity prices and better governance, the debate over aid, which served to distort economic practices and the link of accountability between leaders and citizens, is now secondary. The focus has, refreshingly, shifted to the growth imperative and the need to reduce inequality by creating jobs, especially among the youth.

Of course growth alone is not enough for development, even though sustainable progress is impossible without it. Human development requires growth and, for example, female education and knowledge, perhaps the main driver in reducing child mortality. Sub-Saharan Africa also remains an exceedingly poor continent. The patterns of growth have been highly differentiated between states; some are richer, while others have failed.

This is, however, a positive phenomenon. It indicates that Africa is no longer one single category of countries, but, like other developing regions, is made up of performers, failures, small states (which usually perform much better in Africa) and large ones; along with landlocked, littoral, democratic (by now the overwhelming majority) and autocratic examples. In particular, Africa's larger countries (think of the Democratic Republic of the Congo) have generally had a poor development record since independence, which in part relates to the expanse of territory and complex make-up of their societies – many nations within a single state.

TEN COMPETITIVENESS CHALLENGES

There are other ongoing challenges which cannot be glossed over in the new-found hype about the continent. Addressing these is imperative to sustained growth.

The first challenge is that Africa's middle class is exceptionally small, less than one-sixth of the population in any country. The health of this segment is both an indicator of the spread of wealth beyond a tiny elite and a buffer against pressures from the top and the bottom. Put differently, it is the glue that moderates behaviour. A small middle class is not a recipe for stability and social cohesion, and it is not likely to make much of a dent in all-powerful elites that encourage the patronage-ridden system of government that has been at the heart of Africa's relative underperformance until now.

This relates to a second challenge: the vast majority of Africans, skilled and unskilled, lack formal sector employment. This situation is especially acute among the youth who comprise nearly two-thirds of sub-Saharan Africa's 800 million people. This cohort presents a tremendous development opportunity – large numbers of high-energy young people coming into the market at one time. But, for the opportunity to be realised, they need to be skilled and basic services have to be in place.

Diversifying economies away from natural resources and creating widespread employment remains hard to achieve given low skills levels, high costs of doing business and questionable policy choices. Despite improvements in growth and governance, Africa's ability to attract private investment, especially outside of the natural resources sector, lags behind other developing regions.

Breaking the cycle in which Africa has found itself will go hand-in-hand with a transformation to a high investment, high consumption economy.

Third, basic infrastructure lags. Profound technological changes in the form of digital communications have helped to push up contemporary growth rates. Whereas by the mid-1990s African telephone connectivity was just one-tenth of the global average, by 2010 it was half, even though the global figure had increased fourfold to 70 connections per 100 people.

While digital communication has enabled the 'cut-off' continent to be quickly connected, roads, ports, railways and airports take a while longer. Unlike telecommunications, infrastructure development requires circumventing the biggest obstacle of all to progress in Africa: recalcitrant and sometimes venal authorities. Urbanisation makes building new infrastructure critical. By 2025 more than half of the continent's people will live in Africa's cities.

Again, this offers great development opportunities in terms of economies of scale and concentration of labour, but the infrastructure facilities need to be in place. Africa's population is likely to increase threefold by 2100, to 3.5 billion (or 3.2 billion for sub-Saharan Africa), from just 250 million and 180 million respectively in 1950. The continent's leaders have to be planning now for the infrastructure needs of this number of citizens.

In particular, Africa faces a tremendous energy challenge. The entire electrical generation capacity of the 48 countries of sub-Saharan Africa is about equivalent to that of Spain. Two-thirds of this amount is, however, produced by one country: South Africa. Less than a quarter of the population of sub-Saharan Africa has access to electricity, versus about half in South Asia and more than 80 per cent in Latin America. At current rates, fewer than 40 per cent of African countries will reach universal access to electricity by 2050. This creates a significant development hurdle. Every extra megawatt of power provided can add as much as $3,000 to gross domestic product. Indeed, most high-growth economies are characterised by strong energy sector growth, stable prices and ongoing reforms.

But, fourth, the infrastructure challenge, especially in the short-term, is not just about money for roads, bridges, harbours, railways and power plants. Getting Africa to use more efficiently what it has already is equally, if not more, important. Instead of border posts that close at night, 24/7 operations should become the norm. Achieving this, however, demands breaking the cycle of self-interest that ensures that long queues at borders provide a means of income for those interested in local extortion rather than national trade.

Fifth, a new vision is required for regional integration. Changing such incentives and systems requires going beyond the standard focus on tariff adjustments as shorthand for regional integration across the continent to trade logistics. Summits that create highbrow agendas for common markets are no substitute for hands-on trade facilitation that ensures the free flow of traffic across borders.

Sixth, Africa's growth rates have traditionally tracked commodity prices. These have risen on the back of Chinese and Indian demands. What will happen if this demand, for whatever reason, diminishes? Africa will need to put in place the incentives that encourage beneficiation of natural resources. This should not, however, focus on punitive measures to ensure retention of these commodities in their natural state, but rather on the provision of competitive infrastructure to ensure their transformation, especially cheap and reliable energy.

And while Africa has benefited from the commodity boom, some countries have not done as well as they could have. South Africa stands out in this regard. A 2010 Citibank survey listed South Africa as the world's richest mining country in terms of its reserves, worth an estimated $2.5 trillion. Yet South Africa's mining sector declined at an average of one per cent per annum during the 2000s, when the top 20 mining producers globally grew annually at five per cent.

In 2011 South Africa's global share of greenfield mining projects was just five per cent. Australia's was 38 per cent. Instead of miners being allowed to do their thing, the 2000s' global resource boom became a missed opportunity for South Africa for a number of reasons, including power deficits.

Seventh, on average African countries currently have the highest corporate taxation rates worldwide, at more than 40 per cent. While this might not deter investors in mineral resources, given they have to go where these are, it is a significant disincentive to companies that can take their business anywhere. Labour intensive industries seek, for example, the sort of conditions that encourage employment on a mass scale of the type Africa requires. High tax rates; labour instability and costs, and discretionary systems of personal taxation vulnerable to individual whim and greed are not conducive to attracting the sort of investors countries need.

Much of the above relates, eighth, to the ever-present threat of populist political reactions and policies, especially where politics is fractious, politicians inept and populations impatient. In some cases, for instance Zimbabwe, this is radically destructive, in others less threatening. The further countries get from independence, the less the likelihood of and rationale for such policies. In all, however, it raises suspicions among foreign and some local investors.

Related to this, while democracy has spread, much of the continent remains suffocated by political-economies characterised by graft, cronycapitalism, rent-seeking, elitism and inevitably widening (and potentially destabilising) social inequality. Change from such a system is necessary to open up economic space for business to compete, which is necessary to expand employment.

Indeed, progress in other developing countries has been dependent on three factors: macro-economic stability, improving economic freedoms and the proportional use of government budgets to develop rural areas, hitherto neglected in the concentration of resources and political attention by African elites on cities.

Ninth, high unemployment levels are exacerbated by a lack of local skills in African economies and an antipathy towards importing sorely needed foreign skills. In an era where multiculturalism is not only preached but seen as a great strategic asset to societies, many states in Africa appear to be moving in the opposite direction.

From Côte d'Ivoire to Zambia, questions are posed about what constitutes 'nationality' and there are debates about who qualifies to stand for president. Far from bringing energy and skills and improving competitiveness, immigrants are seen as taking away jobs. Africa remains autistically 'zerosum' in its outlook towards trade and people. Perhaps this is understandable where jobs are scarce and where African states comprise many nations. But countries need to be thinking about how to attract the necessary skills, putting in place immigration ministries to attract the right sort of foreign entrepreneurs.

Finally, tenth, Africa's private sector remains small and vulnerable to political whim. Outside of the natural resources sector, African entrepreneurs battle in global markets. Private capital flows to Africa lag compared to other regions. When African politicians actively promote the private sector without vested interests, the continent could be said to have truly turned a corner.

Tony O Elumelu, MFR, is the Chairman of Heirs Holdings, an African proprietary investment firm that is committed to the economic transformation of Africa by generating long-term investments through economic prosperity and social wealth in a number of sectors, including financial services; healthcare; real estate and hospitality; oil and gas; and agriculture. He is also the founder of The Tony Elumelu Foundation, an Africa-based, African-funded, not-for-profit organisation dedicated to the promotion and celebration of excellence in business leadership and entrepreneurship. Prior to his retirement in July 2010, Elumelu was Group Chief Executive Officer of United Bank for Africa (UBA) in Nigeria.

BUILDING AFRICAN ENTREPRENEURS

TONY O ELUMELU

A population of more than a billion people, with a growing number under the age of 25, opens up the prospect of an exciting future for Africa.

These factors mean the continent is ripe for the entry of global businesses that are clamouring for opportunities presented by millions of new consumers with diverse needs. However, many of these international prospectors have been discouraged by the vast infrastructural and environmental challenges of doing business in Africa. The African private sector is waking up to the fact that Africans themselves should be building businesses and developing the continent. Among these one billion people are many thousands of potential entrepreneurs and business leaders who can positively transform the economic landscape.

For this reason I continue to preach my philosophy of 'Africapitalism', which calls for the African private sector's commitment to economic transformation through investments that generate economic and social wealth. Africapitalism is not capitalism with an African twist, it is a rallying cry for the private sector to take a leading role in driving Africa's growth story and for governments to play their role by providing a sound enabling environment for this growth to flourish.

A DIFFICULT PAST

Africa has had to deal with many crises over the years: political instability in countries led by authoritarian and dictatorial governments; the rise of warlords and sub-regional anarchy; weak institutional structures and endemic corruption within governments; a lack of accountability by leaders and low voter confidence; poor public finance management, and inefficient and rundown state enterprises.

There have also been serious macro-economic challenges. Many countries operated as mono-product economies and some had the worst debt profiles in the world. High interest rates, weak monetary policies and spiralling inflation stifled growth and industries struggled in difficult operating environments.

Countries grappled with some of the world's highest unemployment and lowest literacy rates, weak and volatile exchange rate regimes, and poor internal revenue generation mechanisms. In past decades, this environment made it difficult for investment and entrepreneurship to thrive.

BREAKING DOWN BARRIERS

Things are changing. We now see greater political stability in many countries and the implementation of democratic structures. There has been a significant reduction in political coups and military administrations are now deemed unacceptable. Most of the long-running wars in West and Central Africa have ended.

Corruption and malpractice are being tackled in many places and significant economic reform is taking place with the privatisation of government enterprises and the liberalisation of key sectors, as well as strategic efforts to improve the ease of doing business. Although inflation continues to be a challenge, there has been a broad downward inflationary trend over the past few decades, positive GDP growth for more than a decade and a reduction of debt as a percentage of GDP. More proactive interest rates and monetary policy regimes have been put in place.

A greater commitment to economic reform by business and governments has boosted growth and we are seeing the benefits of increased intra-regional activities. More businesses from West Africa are penetrating East African markets and some from the east are now heading west. Southern African companies are increasing their activities across the rest of Africa and are themselves seeing investment from other parts of the continent.

African companies are playing a role in breaking down the barriers to regional trade that have historically undermined the continent's integration and potential. The new pan-African companies are improving neighbouring economies with capital infusions and the development of products and services specifically designed for the African marketplace.

AFRICANS IN CONTROL

The growth of African multinationals is also changing the way the continent is viewed. We see some of these companies making their mark in the global arena as well. Many local business success stories have become household names, such as United Bank for Africa, MTN, Standard Bank, Shoprite, Dangote Industries, the Bidvest Group, Celtel and Bidco, as well as the Nollywood film industry in Nigeria. The image of a war-torn and epidemic-stricken region with little hope and in dire need of aid is slowly being replaced by images of a continent full of business and investment opportunities.

The economic turnaround in Africa is also changing mindsets. Africans are finally starting to believe in their own continent with many in the Diaspora returning home as the global crisis narrows their opportunities for employment abroad. Many African entrepreneurs are investing at home rather than taking their money abroad and there is a move towards adding value to those investments that has resulted in the creation of more sophisticated businesses, rather than just companies importing finished goods or executing government procurement contracts.

RECONSIDERING THE BOTTOM LINE

The new thinking also looks beyond business deals to the social and environmental impact of economic activity. It is thinking that goes beyond a consideration of just 'doing no harm' and seeks ways for business to create a positive social and environmental impact even while making a healthy financial return.

The Tony Elumelu Foundation is spearheading philanthropic 'impact investing' in Nigeria. Impact investing is the use of for-profit investments to address social and environmental challenges. The foundation's inaugural impact investment, in conjunction with Heirs Holdings, was made in Mtanga Farms Limited of Tanzania. The deal, which may become a model for replication in other countries, touches the everyday lives of hundreds of thousands of low-income people in rural Tanzania by improving farmers' access to inputs, technology and markets. The investment will help to create infrastructure for farmers to get their products to markets and contribute to the development of the Southern Tanzanian Highlands, one of East Africa's most promising but least utilised areas of agriculture production. The investment will also go towards building a seed potato industry in the region, enabling increased yields and incomes for smallholder farmers through access to new seed potato varieties for the first time in decades.

The foundation goes beyond simply supporting profitable enterprises. It uses African capital to create a pipeline of entrepreneurs, while supporting imaginative business leaders whose ideas advance social prosperity. It also seeks to develop African innovation transfer, bringing advances from one part of the continent to solve problems in another.

We have joined a group of major foundations and large investors that have pioneered a rating system to measure the effectiveness of for-profit social enterprises, the Global Impact Investing Rating System. This encourages investment by providing an opportunity to benchmark and measure the social and environmental impact of an investment as clearly as the financial return.

PUBLIC-PRIVATE PARTNERSHIPS

Governments are increasingly seeing the need for a private sector-led model to catalyse growth and development. But African businesses and political leaders must support and learn from one another if they are to establish successful economic relationships and build world-class economies.

This partnership can take different forms depending on the specific sector or industry. But it will only work if it is a two-way conversation.

Three examples of where this has been highly successful come to mind. The first is Rwanda, where the government's focus on improving the ease of doing business has turned a small, landlocked, conflict-ridden, resource-poor and largely illiterate country into an attractive investment destination.

The second is Kenya, where the government's sharp focus on providing the enabling environment for an ICT-based knowledge economy has led to large investments in the country's ICT sector – to such an extent that we now hear it being described as a 'Silicon Savannah'.

The third is Nigeria, where financial sector reforms over the past decade have created a handful of strong banks that have moved beyond Nigeria's borders to drive economic growth across Africa. During my tenure as Chief Executive Officer at UBA we built a single Nigerian business into a pan-African bank with operations in 18 countries. This footprint has had a positive impact on development by creating the much-needed financial infrastructure to facilitate intra-regional trade, payments and investments. For the continent to grow, we need to see at least five similar companies emerging each year. Africa will be the better for it and it is not impossible.

It is important for African governments to put in place policies that incentivise and regulate institutional charitable investment to ensure that wealth created has a strategic social component. This can do for Africa what centuries-old laws, put in place in the US in its early stages of development, did to institutionalise charitable investments, underpinning that country's long-term economic success.

Africa's political leadership must become better aligned to the entrepreneurial aspirations of its people. The African Union (AU), which was founded in 1999 to replace the Organisation of African Unity (OAU) and which give the continent's umbrella body more relevance to present realities, can play a continent-wide enabling role for trade and investment that will throw open the doors of rapid economic development. But, for this to happen, Africa's political leadership must align itself with the entrepreneurial aspirations of its people.

UNLEASHING THE AFRICAN ENTREPRENEUR

Obstacles faced by African entrepreneurs are more onerous than those faced by their counterparts in most other parts of the world. Even if they are able to source equity to build their businesses, the funds may have to be used to buy a generator to provide power, sink a borehole or transport goods over bad roads. These problems, faced by millions of businesses across Africa, are costly and can sink many small companies, or even prevent them taking off in the first place.

But young entrepreneurs can overcome the challenges by working hard, committing themselves to a vision and building strong teams. Africa is in dire need of role models and those who have succeeded need to be elevated so that younger generations can strive to emulate them. We owe it to young, hardworking, intelligent, enterprising Africans to create a good and prosperous future; to give them hope; to allow them to learn from us, and to guide them in making sure they do not make the mistakes we made. One of my greatest joys would be to look back and say I have helped to create a hundred, or even just ten, very successful African entrepreneurs.

I call on all successful African entrepreneurs to start giving back to Africa and making a difference. We must join hands in the 21st century and ask ourselves where Africa will be ten years from now and what role each of us will play in getting it there.

Khanyi Dhlomo, based in South Africa, is Managing Director of Ndalo Media, which she founded in 2007. Ndalo's titles include business and lifestyle magazines *DESTINY* and *Destiny Man* and online offering destinyman.com. She is also founder of DestinyConnect, a women's business network. Prior to launching her own media company, Dhlomo served as Editor of *True Love* magazine for eight years and headed SA Tourism, a government agency, in Paris. In 2011 she made the *Forbes* list of 20 Young Power Women in Africa. She has an MBA from Harvard Business School.

MAKING A NOISE: AFRICA'S WOMEN IN BUSINESS

KHANYI DHLOMO

The past 50 years have been among the most transformative, in terms of changes to the socio-economic, political and technological global landscape. The digital age has accelerated the pace and scope of communication, consumerism and dissemination of information on continents that have the resources and expertise to keep up with the online race.

But this celerity is by no means experienced in all corners of the planet, particularly not in emerging economies in Africa, where poverty, political instability and deeply entrenched cultural values inhibit the access of populations to the global community. And in many of these populations women continue to struggle for equal participation.

AFRICA'S GLOBAL GENDER PROFILE

Research conducted in 2011 by South African research consultancy Intellidex showed a significant discrepancy between the genders among the wealthiest men and women in Africa. While 14 African men on the continent could lay claim to personal wealth of at least $1 billion, not a single woman possessed even half that amount.

In South Africa the wealthiest woman's fortune only just exceeded that of the country's tenth wealthiest man; this despite determined efforts by the government to narrow the gender gap, both in parliament and in boardrooms. What is more, a meaningful percentage of the continent's richest women still ascribe their wealth to inheritance or marriage, rather than to their own efforts. In other words, their money was made by men.

Stumbling blocks to women on the continent achieving true empowerment relate to a variety of factors, which are often interlinked and complex. They range from traditional social values to more Westernised (but equally deep-rooted) forms of chauvinism, patriarchy, lack of infrastructure and low education standards. The 2011 World Economic Forum on Africa highlighted the fact that the current population of the continent is one billion, representing only 15 per cent of the global population. However, this figure is predicted to increase to 2.2 billion by 2050 and 3.6 billion (49 per cent of the global population) by 2100, indicating the urgent need for the continent to catch up with international advances in technology and particularly cyber technology.

Women will have a key role to play in coming decades. However, fully two-thirds of the 774 million adult illiterates in the world are women. The World Economic Forum noted that in sub-Saharan Africa only 24 per cent of women have secondary education – the lowest proportion in the world. At the same time, their labour force participation, at 64 per cent, is the highest in the world, with women spending up to 40 billion hours a year on tasks such as fetching water and firewood.

Another huge obstacle is poverty, which is largely driven by population growth. It was pointed out in forum discussion that, while women globally have an average of 2.5 children, the average African woman has 4.5 children (and more than six in four African countries). Political instability and environmental degradation exacerbate this impoverishment.

Forum participants discussed the widespread existence of a culture of dependency among African women, with one Zambian participant stating that in her country, when a woman speaks out or challenges gender stereotypes, it is called 'making a noise' and inevitably leads to her becoming a social outcast.

In several African countries women still battle for the right to survival, let alone equality. In parts of Sudan and Nigeria, for example, girls are subjugated both psychologically (by being denied access to any but the most basic education) and physically (by being subjected to female circumcision). Further north, in countries such as Egypt, women considered aberrant or defiant continue to be victims of 'honour killings' by male members of their families.

These examples highlight the interface between the spiritual and financial economy in such societies, with women routinely denied a share of either.

FEMALE FOOTPRINTS

Despite – or rather because of – these impediments, advances made by women have been encouraging. A United Nations (UN) report entitled *The World's Women 2010* found while men's global participation in the labour market had declined steadily over 20 years, that of women remained steady. The *2010 World Economic Forum Gender Report* found that in two African countries, Botswana and Lesotho, gender parity had been achieved in education.

While occupational segregation and gender wage gaps remain significant, more and more corporates are including women in their boardrooms. In countries such as South Africa legislation is in place to thwart sexism and promote women, particularly those from previously disadvantaged sectors, into executive positions.

In *Fortune* magazine's 2011 rankings of the most powerful businesswomen in the world, Cynthia Carroll, CEO of mining conglomerate Anglo American, was ranked No 1, while another South African – Maria Ramos, CEO of banking group Absa – was ranked 14th. And on *Forbes*'s 2011 list of the world's 100 most powerful women, Ngozi Okonjo-Iweala, former Finance Minister of Nigeria, credited with liberalising her country's economy and securing a debt write-off of $18 billion from creditors, was ranked 87th. South African, Nonkuleleko Nyembezi-Heita, CEO of the South African arm of global steel company ArcelorMittal, was 97th.

This indicates that, while tokenism still weakens the executive muscle of women in Africa, women at the top of the corporate ladder in leading industries do wield real power, enjoy real credibility and achieve real results.

Nevertheless, female business leaders report the continued existence of a glass ceiling, often underpinned by surreptitious collusion and decision-making in 'old boys' clubs'). Black women executives face not only gender bias but racial prejudice and the problems associated with traditional cultural values, which demand deference towards elders and make it difficult for them to exercise authority in the workplace towards older, but subordinate, employees.

While corporations on the subcontinent are increasingly adopting a more enlightened and tolerant approach towards working mothers and particularly single ones regarding working hours, flexi-time is still far from the norm and remains a sometimes contentious issue that must be negotiated with management. Many women who succeed in making flexi-time a condition of their employment say they experience resentment and ridicule from male colleagues on this score.

One of the most striking impediments to African women's advancement in business – reported by women from all corners of the continent – is a lack of solidarity and support among their own sex. Far too many women who achieve leadership positions fail to play an active part in transferring either their skills or their empowerment to others and, in a disturbing number of cases, actually regard fellow women as professional rivals. There is a growing recognition of the need for mentorship and networking among women. In my own company, Ndalo Media, which offers regular workshops to aspirant and early-stage female entrepreneurs, we have seen a persistent and impassioned call for such guidance.

VIVE LA DIFFERENCE?

A strong case has been made for women's natural aptitude in business leadership, due to their inherent nurturing skills (which temper authority with sensitivity and compassion), their practicality and efficiency (honed over millennia of budgeting and financially managing households and communities), their skill at multi-tasking and their reliability and enterprise.

These natural attributes of women, aligned with their experience of economic and political repression, equip them to promote inclusive growth, eliminate obstructive and costly bureaucracy, streamline channels of command, delegate efficiently and promote corporate social responsibility initiatives within communities.

Nobel Peace Prize Laureate, Muhammad Yunus, who founded the Grameen Bank of Bangladesh in 1983 – an organisation that grants micro-finance to impoverished rural individuals without collateral (98 per cent of them women) – famously noted that indigent female breadwinners, with children and extended families depending on them, are invariably the hardest-working, most resourceful and most inventive recipients of aid. The adoption of women's banks in many countries in Africa echoes this line of thinking and indicates the eagerness of women around the continent to become economically active.

THE WAY FORWARD

The economic empowerment of African women, as well as the economic future of the continent, lies squarely in entrepreneurship. The past two decades have seen a tremendous upsurge of women opening their own ventures across a wide spectrum of activities, including agriculture, crafts, fashion, catering, event management, public relations, IT and tourism. In countries where women have access to the internet and have a functional knowledge of computers, online businesses have proliferated.

Apart from the attractive prospects of being able to schedule their own working hours, operate from simple or makeshift premises and base their businesses on their natural interests and skills, the potential for success and for creating jobs are huge incentives for women to launch their own ventures.

Many problems confront them. Primary among these are accessing financing, particularly in countries which forbid women from owning assets that can be used as collateral; receiving support from government and the corporate sector by way of networking, partnerships and mentorship, and basic training in business skills.

Much could be done by governments to facilitate the growth and confidence of these women:

- National programmes and partnerships should be introduced offering assistance and encouragement. In South Africa, a growing number of projects have been introduced for this purpose, from small business financing institutions to women's empowerment initiatives. A private-public partnership (Y-AGE) offers funding, membership and continued

support to entrepreneurs, with the proviso that successful candidates create at least 15 jobs in a specified timeframe.
- Cultural stereotypes and prejudices could be countered by education programmes, both at school and at community level, explaining the economic potential of women and their right to realise it. There might be stiff resistance, particularly from traditional ethnic and religious groups, but building just one generation of enlightened schoolchildren would be sufficient to effect a transformation.
- Government ministries can be created to focus on and promote the economic and educational empowerment of women in Africa. These do exist in a number of countries and are doing much to close the gender gap and fast-track female access to meaningful roles. In addition, awareness of women's empowerment is raised by initiatives such as the African Union's African Women's Decade, which kicked off in 2010 and has put women's issues on the front burner of legislation. However, the success of such initiatives depends largely on the buy-in and co-operation of other government bodies, the corporate sector and the public in order to create the required credibility for women advancing into prominent positions.
- As mentioned above, in my own company, Ndalo Media, we devote much of our energy to promoting entrepreneurship among women. This is reflected in *DESTINY*, our monthly national business and lifestyle publication for women in business; in our website, www.destinyconnect.com, which offers networking and forum capabilities for existing and aspirant businesswomen; in our regular workshops, where start-up and early-stage entrepreneurs are given practical, strategic advice by business experts and mentors, and in our involvement in initiatives aimed at uplifting and empowering women around South Africa. The response we have received from women of all ages who are eager for guidance and encouragement has been overwhelming. Adopting such a focused, purposeful approach to empowerment is crucial, both as an entrenched part of corporates' social responsibility initiatives and as a priority in both state and non-governmental institutions.

Finding a place in the sun begins with finding the confidence to believe in it, the courage to insist on it and, crucially, the voice to claim it. It is time for the women of Africa to make a noise.

Doug de Villiers is one of Africa's leading brand and reputational experts. As the CEO of Interbrand Sampson de Villiers, part of the global Interbrand group, he heads up brand reputation delivery in more than 23 countries in Africa. With multiple country brand projects in his portfolio, he has lived and worked in Australasia, Europe, North & South America and Africa and is a regular lecturer, researcher and commentator on brand building.

THE MAKING OF THE AFRICAN BRAND

DOUG DE VILLIERS

It is largely a fallacy that governments have the capability or responsibility to build country brands. If anything, governments are better at destroying a country's reputation along with its brand. A government's primary responsibility is to *enable* citizens and the private sector (through the provision of applicable systems, resources and skills) to perform optimally; and from optimal performance comes a positive reputation. In the BE>DO>SAY formula, it is the BE. It is a fact that reputation is built on what is done (BE) not what is said (SAY). So what is it with the continuous dialogue around 'Brand Africa'?

In talking about African brand issues, we need to look at how to change the reputation building approach from SAY>DO>BE to BE>DO>SAY.

When we look at recent research conducted by Interbrand Sampson on the reputation of Africa, we can clearly see that the global audience perceives that some countries generally contribute positively to the continent's reputation, while others do not. And some countries switch roles. In the survey, South Africa comes up as the most positive continental brand asset in Africa. But political activities and statements that reflect badly on the country's ability to manage itself and progress and the regular reports about corruption, for example, may quickly erode the image of the country, and therefore its brand.

Countries which build a positive image of Africa

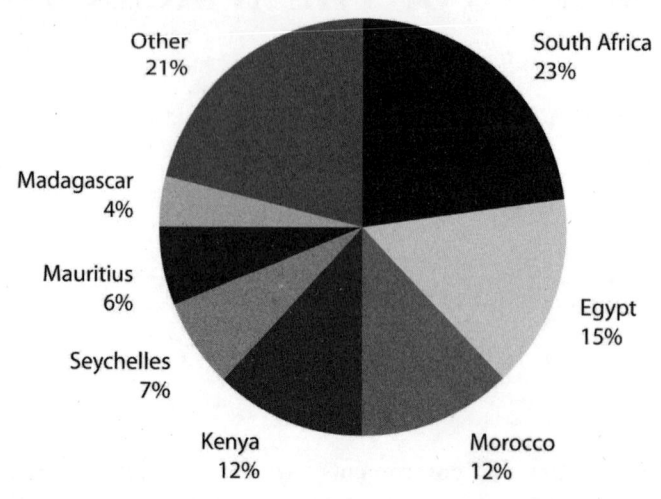

- Other 21%
- South Africa 23%
- Madagascar 4%
- Mauritius 6%
- Seychelles 7%
- Kenya 12%
- Morocco 12%
- Egypt 15%

Souce: Interbrand Sampson Survey

Like all brands in any category, the branding of a continent is made up of the collective country brands, which in turn are made up of a host of elements such as natural features (the beaches of Mauritius, Table Mountain in South Africa, Mount Kilimanjaro in East Africa, the Great Barrier Reef in Australia, etc); individuals (Nelson Mandela, Haile Gabreselassie, Richard Branson, Elvis Presley, etc); products and services (BMW, pasta, Sony, Chianti, Harvard, De Beers, Tusker, etc), and a host of historic places and activities (first man on the moon, apartheid, Machu Picchu, etc). In turn, each of these has specific attributes that define the brand.

Take Europe. Most of the countries there have very little in common other than geography. But the country brands are clear. Let us take Germany, for example. Germany – German engineering – precision – cars – BMW – luxury – wealth – 7 series. In the above example, the country brand was primarily built by the people of Germany and the products and services they delivered. Germany's vehicle brands have become so interlinked that just the vehicle brand alone can bring to mind the country: BMW/ Mercedes/Audi – cars – German engineering – Germany. These three brands alone have done more to build 'Brand Germany' than any government advertisement has. The government has, of course, provided and supported the growth of the brand reputation but it has acted as an enabler, not a controller.

In the case of Italy (or France), the country's brand is less tangible but equally distinctive. The country is associated with a passion for life, food, wine and romance. But it also has a positive vehicle brand in Ferrari. If anything, the government brand attributes, certainly in the person of the former Prime Minister, Silvio Berlusconi, who left in disgrace after 20 years in power, have been negative.

With a much shorter economic history, African countries have more in common perhaps than European countries, but many of the commonalities are negative continent brand factors and include disease, poverty, colonialism, racism, dictatorships and conflict. Some of the potentially positive attributes have a negative downside, for example 'blood diamonds' or the 'curse' of oil.

A continental reputation survey conducted by Interbrand Sampson in Africa showed that the world still views Africa in a primarily negative light. The results from respondents of what comes to mind when they think about Africa is indicated in the graphic below.

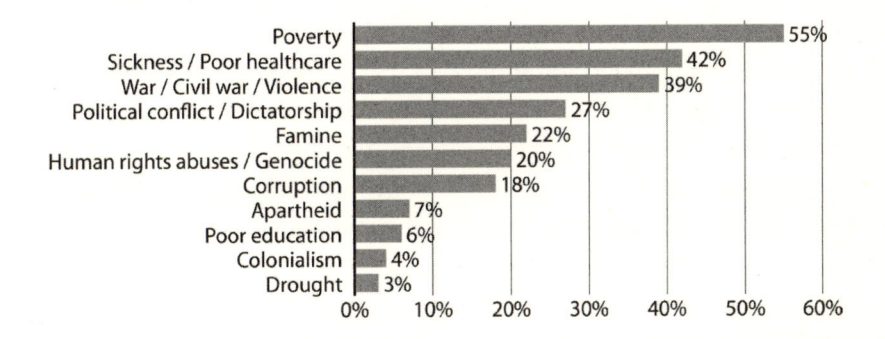

Attribute	Percentage
Poverty	55%
Sickness / Poor healthcare	42%
War / Civil war / Violence	39%
Political conflict / Dictatorship	27%
Famine	22%
Human rights abuses / Genocide	20%
Corruption	18%
Apartheid	7%
Poor education	6%
Colonialism	4%
Drought	3%

That said, there were still a host of positive natural attributes listed by respondents, with tourism way out in front. Sport and cultural issues are also top of the list, but business sectors, companies, and African manufactured products hardly feature. Simply put, Africa is known for what it has always had, natural beauty, and has added very little to its basket of attractions in recent times.

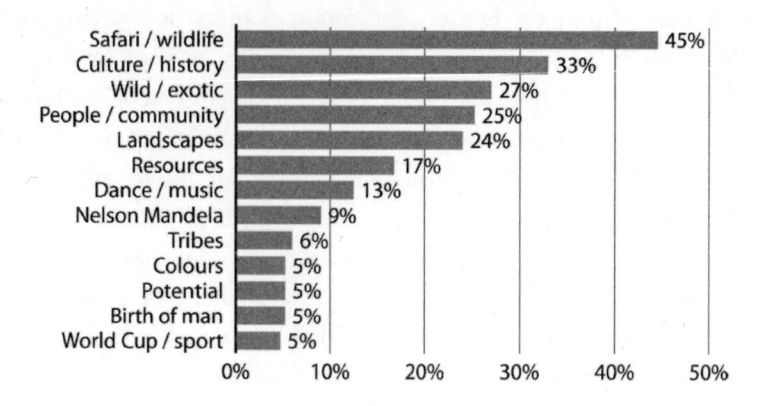

Category	Percentage
Safari / wildlife	45%
Culture / history	33%
Wild / exotic	27%
People / community	25%
Landscapes	24%
Resources	17%
Dance / music	13%
Nelson Mandela	9%
Tribes	6%
Colours	5%
Potential	5%
Birth of man	5%
World Cup / sport	5%

The reality is that Africa's brand can and will only be positively developed by the activities of individuals who have been enabled by governments and resources to build brands and reputations from the bottom up. The African brand cannot be built by an advertising campaign (the SAY) despite the high spending on glossy country features in international books and magazines by many governments.

Many nations around the world have put 'country brand' campaigns in place in order to position their countries in a competitive manner for multiple audiences such as investors, tourists and citizens. These country brand units are critical in providing the basis for the development of a country's reputation. But, it is important that they do not become propaganda machines and that they can back up what they reflect as being the advantages of their country.

History has shown time and time again that propaganda is not a relevant, believable or sustainable option to promote anything. In fact, any brand that purports to be something that it is not makes a promise it cannot credibly deliver. This is likely to have the opposite effect of what is intended and could instead incur serious reputational damage that it may take a while to recover from.

So the 500 kg gorilla in the room is not what the country says about itself but what the target audiences say about the country. Until such time as countries in Africa show believable and positive brand promise delivery, most advertising will come across as a bandage on a severed head.

Africa's burgeoning reputation as a sustainable investment destination will be undermined as long as corruption is one of primary reputational indicators; high value citizens will emigrate from Africa as long as crime is a reputational indicator, and so on. Unfortunately, many governments have failed to deliver on promises to deal with serious challenges facing the continent and this has affected country brands and even the broader continental brand. Taking action on its own is a brand issue, but especially acting on promises made to an electorate is a primary brand reputation delivery mechanism.

It does not always take that much to change the perception of a country or a sector through bold and positive action. Nigeria's Central Bank Governor, Lamido Sanusi, is one individual who has proved that actions speak louder than words. His effort in managing the Nigerian financial sector and its financial institutions has changed the way the world perceives the previously negatively positioned Nigerian financial sector, which had been battered by poor corporate governance, financial stress and other problems.

By the same token, citizens and corporate bodies in any African country have a direct role in building their own country's reputation. South Africa's commercial successes have had a significant and positive effect on South Africa's brand and, to some extent, also the continental brand.

Take South African-based mobile phone operator MTN, for example. It is not only a great commercial success, it is also a continental player of global significance and delivery capability. Its sponsorship of the 2010 football World Cup not only contributed massively to the value of the MTN commercial brand on an international platform, but also provided a stage for Africa to show a positive commercial brand image that went well beyond South Africa and even Africa.

Standard Bank, too, has become a large African player, but one which has significance and reach well beyond Africa. SABMiller, a globally dominant and still fast growing brand, has without doubt helped to position South Africans as 'can do' global business people. Its brand remains African despite its offshore listing and global activities.

South African restaurant chain, Nando's, has spread its wings across emerging markets and in the likes of the UK and the US. Then there is Discovery Health. The company, largely through the perseverance, attitude and presence of founder and CEO, Adrian Gore, has led the global community to take notice of yet another clever and driven African company.

Emerging multinationals are coming out of other African countries too, all helping to build Africa's business brand. This is particularly important in an era of increased investor interest in the continent.

Even the NGO arena has played its part in contributing to 'Brand South Africa' and, by extension, the continent with the appointment of Kumi Naidoo as Executive Director of Greenpeace International. In a world where our environmental future is under constant threat, he is a good brand ambassador to have.

A host of other individuals contribute effectively to both country and continental brand in a positive manner: the obvious one is former South African President Nelson Mandela, but human rights figure Archbishop Desmond Tutu, Oscar-winning actress Charlize Theron, Olympic swimmer Roland Schoeman, golf legend Gary Player and singer and malaria campaigner Yvonne Chaka Chaka have all built a positive reputational image for themselves and South Africa. Apart from Mandela, these people represent private excellence that has had little or nothing to do with governments.

What about the reputation breakers? The world is full of them and Africa has its fair share. But with the continent under the spotlight currently as a business destination, we could certainly do with more reputation builders and fewer brand assassins.

The obvious individuals in the latter category include the usual dictators and their ilk, and in South Africa's case, a couple of embarrassing public figures whose comments and actions have negatively affected the positive South African brand. The continent still needs leaders who can stand head and shoulders above the pack in global politics by creating excellence in their countries. This would help to build the continental brand even as it builds their country brand.

On a continent obsessed with all the things that separate and divide us (specifically race, ethnicity, language and religion), it is time for individuals to look to things that unite us. We can then use these to start, from the bottom up, growing the brands that affect our lives in different ways – our personal brand, our organisation's brand and, through that, our country brand – through to the reputation of the continent as a whole.

The sooner governments realise that they are responsible for enabling African countries and peoples to formulate and deliver tangible promises, the quicker we can have a positive and meaningful continental brand. To really build the African brand we need to get the world talking about us — about our people, our natural beauty and our history, but also our economic brands.

Ultimately building a brand reputation is easy, really easy: BE > DO > SAY.

Actis is a global emerging markets private equity firm with more than 60 years' experience of investing in Africa. The firm operates in Asia, Latin America and Africa, with its African offices in Johannesburg, Lagos, Cairo and Nairobi. Actis was established in 2004 when it was spun out of the CDC, the UK's development arm established in 1948 to invest in Commonwealth countries.

Actis has $4.6 billion under management, it is invested in more than 60 companies that employ 100,000 staff. Africa represents a major part of Actis's business with $1.5 billion of its funds invested across the continent.

PRIVATE EQUITY

ACTIS

Investor interest in quality African companies has been growing noticeably from Europe and North America, as well as increasingly from other emerging markets, says Simon Harford, Partner at British private equity firm Actis.

'The strong historical links with corporate investors from developed countries are still there, while more recently we have seen greater acquisition appetite from India and other emerging markets,' notes Harford.

'Private equity is playing an important role in building quality companies in Africa by assisting African businesses to develop to the next level and position themselves for greater competition and international linkages.'

The African private sector has grown rapidly during the past decade of economic, political and policy reform in most countries. The number of home-grown multinational companies has mushroomed too, particularly in large economies such as Kenya and Nigeria, where deepening regional ties provide ready expansion opportunities.

In 2012 there were about 40 private equity firms investing in African businesses and new money is continually being raised for African deployment. Pan-African opportunities are also increasingly on the radar of African pension funds, including South Africa's giant Public Investment Corporation which announced it planned to invest up to $3.8 billion in African private equity over a few years. The number of corporate mergers and acquisitions has risen sharply, reflecting the increased need for business growth beyond the home economy as well as an increased supply of quality acquisition targets within the continent.

Actis, which also operates in Asia and Latin America, is one of the few investors that is genuinely 'on the ground' and pan-African. The firm has a decades-long track record of investing in Africa, has more than 20 staff based locally in multiple African offices and in 2012 held $1.5 billion of investments in 15 African countries. The firm aims to continue investing some $300 million a year in Africa, mostly in the continent's biggest economies of South Africa, Egypt and Nigeria, as well as in the East African region, in the Maghreb and elsewhere.

It focuses on a core of five sectors in Africa that are central to broad-based economic growth: financial services, consumer businesses, industrials, power and real estate.

Actis's most recent African investments include the South African vehicle tracking equipment firm, Tracker; the West African fabrics manufacturer, Vlisco; pan-African card payments platform, Emerging Markets Payment Holdings; Egypt's leading private sector bank, Commercial International Bank; and the two flagship retail/office malls in Nigeria, The Palms and Ikeja City Mall.

THE ROLE OF THOUGHTFUL CAPITAL

Private equity's role in this crucial African evolution is not just about funding businesses but providing what Harford calls 'thoughtful capital'.

A lot of African businesses, are private companies that find it difficult to access long-term quality capital. But, even more critically, many if not most growing African businesses observe that their major obstacles are not actually capital but other issues such as management skills, corporate governance development, international connections and environmental/social practices. Harford confirms this and identifies the high proportion of family-owned and owner-manager businesses in Africa as prime examples of this challenge. African companies do not simply require capital, they ideally require from their funder additional support and value creation, or 'thoughtful capital'. Private equity can provide this package of support in a unique way.

A large number of Actis's investments around the world are in family-owned businesses and the picture is no different in Africa. 'Family-owned companies are a very important part of the economy in many emerging markets and they are particularly important in Africa. We help these family and owner-manager businesses transition to a more corporate structure that can survive beyond the immediate leadership.

'Even if they can get the capital, these family and owner-manager businesses need access to skills to "corporatise" their business and create a more sustainable company beyond the immediate family or manager. African firms are operating in an increasingly global market where they have to deal with global competitors, regulators, customers, suppliers, management and other stakeholders. All of these factors put pressure on owners and managers to raise the competitive skills of their operations beyond what the narrow family team can sustain.

'Actis will normally invest in a company as a major shareholder, often with the family retaining a stake, and we then help them to attract professional management to senior positions beyond the family managers. We then help them systematically to institutionalise all aspects of the business. This includes establishing and running a robust board; incorporating good corporate governance principles; operating thorough financial systems and practices; introducing high standards of environmental and social practices, and any other elements that will make the company more attractive and competitive.

'I've spent the past seven years sitting at boardroom tables in West and South Africa and I have seen consistent and big changes in the companies' priorities and business needs. For instance, there is a much greater recognition of the interconnectedness of business and opportunity within Africa, and that businesses must become less parochial and more proactive.

'There's also more recognition of corporate governance obligations than there used to be, as well as ever more frustration with governments that still have not tackled infrastructure, regulatory and other deficiencies to an enabling environment for business to operate in. As a consequence, there is a growing assumption that companies operating across Africa must set and adhere to their own high standards and not wait for an external body to impose standards on them,' says Harford.

'We are also seeing more demand from African companies for us to assist them with building connections to businesses in other emerging markets, notably India, Brazil and China. As we operate in all those countries this is an easy and important role for Actis to play.'

ACTIS'S PRIVATE EQUITY MODEL

A growing African economy is going to be driven predominantly by a flourishing private sector, says Harford. 'For the private sector to flourish, it needs capital from lots of different sources, depending on the need and nature of the business. But in many cases it's not just capital that is required, it's the development of sustainable business models, building the right skills and having the right soft and hard infrastructure.'

Where does private equity fit in? 'We don't focus only on business funding or indeed earnings growth; we bring explicit requirements for the running of a business in terms of ethical conduct, corporate governance, environmental and social issues as well as health and safety issues, with a focus on the company's impact on the wider society. We care about how a company grows, not just that it grows.'

Because there is such a strong alignment between what private equity offers and the needs of the African private sector, it makes sense to have more of this equity available to develop the continent, especially outside South Africa, which has the most mature and sophisticated private sector (albeit one that still benefits strongly from the availability of private equity funding).

'Stock markets might provide equity capital but there's no value addition or business support with that type of funding. And it often comes with a short-term perspective. In any case, the majority of African companies are privately owned and are not ready or willing to go public. We're not just a consultancy providing advice and then walking way. If we get it wrong we suffer. If we succeed in helping companies in which we invest, everyone benefits.'

At the end of the investment period, typically four to five years, Actis sells its stake in the company in order to return funds to its own investors, with the aim of at least doubling its original investment. The exit strategy is critical. 'It is important that our exit is conducted in as responsible a manner as the original investment,' says Harford. 'We must leave the company in a much stronger state than when we arrived and we must leave it in a way that ensures it has a sustainable and growing path for all its future owners. If we don't deliver this, it undermines the viability of our own model.'

Buyers of Actis's investments are most typically trade corporates or similar strategic acquirers. They might be other African companies, or international acquirers in the same sector who are attracted to buying a business with a strong track record as well as the rigorous governance and other practices of the Actis-owned business. Exits via stock exchanges do occur but are less common, as it is rare that a trade buyer does not outbid what a stock market placing would achieve. But, says Harford, the exit strategy also depends on what the other shareholders want.

'We will always take care to reflect the wishes of our fellow shareholders, which might be for a market listing. When our investment has gone well, buyers and exits are easier to find precisely because the company is growing strongly and demonstrates a positive future.'

The increasing interest from Brazilian, Chinese and Indian buyers looking to get a foothold in the African region is likely to give private equity firms more exit options in the future. Harford notes though that China's recent interest seems very much still driven at a government-to-government level and primarily involves natural resources. In contrast, there is growing interest in African opportunities from Indian companies, particularly in the consumer goods industry, and many of Actis's current Indian clients have asked the firm to assist them in finding African growth opportunities to acquire.

THE SOUTH AFRICAN ANGLE

South Africa is obviously also a major player elsewhere in Africa. However, despite the growing geographic footprint of South African companies, says Harford, until recently many executives of South Africa's top companies were still ambivalent about investing on the continent. 'Many were not getting the real Africa story and were still constrained by outdated views or by their own mistakes in executing African growth. But I see this changing. Companies are recognising that they have no choice but to widen their African business beyond South Africa. They have no choice, not just because of softer growth in South Africa itself, or because their competitors are doing so, but because so much of the rest of Africa is progressing really well.

'The market opportunity is there, even though the execution challenges remain significant. It's at the inflexion stage where it's becoming untenable *not* to have an Africa plan, or *not* to be demonstrating clear progress in executing upon it.' While it is still daunting to deliver, reaching this inflexion point is exciting for the future of the African economy and pan-African businesses.

'But, understandably, companies often still don't know how best to go about it. They may lack the managerial expertise for these markets, have had bad previous experiences, or be anxious about who to do business with and how to navigate governments and other ethical issues,' says Harford. 'As a seasoned operator across Africa, with many scars on our back, Actis is having more and more discussions with South African corporates about how we can help them in this respect.

'The strong interest in acquisitions within Africa also talks to the point of whether South Africa is the right landing place for companies coming to the continent from elsewhere. Personally, I don't think it needs to be South Africa and indeed sometimes it can be riskier to use South Africa as your base. The South African business environment is so very different to that in North and sub-Sahara Africa that, if your ultimate goal is doing business mostly in those regions, you might need to choose a base that gives you a more relevant pool of management and business insight into those markets. Depending of course on what sector you are in, you may not find that South Africa offers this and that elsewhere, such as Accra or Nairobi, gives access to more relevant management, advisory and support capability.'

AFRICA IS NOT A COUNTRY

The challenges of operating in Africa vary enormously depending on what African market one is talking about.

'The challenges in South Africa will be very different from those in West

Africa, for example. In one country the economic context might be more around growth, government policy and long-term planning, workforce and trade union issues and soft infrastructure issues such as health and education.

'In other countries, such as those in sub-Saharan Africa, the economic context might well be more affected by factors such as physical infrastructure, management and skills availability, security and political outlook. If your business is reliant in some way on the government, you would likely be very concerned about the nature of issues such as government policies, transparency, corruption, due process and credit worthiness.

'Of course there are many commonalities but you need to be careful about generalisations. Doing business in Africa is not doing business in one country but in 54 states. You have to look past the common challenges and opportunities to look for country-specific issues otherwise you could fail in a market by replicating business practices from elsewhere.'

Corruption remains an issue of great and legitimate concern to most companies, Harford says. However, he adds, a new development is high-profile cases of companies themselves being guilty of fostering corruption by offering bribes – but being brought to book.

'Encouragingly in the past few years a number of prominent international companies have been found in court – interestingly more in the US or Europe than in Africa itself – to have behaved unethically and have been materially fined. This thankfully is leading to a greater awareness among companies that operating corruptly is becoming harder to get away with, quite aside from the continuing moral repugnance of it. The whole issue is becoming more visible, which is very positive for Africa and all other markets where this remains a thorny problem. For too long it has been conveniently ignored that a significant element of government corruption has been fed by international companies doing the bribing.'

Harford says the state of the business climate in African economies is constantly being evaluated against global indices devised by organisations such as the World Bank and World Economic Forum. 'Of course the picture is not always consistent and one can quibble about the methodology. But, if one looks at trends and multiple data points, it's evident that some African countries are progressing well over many years, while others are going sideways or even backwards.

'For example, in infrastructure funding (power, transport etc) such long-term trends in the business climate are essential data as the funding lifespan can easily be 15 or 20 years. In the power sector, governments are unlikely to attract quality private capital unless they indisputably embed a multi-faceted business climate that incentivises private funders, including but certainly not limited to the right regulatory framework, transparent and commercial off-take pricing and input tariffs, and processes that are predictable and corruption-free. Returns have to be predictable and sustainable before a private funder will commit 20-year capital.' He says Actis is a committed provider of capital to power infrastructure and yet it continues to find significant variations between African countries when it comes to their genuine commitment to establish good enabling environments.

It is important for governments to become more effective enablers of not just general economic growth, but private sector growth, he says. 'Governments need to enable the private sector where it is their responsibility and in their power to do so, and then step aside to allow the private sector to drive that segment of the economy. No government can or should try to do it all themselves, especially in African countries where the starting position still presents major challenges. They need to adopt explicit strategies to tap the deep pockets of private capital that is definitely available for Africa. But that capital will not be deployed without the critical pre-conditions and enablers in the business climate. Capital is mobile and will inexorably flow elsewhere in the world if Africa doesn't make itself competitive. It is hard to generalise on how governments are stepping up to this reality. Some are totally aligned with being competitive and delivering genuine reforms, while others talk but sadly don't deliver. As a provider of capital and skills into African business, one has to differentiate carefully between the talk and the action.'

AFRICA'S FUTURE

Harford believes the problems in the eurozone countries have presented opportunities for companies with operations in emerging markets, including Africa. 'Business confidence and uncertainty in Europe is affecting business everywhere, but in Africa the direct effect is relatively limited for most sectors. For example, while a European bank with activities in Africa will probably have been negatively affected, a European consumer business will have found its African business to be an advantage during the slowdown in its developed markets.'

The outlook for Africa can be said to be generally positive. Clearly there are many challenges ahead and the continent is coming off a low base in terms of competitiveness and trade. There are still relatively small investment inflows to Africa – about four per cent of the foreign direct investment total in 2011 – and its countries have to compete effectively to secure a bigger slice of those flows. There is demonstrable progress but the continent needs to build on that and accelerate it. Both the private sector and governments face this task.

The positive changes taking place on the continent are also luring African Diaspora skills back from other regions, a trend that has been particularly noticeable since the mid-2000s. These are often highly skilled, passionate, committed and valuable people who have seen opportunities in their home countries and want to return.

This trend has been aided by the impact of the international crisis on developed economies, says Harford, and Africa is now widely seen as a place with a bright future and plentiful opportunities for entrepreneurs and others. 'It's got high growth, almost unlimited opportunity and Africans have a chance to make an impact on their countries and on the continent. That is exciting for everyone who is working in Africa, which feels somewhat of a contrast with the rather gloomy environment and outlook in developed markets.'

AngloGold Ashanti, a leading gold mining company based in South Africa, has 20 operations on four continents. It has mines in six African countries – Mali, Tanzania, South Africa, Namibia, Guinea and Ghana – with exploration under way in the Democratic Republic of Congo. The company has a primary listing in Johannesburg and secondary listings in London, Paris and Ghana, depositary receipts in Brussels and depositary shares in New York and Ghana.

MINING

ANGLOGOLD ASHANTI

One of the key debates in the mining sector is about what degree of government shareholding in mining operations is appropriate, says Richard Duffy, former Vice President of Continental Africa, AngloGold Ashanti, who was appointed Chief Financial Officer in May 2013. In an era of high commodity prices, governments globally are looking for ways to extract more revenue from resources in a variety of ways, he says.

Commodity producers operating in Africa are facing changes in the legal frameworks in which they operate. This includes mandatory government stakes in projects or, where these already exist, an increase in the stakes. It also includes the imposition of windfall taxes on profits, the raising of royalties and increases in corporate taxes.

Some of these changes are taking place or are under consideration in key African markets in which AngloGold Ashanti operates. For example, Guinea's mining code, passed in late 2011, gives the government an option to buy an additional 20 per cent stake in mining operations in the country over and above the original 15 per cent. In the Democratic Republic of Congo, where AngloGold Ashanti had to renegotiate its contract with the state as part of an industry-wide review of all mining contracts, there is also provision for state ownership.

Ghana and Tanzania have found other ways to raise their share of the commodity pie. In 2011, Ghana raised the corporate tax for miners to 35 per cent from 25 per cent , and announced a separate 10 per cent windfall tax on mining profits, while Tanzania has proposed a super tax on mining profits and a hike in royalties.

Duffy says the company has fiscal stability agreements with governments that were put in place at the time of the original investment. 'In terms of these agreements, taxes will not go beyond a certain threshold and royalties are capped. From time to time, we have been pressured to change the fiscal arrangements and there has been some robust discussion. One of the benefits of operating in Africa is that we are able to engage with government officials quite easily – there are many countries outside the continent where this is not the case.

'In some instances, we have agreed to amendments, but we haven't had a situation where a government has ignored the agreement or breached it.

'In African countries we are one of the biggest taxpayers and our operations have a large knock-on effect in the economy. This is not always taken into account in determining factors such as royalty percentages. There is this perception that we are making money hand over fist and getting the lion's share.' But, he says, the investments are a long-term liability. For example, the Geita mine in Tanzania operated for 11 years before the shareholder loan for setting it up was paid off at the end of 2011.

In Tanzania, 70 per cent of spending stays in the host country, through wages and salaries, payments to local suppliers, reinvestment of surpluses and other expenditure. The state also receives more in various taxes than the total dividends paid to shareholders.

'The government takes by far the biggest slice of the pie and the shareholder slice is very small. But, because we haven't told our story well, it is sometimes difficult for governments to see the benefits we bring beyond the taxes we pay. We need to better communicate the actual size of our contribution to local economies in formal stakeholder engagement.'

Local beneficiation is a new demand on many governments' wish lists. 'There is a perception that having a refinery in your country is important because if you export the raw material you are giving away value. But the margins in this industry are in mining, production and retail, not in refining, which is low on labour and high on technology. Building a local jewellery industry around gold would generate more value.

'There is also a definite trend towards localisation in terms of hiring practices, procurement, buying consumables, services and other areas where greater linkages to local economies can be created. But the benefits of this strategy are limited at this stage because of supply side constraints.

'Africa has a very high dependence on mining. It is important for governments to identify how they can leverage that and do more than looking at ways to extract rent. That is the common ground we are looking for.'

CHANGING THE STAKEHOLDER MODEL

The emphasis on greater benefits for the countries in which mining companies operate in developing regions has led AngloGold Ashanti to change the model it uses in mining areas, says Duffy. 'We are moving away from a dependence relationship to a strategic engagement with the communities around the mines.

'The old model was to ask the general manager, who was running a tough mine under tough conditions, to deal with a lot of complex community issues as well, and we were surprised when it didn't work. We would just build a school and feel good about it but we didn't understand what the community actually needed.

'A mining company going into a rural area and building a small town quickly creates a dependence on the mine, particularly for jobs. As a result, we have much higher employment levels in African operations than in Australia, for example. But you can't employ entire communities. This dependence is very difficult to sustain.

'Technology is changing the way business is being done in Africa. There is nowhere where we operate, even in the jungle in north-east Congo, where people don't have mobile phone access. There is no longer anywhere where communities are cut off from the rest of the world and this raises expectations and puts pressure on governments and on companies to respond to this changing dynamic.

'So a new model is very important. We see ourselves as a catalyst for development, rather than the sole source of opportunity. We want to sit across the table from community leaders and discuss relevant issues. It sounds like common sense but it takes a lot of time and effort because you can't just create relationships out of nothing. You have to work at them,' says Duffy.

'There has been a high degree of mistrust around mining and it is something we need to address. We can't step into the government's shoes but neither can we ignore community imperatives. We have to be proactive as there is a fairly small window of opportunity to do something before things can go wrong.

'We have brought in a team from the development side of the business to work with the communities. This provides a very different skill set and gives us capability where we haven't had it before. We also bring in other parties to build capacity if necessary.'

AngloGold Ashanti is piloting a 'millennium village' at its mine in Guinea in West Africa. The millennium village model was developed by the Earth Institute at Colombia University in the US, the United Nations Development Programme (UNDP) and Millennium Promise, a private initiative. It uses the millennium development goals (MDGs) as a framework to invest in different sectors, such as agriculture, infrastructure, the environment, health, education and business development. Brazilian miner, Vale, is another company using the model in Africa.

'Typically in the mining industry sustainable projects have been ad hoc and project-based without being systemically linked to any strategic outcome. We have changed that to become aligned to the country's national strategic agenda and the MDG framework provides us with a basis for measuring our impact,' says Duffy.

'We sat with the government in Guinea and explained what we aimed to do. We will also meet local authorities and community leaders to come up with a development plan. We want communities to see the benefit of our being there, not just because we have built schools and hospitals but because we are a catalyst for broader development. This is one of the key differentiators going forward if you want to succeed.'

Apart from providing agricultural outlets, the company is looking at ways to formalise the artisanal miners at its sites. 'This is another part of our strategy. You can't just relocate artisanal miners and expect they will stay away. We see an opportunity to engage constructively with them to see if we can provide some basic safety and environmental good practice.'

RISK AND COMPLIANCE

The company has a footprint in some challenging markets in Africa, such as Guinea (Siguiri mine) and Mali (Morila, Sadiola and Yatela) but also in more stable economies such as Tanzania (Geita), Namibia (Navachab) and Ghana (Obuasi and Iduapriem). The combined output from the African mines, excluding South Africa, contributed 39 per cent to group production in 2012 and employed 16,600 people, including contractors. It operates six mines in its home market, South Africa, which contributed 31 per cent of total production in 2012.

It has two exploration projects in the DRC. One is Kibali, in partnership with Randgold Resources, in which each company has a 45 per cent shareholding, with ten per cent owned by the government. The other is Mongbwalu concession, in which AngloGold Ashanti has an 86 per cent share and the government the remainder. Exploration rights were secured in 1996 but the company waited until the country's long civil war ended and a peace agreement was signed before proceeding in 2003.

AngloGold Ashanti plans to produce up to 2.3 million ounces of gold by 2015 from new operations in Africa outside South Africa. 'Africa is highly prospective so it's an obvious destination for us,' explains Duffy. 'We are an African company so that is another reason why we look to invest in Africa. We go where the gold is and where we think we can generate a return for shareholders.

'We look at the opportunity and the risk, not only on a country by country basis but also on a region by region basis as risk within countries can be quite localised. For example, in DRC, the risk in Kinshasa is different from risk in the north-east of the country which is different again from the North Kivu region.'

There are some non-negotiable risks. 'One of these is the safety of staff. If the security situation suggests they would be at risk in an area, we wouldn't operate there.' The company has contingency plans in place for insecurity arising out of events such as elections, which in some countries can lead to violence.

There have been a few occasions when the staff at a mine has either been evacuated or had numbers reduced for a period of time in the face of a perceived threat. 'It was not about specific incidents or anything involving our staff but was rather about the security situation around our camps. But this has not been necessary for the past few years.

'We would also not consider going into markets where it was impossible to operate without paying bribes or to do business in accordance with our values. We are pretty clear about how we operate. If we felt that the political risk from a shareholder perspective was too great, we would think hard before we invested. But this hasn't happened as yet.'

The company has to consider not only shareholders and staff in its investments, but also compliance with a raft of regulations, rules and global compacts. These include regulations on the five stock exchanges on which it is listed and other guidelines it has signed up to, such as the UN Global Compact, which comprises ten principles relating to issues such as human rights, labour, the environment and corruption; the US's Foreign Corrupt Practices Act (FCPA); the Global Reporting Initiative, and the Extractive Industries Transparency Initiative (EITI).

Of the countries in which AngloGold Ashanti operates, only Ghana has achieved full compliance with EITI membership provisions. Tanzania, Mali and the DRC are candidate members. But AngloGold Ashanti does disclose payments made to governments in all countries in which it operates. And the amounts are increasing. In 2012, it paid $15.9 million to the DRC government, up from $2 million in 2008; in Ghana it paid $75.5 million ($42 million); Guinea $101.4 million ($37.6 million); Mali $132.3 million ($118 million); South Africa $250.8 million ($91 million); Namibia $10.9 million ($9.2 million) and Tanzania nearly $214 million ($38.4 million).

It has also engaged the World Gold Council and the Responsible Jewellery Council to develop industry standards for responsible gold production in the wake of legislation passed in the US in 2010 that gives consumers more power to demand transparency over products produced from gold mined in central Africa, particularly in the DRC.

'From a compliance point of view, Africa is not more difficult than anywhere else we operate. And there is a positive aspect in that some of these global compacts and guidelines also put pressure on governments to be more transparent and to focus more on democratic governance, which makes it easier for us to comply with them. In fact, there is probably less impact on companies than on governments.'

CORPORATE HEADACHES

In addition to the macro challenges, mining companies face many logistics problems in remote areas. 'Infrastructure is always a problem. We generate our own power in a number of sites, such as Geita in Tanzania, Siguiri in Guinea and Sadiola in Mali. In South Africa, Ghana and Namibia we are on the national grid. In DRC we plan to generate hydro power for the mine and some of the communities around us. If you're able to lock in reliable power supply at a competitive price, you have a big advantage.'

Transport routes are another potential problem. For example, in DRC, the nearest town, Bunia, is 90 km from the site, a journey that used to take three to four days before the company rehabilitated the road. It now takes four to five hours. Apart from the obvious benefits for the mine, it has advantages for the villagers. Facilitating access to infrastructure lays the ground for developing an entrepreneurial base and it also reduces costs of food and other goods going to the communities along the way.

Most of the company's sites have reasonable road access and nearby airports. During the war in the DRC, Bunia was the local headquarters for UN peacekeepers and has a large airport, which benefits the mine. But, however goods get to the mine, the high cost of transport from any port in Africa to anywhere inland makes it an expensive exercise.

Another headache is finding and retaining skills. 'In some countries where mining is relatively new, such as Guinea, it is difficult to source goods and skills locally. There is a real squeeze on technical skills and as we train people they get poached by other companies. So the challenge is to have retention mechanisms in place to keep the skills in the company.'

Health is a big issue, particularly the incidence of malaria in tropical regions, which can result in millions of man hours lost every year among workers. Ghana has a particularly high incidence of malaria and the company has received funding from the Global Fund to Fight AIDS, Tuberculosis and Malaria (GFATM) to extend its integrated malaria control model, implemented at Obuasi mine, to 40 regions in the country. This is due to run for five years from 2011 and has created about 3,800 jobs.

The success of the company's malaria programme is indicated by the figures. In 2005, the Obuasi mine hospital treated an average of 6,800 malaria patients a month out of a total workforce of 8,000 with the monthly cost of treatment amounting to more than $55,000. After the mine invested several million dollars on a control programme in the mine and surrounding town, the number of cases at the mine hospital was reduced by 75 per cent over five years. Medication costs were reduced to $9,800 per month and lost days to malaria from 6,983 a month in 2005 to fewer than 300.

Security is also an issue, which is to be expected given high poverty levels in African countries. Numbers of staff injured in security incidents have risen, a fact that the company attributes to a higher level of organisation among criminal elements and syndicates. In December 2011, for example, heavily armed robbers with masks, sub-machine guns and hand grenades tried to steal 587 kgs of gold bars from a plane on an airstrip in northern Tanzania, but were thwarted by police.

Political risk remains a significant challenge and AngloGold Ashanti has had its fair share of it in markets such as Guinea. The 2008 death of Lansana Conte, who had been Guinea's leader for 24 years, resulted in a military coup by Captain Moussa Dadis Camara who, on assuming power, quickly focused on the mining industry, saying he would withdraw the rights of any company found to have done deals without following due process.

While AngloGold Ashanti, which operates the country's biggest gold mine, did not fall foul of this review, it had other problems. On one occasion a major issue was made of the failure of the mine's general manager to attend a meeting with the president at short notice. Camara's officials also briefly halted the company's gold exports while officials ostensibly disputed the nature and protocols of the mine's $35 million environmental rehabilitation provision.

Exports were permitted to resume after AngloGold Ashanti paid $10 million of the amount in an advance payment to the government. The company stipulated that the money should be used solely for environmental rehabilitation of Siguiri mine with the balance offset against the company's future liabilities. In another incident, a government delegation accompanied a gold shipment to Rand Refinery in Johannesburg in order to satisfy itself that there were no undue aspects to the shipment process. 'We have had some turbulent times but we have never had any significant issues we could not deal with.'

THE NGO PROBLEM

The company has also bumped heads with local and international non-governmental organisations (NGOs). In the most prominent case, Human Rights Watch accused AngloGold Ashanti of providing financial and logistical support to a rebel group in north-east Congo. It refused to accept the company's defence – that contact with the rebels was made under duress – saying the company should have waited until it was able to work in the area without having to deal with abusive warlords.

'What happened is that a group of our men on the ground were threatened at gunpoint for money. We were certainly not financing a local militia – it was an act of extortion and we disclosed that. But the question is really whether, if people have to do something that contravenes the company's values, you should have put them in that position in the first place.

'NGOs are stakeholders. We can't pretend they are not there. We actively seek to involve them in some of the work we do and get their advice. We have engaged with the people who vilified us in the DRC report and have invited them to be part of our community stakeholder engagement. In many cases NGOs make some very good points. But it is frustrating that we are subject to compliance with a whole range of rules and regulations and they aren't,' says Duffy.

LOOKING AHEAD

'There is always pressure from governments to raise additional revenue. We do see increases in taxes and royalties continuing as the demand for African commodities increases and it will probably continue until we can show governments a different model and engage with them on this issue going forward.'

The push for carbon taxes is mounting, but Duffy is sanguine about the likelihood of increasing pressure on resources companies in a greener world. 'For us the situation is more of a potential benefit than a threat. For example, there is plenty of hydro potential for green energy and biomass in agricultural projects the mines are developing. There are forests in many of the areas in which we operate so there is potential for reforestation or preventing deforestation. All of these now have value in the carbon credit world.

'So it is a threat but I think Africa is going to lag other areas such as the US and Australia in imposing carbon taxes, and we can potentially benefit in the carbon trading market by doing things that offset the carbon footprint from an Africa perspective.

'There is also a big opportunity for African countries to use technology to develop best practice and thus become more globally competitive. That will help to make Africa a much more attractive destination for international investors.

'I am an Afro-optimist. I do believe activities in natural resources will increase whether they are in agriculture, mining or the oil industry. But it is not suddenly going to become easy to operate in Africa. While I think it is getting better to do business in DRC and Guinea, for example, to say that it would be a smooth transition to stability is unrealistic and naïve. There will still be some bumps along the way.

'But African countries' dependence on mining will require them to find a workable way forward to optimise the benefits from the industry and hopefully we will be able to play a part in that.'

The Carlson Rezidor Hotel Group is one of the world's largest and most dynamic hotel groups, employing more than 80,000 people. Its portfolio includes more than 1,300 hotels. It is a strategic partnership between the US-based global hospitality and travel group Carlson and the Rezidor Hotel Group. 75 per cent of the 100 plus hotels currently under development are in emerging markets including Africa.

It has a global footprint spanning 80 countries and a set of international brands such as Radisson Blu, Country Inns & Suites by Carlson, Park Inn by Radisson, Hotel Missoni and Park Plaza. In most of the group's hotels, guests can benefit from the Club Carlson loyalty programme.

HOSPITALITY

Carlson Rezidor Hotel Group

As growth slows down in developed countries, international hotel chains are scrambling for a piece of the action in the African markets where the supply of rooms has not kept pace with demand. In 2010 there were 41 hotel brands operating on the continent; in 2013 there were more than 70, says Andrew McLachlan, Vice President of Business Development, Africa & Indian Ocean Islands, for the Carlson Rezidor Hotel Group.

'Sub-Saharan Africa is in the best place it has been in 30 years and more and more international brands are going to have a presence here in future because they are looking for growth and Africa is only getting started. Some of the fastest growing economies in the world right now are in Africa.'

Carlson Rezidor is one of the fastest growing hotel chains in the world with a global footprint spanning over 80 countries and it plans to be in every major African city and financial centre in time. McLachlan, who spent 15 years with South Africa's Protea Hotel Group, says changes in recent years make it much easier to operate on the continent.

'There are more flights – you can now get anywhere in a day and back the next day. Five years ago you were looking at a week's turnaround between destinations.

'Telecommunications has improved beyond recognition, which has made it much easier to do business. African business owners tend to have two or three phones on them so you can reach them at any time, which has significantly improved the ability to make decisions and do deals.

'Technology has also made things easier. For example, online booking systems allow customers to plan properly and credit cards can be used in many countries. In some places you can now draw money from ATMs. Previously, you had to arrive in an African country with wads of US dollars and hope corrupt officials didn't find a way to take them off you. The experience of being harassed by officials at airports has also diminished recently and the whole airport experience is not nearly as stressful as it used to be.'

ROLLING OUT THE BRAND

In 2007 Carlson Rezidor opened its Africa office in Cape Town, the city where the first Radisson Blu hotel on the continent was opened. At the time, the group had eight hotels open or under development across five countries on the continent. By mid-2013, it had 51 hotels open or under development in 21 African countries.

'We always believed we should enter the African market through South Africa because there is decent infrastructure, a reliable legal system, a relatively high standard of hotel product and good staff levels from a training point of view. The added advantage when we entered Cape Town was that the market mix was predominantly higher international, versus domestic, custom. Being a European hotel group, many of the international customers were already familiar with the brand so we could make a positive impact immediately.

'As our competitors did, we originally tried to grow our African operations from Europe, but in the first six years we only developed eight hotels. In 2006 the company decided that if it was going to be serious about Africa it needed to open an office in Africa to position the group to quickly pick up information and react faster to opportunities.'

The biggest market gap in Africa is in the business hotel segment. Rapid economic growth is attracting a lot more people to the continent and demand is quickly outpacing supply. One big event in an African capital can create an instant shortage of hotel rooms.

Carlson Rezidor has recognised this and is focusing its African expansion on business hotels. The upmarket Radisson Blu brand dominates the Africa roll-out, while the mid-market Park Inn by Radisson brand is mostly in South Africa, Nigeria and the East Africa Lake District. 'We see the Radisson Blu as our heavyweight boxer that goes into a market first to fight for our market share. In certain markets we will then think about putting in Park Inn by Radisson.' The lifestyle fashion brand, Hotel Missoni, and luxury brand Regent Hotels are only considered for a few select African markets, including city locations in Abuja, Nairobi, Johannesburg and Lagos and resort locations in Mauritius, Seychelles and Morocco.

'The size and quality of the local service industry is a consideration in choosing which brand to take into a place. The more underdeveloped the city is, the more there is a requirement for a full-service hotel that is self sufficient. It becomes everything to that city – the best residence in town, the place with the best restaurant, the best meeting rooms and so on.

'A hotel in such markets must cater for all its own needs and those of its guests internally, unlike more mature markets where there are many restaurant and meeting options and we can outsource certain functions and generally have a leaner offering from a staff and facility point of view.'

McLachlan says the group has found that mixed-use developments are a good model for Africa as they provide a secure environment for retail, residential and even medical facilities. 'Given the difficulty of getting municipal services in many countries, this model also allows shared services and cost rationalisation.'

In line with global trends, the company has no investment in real estate and operates hotels under management contracts, leases or franchises. In Africa, the business model is purely management contracts. 'This enables us to grow faster than if we had to secure property and deal with the challenges that go with that. But we are very involved in the hotel, right from the conceptual design stage to the quality of finishes.'

Being involved at an early stage allows the group to keep costs in check. 'From the day the hotel opens, the owners look to us to make a return on their investment so it would be irresponsible to let the costs run away during the development stage. It's mandatory that we commission background checks on the proposed hotel owners and important that we understand their debt to equity ratios in a new hotel project. We don't want to enter into a development that is over geared and the hotel collapses in the early years because there is too much debt to service while the hotel is still ramping up and has not stabilised.'

In a top hotel, security is a key consideration and, during the development process, the group brings in security experts internally and externally to advise developers on this important aspect of hotel design.

'Across Africa we maintain first world security and safety standards, particularly as this is a way to attract international guests.' US first lady, Michelle Obama, stayed at the Radisson Blu Hotel Sandton in Johannesburg during her South African visit in 2011 and the hotel was checked by US security staff beforehand. As a result, in 2013, fourteen African heads of state were all accomodated in the same hotel during the Africa Cup of Nations Football Tournament. 'It is important to get onto the list of security agencies' approved hotels as foreign diplomatic missions and multinational companies contact them to find out where the safest place is to stay for their executives. And, in the case of unrest in a city, safe hotels are a first port of call for many people.'

In Africa, many hotels that Rezidor manages are owned by local wealthy individuals with title to land. 'Hotel real estate is a high-performing asset class, a fact that is reflected in the interest shown in it by listed property funds and pension funds as well as private investment. For wealthy individuals, owning a hotel is highly prestigious, especially if it is under an international brand. It is the best kind of business card to have and they can use it to leverage their other businesses.'

McLachlan says some governments recognise the advantages of having a quality hotel brand in their cities and get involved in the hotel business through PPPs. 'People going into new markets want to know two things – can they fly in on a safe, reliable airline and can they stay in a safe, reliable hotel. Some governments recognise this and want international hotels to attract foreign investors to do business in their country.

'Most of our growth comes through new-build hotels because converting existing hotels in Africa to meet our standards is very difficult. However, there are occasions when we come across an old hotel carcass which was built solidly and has the potential to be rebuilt to its former glory. This type of hotel project gives us a head start in time versus a new build and provides a saving of more than 30 per cent for the hotel owner.'

Although Rezidor is very involved in the look and feel of the hotels it manages, the final choice lies with the owners. 'Our interior design style follows a modern, minimalistic trend and styling with a local accent. An international customer wants the comfort of being in a quality hotel, with all the security and safety features, but still feels he or she is in Dakar or Lagos and not in Copenhagen or London. We have to get the design balance right.'

INTERNATIONAL ROOTS

Rezidor has a long and complex corporate history. The hotel group emerged out of the catering services of Scandinavian Airlines (SAS) to become SAS Catering and Hotels. The airline diversified into the hotel industry in 1960 to complement its flight network, starting with a hotel in Copenhagen, which was one of the first 'designer' hotels in the world – the creation of legendary designer Arne Jacobsen. Today the hotel, renamed Radisson Blu Royal Hotel, Copenhagen, is one of the city's prime attractions.

After various incarnations and name changes over decades, the group went public in 2006 as The Rezidor Hotel Group. The company is listed on the Stockholm Stock Exchange and Carlson Companies is its largest shareholder with 50.1 per cent of the stock. Rezidor has changed the name of its core brand, Radisson SAS, to Radisson Blu, reflecting the end of its links with the SAS Airlines Group.

The Rezidor portfolio has expanded to more than 430 hotels and 97,000 rooms in 70 countries across Europe, the Middle East and Africa, reflecting year-on-year growth of 17 per cent since the late 1990s. Of the 100-plus hotels under development in 2013, more than 80 per cent were in emerging markets, including Africa, Russia and the Middle East.

'In 16 years Radisson has become the largest upscale brand in Europe. It is bigger than all the older well-known competitors such as Hilton, Marriott, Intercontinental, Sheraton and Sofitel. We have a flat organisational structure and can move fast. We have empowered people on the ground to make decisions,' says McLachlan.

A LOOK AT THE COMPETITION

'The level of competition depends on where you are and what segment of the market you are trying to enter. In the five-star bracket, our competition is from premier global brands. In the mid-market bracket, the main competition is from growing regional African brands. These include Southern Sun, Protea Hotels, Three Cities and Legacy Group from South Africa; African Sun from Zimbabwe, and Senova and Serena from East Africa.

'In Francophone Africa, where we have nine hotels, our main competitor is the French chain Accor with brands like Ibis, Novotel, Sofitel and more recently Pullman. But there is a lot less competition because of the language issue. We have a strong presence in France and Belgium so French-speaking travellers already know our Radisson Blu and Park Inn by Radisson brands. At one time if you didn't have a presence in Paris, Francophone Africa didn't want to talk to you but now we find they want something new and they like the fact we aren't a French company.'

CHALLENGES

A key challenge in the hotel industry is the high cost of building and availability of local construction skills. 'We try to use a main contractor with a presence in more than one market and put together a professional team that we can use across markets. Once the hotel is built, we have to train staff as there is no ready pool of local people trained in the international hospitality industry to draw on.'

Building costs in Africa are typically higher than in most other regions because the operating environment tends to be more expensive. Costs are evaluated on a 'per key' basis, which is the total cost of development divided by the number of rooms, excluding land as this is always the biggest variable from location to location.

'The cost per key of a Radisson Blu can vary depending on the location. We have this brand being developed from $200,000 per key in parts of East Africa, $250,000 in South Africa to as much as $400,000 in Nigeria. On average though a typical Radisson Blu Hotel will cost $250,000 per key.'

Another challenge is the loophole opened up by the fact that many international brands have not registered their trademark in countries where they do not have a presence. This allows local operators to 'knock off' these brands and lure custom from travellers who think they are dealing with international chains. For example, Addis Ababa in Ethiopia boasts a Marriot (spelled with one 't') and an Intercontinental Hotel, neither of which has a link to the international groups with those names. In Nigeria, there is a Crowne Plaza that has no link to the US's Intercontinental chain and a Citilodge group that is spelled slightly differently to the well-known South African City Lodge chain.

The implication is that international groups may not be able to trade under their own brands in certain countries should they want to enter those markets. There are also potential reputational issues if the local hotels are not run to international standards.

McLachlan says Rezidor has thought ahead on this issue. 'Quite early in our regional development strategy, we decided on which countries we wanted to be in and, even if we didn't have a deal in place, we registered our brand and trademark there. So these are not issues when we do enter.'

He says that in emerging markets the time taken between signing a deal and opening a hotel is a lot longer than it is in Europe, or even South Africa. 'Shortening this time can be difficult given that a lot of product is imported and there are often lengthy delays getting cargo out of the harbour.' Key staff, such as the hotel manager, are appointed earlier in the development process in Africa because it can take longer to source skills, do training and complete other pre-opening processes. The full staff complement comes on board two months before opening.

Another challenge is stretching budgets. 'Due to time, cost of funding, importation and transportation, we are always rationalising our designs so we get the very most for our buck.

'In the Middle East, there aren't the budget constraints you have in Africa but there are more religious and cultural issues to consider. For example, in certain countries you have to provide separate swimming pools for women and men, separate banqueting facilities and two sets of bathrooms. We don't have that problem in African countries.'

Government bureaucracy and unnecessary red tape are hurdles experienced by any business setting up in an Africa country and Rezidor is no exception, says McLachlan. 'There can sometimes be government interference in a deal. For example, if a hotel owner has links to a top government official or minister and that job changes hands, the new official sometimes wants to re-examine the deal or the land lease, delaying the project or shutting it down.'

Access to debt locally has improved as local and regional financial institutions have grown. 'A few years ago in many parts of Africa local banks only provided debt in local currency on two and three terms with interest rates of more than 20 per cent. You couldn't build a hotel in this timeframe, so the owner had to either refinance or start servicing debt before the hotel was open. It sometimes resulted in hotels being built on a piecemeal basis as money became available.

'It is now possible to get dollar loans at much more attractive interest rates with terms of seven to ten years, which has made it feasible to build bigger and more sophisticated hotels.'

FUTURE PLANS

Rezidor is keeping its foot on the expansion pedal with new hotels in Libreville (Gabon), Conakry (Guinea) and Freetown (Sierra Leone), the latter being the only new international hotel built in the West African country since civil war began there in the 1990s. 'As a first mover, we expect to control these markets for a number of years as they are big enough for one international hotel to do well but not big enough for a second high-end brand.'

High demand for hotel rooms in resource rich countries, which often have limited infrastructure, has caught Rezidor's eye and it is looking at opportunities in Uganda, DRC and the Republic of Congo, economies that are growing rapidly on the back of mining and oil.

'South Africa and Nigeria remain key markets and we are looking for opportunities in Durban, the one main city we don't currently have a presence in within South Africa - and at smaller urban centres. We have more than ten negotiations under way in Nigeria, mostly in the Park Inn by Radisson brand.

'An area of future expansion in Africa is in leisure tourism. There are great resort opportunities on the continent. Our resort portfolio is currently only ten per cent of the total and we would like to grow it to 15 per cent through opportunities in the Indian Ocean Islands, Mozambique, South Africa, Tanzania, Kenya and North Africa.'

Leisure options can enable the company to keep loyal business customers within the brand for their holidays. 'If we don't have an offering that allows them to burn off their loyalty points, there is a chance they could stay with the competition. Resorts are very brand enhancing – it is easier to get media coverage and people tend to talk about their holiday accommodation but not the hotels in which they stay on business trips. Word of mouth is still the strongest form of advertising.'

A new growth area is the conference circuit. In Rwanda, for example, the government has commissioned not only a 292-room Radisson Blu hotel but also a 34,000 m^2 world class conference and exhibition centre as a catalyst for growth in the capital Kigali. 'The largest such facility in the region at the moment is in Kenya, but it is more than 35 years old,' notes McLachlan.

'Global international brands have gone into all major emerging markets in the world. There may be an opportunity for realignment between overseas and regional brands in joint ventures, for example. Regional companies understand their home market very well but don't always have the same marketing reach as international companies. Rising competition will force everyone to up their game.'

The Coca-Cola Company has a presence in more than 200 countries worldwide and markets more than 3,500 beverage products, including water, juice drinks, teas, coffees, sports drinks and energy drinks. It directly employs some 68,000 people in Africa and the Coca-Cola system comprises the company and more than 300 bottling partners worldwide (46 in Africa). Coca-Cola entered Africa in 1928 and today has a presence in all 54 countries on the continent.

RETAIL AND SERVICES

THE COCA-COLA COMPANY

'We see Africa much more in terms of opportunities than risks. In fact, the risk is not having a presence here,' says William Asiko, Director of Public Affairs and Communications for Coca-Cola Africa and President of The Coca-Cola Africa Foundation.

The US-based global company has an ambitious strategy to double its number of 'servings' per day worldwide, from 1.5 billion (2010 level) to three billion by 2020. 'In other words, we will achieve what we have done in the past 125 years in the next ten.' At a time when developed markets are slowing down or showing only moderate growth, African markets are critical to pushing up growth.

In recognition of this, the Coca-Cola Africa system (the company and its bottlers) wants to double the investment it has made in the continent over the past ten years through the course of the next decade. These investments will go into addressing new demand by urbanising middle-class consumers for different products.

The Coca-Cola system is well established across the continent, with a presence in every market.

The company markets and distributes some 80 brands to 925 million African consumers across the continent through a network of 46 bottlers, operating 160 bottling and canning operations and serving 900,000 retailers across the formal and informal sectors.

'We are optimistic and committed to Africa as an increasingly important growth market,' says Asiko. 'Studies suggest that soft drink sales volumes will continue to grow. In South Africa, we foresee solid single digit growth and in Tanzania we are looking at double digit growth over the next few years, to name just two examples.'

South Africa is Coca-Cola's oldest African market. It was established in 1928 when the first bottling plant and distribution centres were opened in Durban and Cape Town and shortly thereafter Johannesburg. It is now the company's biggest market in Africa and one of its top 20 performers globally. Coca-Cola bottlers in South Africa sell an average of 235 beverage servings to each person every year – about ten billion units. The world per capita average is 77 servings. Other top performing markets in Africa are Nigeria, Egypt, Morocco and Kenya.

Finding a Coca-Cola product is easy in Africa. From upmarket restaurants and supermarkets in cities to sprawling informal settlements, Coca-Cola products are readily available wherever one goes.

The company's trademark red signage pops up in the most remote villages and towns across the continent as thousands of small entrepreneurs take beverages into little stores and sidewalk stalls in a supply chain that is the envy of consumer companies across the globe.

Coca-Cola says there is no secret to the success of its supply chain. It is the result of the system's ability to reach into communities and leverage local partnerships. Local entrepreneurs are the key to getting products into remote areas. They are supported with signage, coolers and training and have the added benefits of a consistent supply of stock and being associated with a global brand.

'In general terms, the stand-out feature of Coca-Cola's presence in a market – and Africa is no exception – is that, while the brand is global, the company is local in every country in which it operates. Local manufacturing and distribution are hallmarks of the roll-out in Africa.

'Based on our long-term investment approach and local partnerships, we are highly optimistic about the relevance of our African business – and we have not reduced or revised our growth plans because of global economic conditions in any of our markets.'

Coca-Cola's 2020 Vision is supported by a very positive economic picture of Africa in 2020. This includes the following facts:

- Ten million of Africa's youth will be entering the job market annually
- Africa's collective GDP will be $2.6 trillion
- African consumers are predicted to be spending $1.4 trillion annually
- 1.1 billion Africans will be of working age
- 50 per cent of Africans will most likely be living in cities by 2030
- Africa will have 60 per cent share of the world's total uncultivated arable land.

'Africa is not a market waiting to develop, it is a market already in development,' says Asiko. 'The opportunity to grow and contribute is there for businesses that are prepared to function in partnership with Africans. The Coca-Cola Company has been committed to the future of Africa for many years and we see recent developments on the continent as a welcome affirmation of our confidence.'

Positive developments that have taken place in recent times include improvements to the business climate. This includes legal reform, administrative improvements, infrastructure investment and business registration. 'This overall development of a more conducive business climate stands out as one of the most important changes in Africa over the past five years or more – changes recognised by rapidly improving rankings in indices developed by the World Economic Forum, the World Bank and others.

'The youthful profile of the African demographic and rapid urbanisation are powerful catalysts for African business growth. If one simply looks at the numbers, the potential is enormous. Without exception, we see every African market holding the prospect for growth,' says Asiko.

SUSTAINABLE COMMUNITIES

'One reason for The Coca-Cola Company's long and successful history is our approach to doing business in a way that benefits the long-term interests of the communities in which we operate. At the same time, the economic value of our local businesses is growing. For our business to be sustainable, local communities need to be sustainable.'

The framework for Coca-Cola's commitment to sustainability is called

Live Positively. Through Live Positively its says it is able to 'think holistically and globally about sustainability efforts throughout the Coca-Cola system'. The framework includes goals, metrics and 'principles for work in developing benefits, supporting healthy living programmes, building communities, improving environmental programmes for its operations and creating a safe, inclusive work environment for associates'.

'When I was a young boy growing up in Kenya, it always struck me how naturally entrepreneurial people can be,' says Asiko. 'However, what they often need is a bit of training and guidance to take their ideas to the next level.

'Most of the people you come across in the villages of Africa understand how to trade. Through programmes like our Micro Distribution Centre (MDC) project, we are getting them to think about their business as a provider of income and employment, not just for themselves but also for other members of their community. To me the mark of a successful business is one that assists people to do what they are good at, just better.'

CORPORATE EVOLUTION

The history of Coca-Cola has two hallmarks – one, that it is a local company with local partners in every market, and two, that global standards of quality are applied everywhere in the world.

The success of the supply chain in developing countries is typified by the MDC model. 'This was developed out of a business need – to distribute our product in hard-to-reach markets,' explains Asiko.

MDCs are small product distribution centres managed by local people. In Africa there are more than 3,200 of these small businesses, directly employing more than 19,000 people. More than 800 of them are exclusively owned and managed by women and an additional 800 are managed by women as co-owners.

'To succeed in Africa, companies must explore new models of collaboration that focus on shared values that recognise the connection between business success and sustainable communities.'

Coca-Cola has used the same model of small entrepreneurs effectively in Latin America and Mexico, which currently has the highest per capita consumption of Coca-Cola in the world.

In 2009 the company made a commitment to empower women in its businesses as part of the Clinton Global Initiative interventions, which aim to build a community of global leaders to forge solutions to the world's most pressing challenges. Since then, more than 50 per cent of new MDCs created have been owned and run by women.

These small operations get Coca-Cola products to consumers in remote areas. They also mean jobs, income and more stable lives. 'It is important to note that MDCs are localised and community rooted – they are not imposed by the business, but rather have risen through collaboration,' adds Asiko.

The use of micro distribution continues to grow. In countries such as Kenya, Tanzania, Uganda, Ethiopia and Mozambique it represents the majority of sales, while its use is growing rapidly in North and West Africa, particularly in Nigeria and Ghana, where more than 70 per cent of the micro distributors are owned by women. Similar models are now being replicated in other comparable markets in Coca-Cola's business worldwide.

'I'd recommend that when doing business in Africa, be local and involve local communities in your work,' says Asiko. 'Provide consistent quality, take a long-term view and do business in a manner that benefits and sustains the local communities that you touch. We have learned that partnerships are a key factor for success.'

American multinational, DuPont, founded in 1802, applies science and innovation to solve challenges in the commercial market, working across many sectors, including agriculture, nutrition, energy, construction, protection and the automotive industry. It operates in approximately 90 countries, employs 8,500 scientists and engineers and has more than 75 research centres and 250,000 products. It is the 75th-largest US industrial service corporation on the *Fortune 500* list. Its sub-Saharan African headquarters are in South Africa and it has operations in ten countries on the continent.

SCIENCE AND TECHNOLOGY

DUPONT

'The biggest opportunity in Africa for the future lies in the agriculture sector,' says Carlman Moyo, Regional Director, sub-Saharan Africa, for American multinational company, DuPont. 'The current average maize yield in Africa is less than two tonnes per hectare. We need to double or even triple that to feed the growing population. In the US, for example, the average maize yield per hectare is nearly ten tonnes.

'The same hectare of land that fed two people in 1960 will need to feed five by 2025. Put simply, we need to grow more food on less land if we are going to feed more people without using more natural habitats and biologically diverse, unfarmed land for agricultural use. We need to do this while emitting fewer greenhouse gases and using less water,' says Moyo.

'There are examples that prove this can be done, but it takes serious investment in targeted, effective agricultural policies based on best practice and local needs. It's also been proven that when you raise agricultural productivity you see tangible benefits to society.

'According to the World Bank, growth in agriculture is at least twice as effective in reducing poverty as growth in other sectors. It reduces poverty by raising farm incomes, by generating employment and by reducing potential for volatility in food prices.

'There are also environmental benefits from raising agricultural productivity. The environmental challenges we face are formidable: climate change and hotter, drier conditions for much of Africa, increased water scarcity and diminishing biodiversity. Huge population growth means more people to feed, protect and provide energy for.'

Science, he says, can play a role in increasing yields and improving farming methods through innovation, producing hybrid seeds that can better withstand drought and disease and increasing technology options in farming. The company has invested millions of dollars in research and development to improve food quantity and quality. 'In Ethiopia, where DuPont has worked with farmers, small-scale local producers have increased their yield by more than 300 per cent over the past 15 years by using new agricultural technologies.

'DuPont is also focusing on ways of increasing nutrition, especially in Africa, where there has traditionally been a reliance on meat as a source of protein. There is not enough meat to go around and we are looking at soy as a more sustainable source of protein. To extract 1kg of protein from soy costs nearly ten times less than the same amount of protein from a cow.'

THE CASE FOR AFRICA

Moyo says three key trends are driving sub-Saharan Africa's economic growth. 'One is economic and geographic diversity within the region, which comprises many markets, each with varying degrees of economic and political maturity. There are also varying degrees of growth and economic contribution by different sectors. According to the United States Embassy in South Africa, the following sectors contributed to South Africa's GDP in 2011: agriculture and mining (12.2 per cent); manufacturing, construction and utilities (20.8 per cent) and trade, transport and services (67 per cent).

'The second trend is political stability and improving governance. According to the 2011 Ibrahim Index of African Governance, just over half the countries in Africa have improved in overall governance quality over the last five years. The countries that have consistently ranked in the top five are Mauritius, Cape Verde, Botswana, Seychelles and South Africa. There's been a notable decrease in armed conflict and corruption and a strengthening of the rule of law and transparency.

'The third trend is demographic change under way in the region, with a growing youthful population, more people in the work force and a dramatic growth of the middle class that has triggered more disposable income and an unprecedented demand for goods and services.'

Moyo says DuPont has also identified three 'megatrends' that are driving growth globally and these have been aligned to 86 per cent of the company's annual research and development spend, which topped $2 billion in 2011.

'The first is increasing food production. Supply and demand in the growing needs of the world's more than seven billion people are significantly incongruent. Africa's population is one of the fastest growing and it is predicted to double its population to nearly two billion people by 2050 – more than 20 per cent of the world population. Feeding this population is a significant challenge. About a quarter of the world's nearly one billion food-insecure people live in Africa,' says Moyo.

However, the continent's favourable climatic conditions and natural agricultural resources can be turned into a competitive advantage, allowing the region to contribute to addressing these global challenges. Food supply can be improved using biotechnology, which, in some cases, has increased larger local farmers' yields by 20 per cent to 30 per cent per hectare and small-scale farmers' yields by up to 40 per cent.

'The second megatrend is decreasing dependence on fossil fuels. By 2030 the world will consume 60 per cent more energy than it does currently and the supply of fuels will not last at this pace. Africa is endowed with abundant natural resources that can be harvested for energy.

'We are working with several major oil suppliers to introduce innovative solutions and new technologies. We use our science to help transform the sun's potential into clean, efficient energy, providing innovative materials for photovoltaic applications and modules and offer materials that contribute to the performance, reliability and operation of wind turbines.

'A decade ago we pledged to hold our total energy use flat, on absolute terms, at 1990 levels. Our current annual energy use is 13 per cent below those levels despite a 45 per cent production increase. We have products and solutions in the market that also help our customers and value chains to reduce energy consumption. These three areas – energy efficiency, more effective oil and gas extraction and use, and renewable sources of energy – will significantly contribute to reducing our dependence on fossil fuels.'

Biofuels is another area of energy specialisation. DuPont is developing technology to generate energy from the stems of plants, rather than the grain. 'If you can do this commercially, the sky is the limit,' he says, adding that such a process addresses the criticism about biofuels crowding out food crops.

The third megatrend is protecting people and the environment, a major challenge given rising population rates.

Moyo offers a few quick facts on why he believes opening Africa's markets for international business and global trade is a step in the right direction.

- Six of the top ten fastest growing economies are in Africa.
- By some estimates, Africa has ten per cent of the world's oil deposits, 40 per cent of gold deposits, 90 per cent of platinum/chromium deposits and 60 per cent of the world's uncultivated arable land.
- Africa has the largest growth rate of mobile phone subscribers. The 500 million subscriber total in 2011, driven by growth in Nigeria, South Africa, Kenya and Ghana, was double that of 2008.
- There is a growing desire and aspiration by Africans to compete. Africans are now among the biggest investors in Africa.
- Disposable incomes are growing.
- There are improvements in the regulatory space.
- The gradual removal of cross-border trade barriers and the establishment of free trade areas is making doing business easier and creating larger markets.
- There is an increase in political stability and the number of democratically elected governments.

THE AFRICAN FOOTPRINT

DuPont has been involved in Africa's agricultural industry for more than two decades. In 2010 DuPont in South Africa upgraded to a wholly owned subsidiary to serve as the headquarters for expansion into sub-Saharan Africa.

'Previously, 90 per cent of our sub-Saharan African sales were coming from South Africa and the company was happy with that. But now that other countries in the region are more open to business and investing is easier, it makes sense to be there,' says Moyo.

The company, which saw growth in Africa at a steady rate of 21 per cent over the five years to 2012, has operations in ten countries, production sites in four and research stations in Kenya and South Africa.

'We are focused on the top ten economies of sub-Saharan Africa by GDP. These constitute 80 per cent of Africa's overall GDP. Within these, we've prioritised the three biggest and most influential markets in each of the sub-regions – South Africa for Southern Africa, Kenya for East Africa and Nigeria for West Africa.'

Much of DuPont's work in agriculture is conducted through its subsidiary company Pioneer Hi-Bred, the world's leading developer and supplier of advanced plant genetics. Pioneer provides agronomic support and services to help increase farmer productivity and profitability and strives to develop sustainable agricultural systems.

Moyo says relationships with governments are changing in nature. 'Government relations traditionally have been focused on permits and the right to operate. But increasingly they are becoming more about investment and job creation.

'Getting governments to understand the work we are doing to solve problems is part of the infrastructure that we are developing here in Africa. It's a capability that we need in every key country. They need to be more aware of scientific developments and how they can improve access to new technologies. Science is available but if you don't know how to use it it is not of any benefit.

'Sub-Saharan Africa is among the top ten markets in terms of revenues for DuPont in our Europe, Middle East and Africa region. Our target for the region is to grow sales at 15 per cent CAGR (compound annual growth rate) over the next three to five years. We hope that sub-Saharan Africa will be among our top revenue contributors in the near future.'

In deciding which markets to enter, DuPont looks at a combination of macro-economic factors such as population growth, infrastructure, risk profile, regulatory environment, skills, liquidity and the business environment as well as microeconomic factors including the availability of partners the company can work with.

'One of the factors contributing to DuPont's success over the years is working very closely through the supply chain and the value chain. A good understanding of the market is critical to ensuring our products are tailored to meet the market's real needs, as opposed to what the transactional customer thinks the market needs. This means we are focused on having the right people in the right positions and looking for solutions locally by collaborating with customers, governments, NGOs, universities and other stakeholders in a market.'

CHALLENGES

Moyo acknowledges that, while emerging market economies present growth prospects, many challenges exist. One of these is the diversity of markets. Africa is not, as it is sometimes perceived to be, a homogeneous market. This complication is exacerbated by the distances between countries and a lack of infrastructure development.

'Then again, risks in Africa are lower because the continent is not one single market. If there is a downturn in one country, it doesn't necessarily mean that other markets are affected. By and large it's a cash-driven continent and when there's a downturn we're not affected by credit on our hands. But there are specific challenges related to cash-driven economies too.'

Another challenge is the need to tailor global technology and materials to meet local needs and environments. Skills shortages, competition for the investment dollar and increasing competition from China and India are others. And Moyo says little is being done in Africa about standards and policies to ensure food safety.

Sometimes small issues can have a big impact. 'I find it frustrating when one is invited to invest in a country but then find you're challenged with getting the required work permits to set up your business. In some instances this can take years, which has an impact on the speed of take-off in that market.'

Moyo adds that one of the insights gained from doing business in Africa is that reality is very different from written theory. 'I've learned that in some of the highest risk markets you have some of the greatest returns, as long as you mitigate your risks. I've also learned that timing is critical – if you don't penetrate a market early, it may be difficult to enter that market later. It is important to use local people with local market knowledge; and it's possible to do business in Africa without giving in to corruption. This reinforces the importance of sound core values and sticking to them – that is critical to long-term sustainability.'

What needs to be put in place to unlock Africa's potential? Moyo lists his priorities:

- A continued drive to open up trade between African countries
- Improved regulatory space and policy framework and policing of that environment
- Investment in infrastructure
- Maintenance of democracy
- Investment in education
- Growth in the industrial base
- Exploitation of science to improve agriculture and energy availability
- Commitment to sustainable development
- Capitalising on country strengths and resource richness
- Focusing on governance. This should include putting in place clear strategies for investment in infrastructure, education and security

'Emerging market economies present lucrative opportunities and Africa is growing rapidly with many global players keeping an eye on African prospects. The continent has become a critical factor in DuPont's future expansion.'

General Electric (GE), one of the world's biggest companies, operates in the services, technology and manufacturing sectors in more than 100 countries and employs 300,000 people worldwide. Its business segments include Energy Infrastructure, Aviation, Healthcare, Transportation, Home & Business Solutions and GE Capital. Established in 1892, today GE is the only company listed on the Dow Jones Industrial Index that was also included in the original Index in 1896. It is one of the top US companies in the *Fortune 500* and is ranked as the eigth largest in the world, based on revenues. In 2011 it established GE Africa, which has its headquarters in Nairobi, Kenya.

DIVERSIFIED INDUSTRIAL AND FINANCIAL SERVICES

GENERAL ELECTRIC

Africa is a key driver for General Electric's future growth strategy, says Lazarus Angbazo, President and CEO for East, Central and West Africa. Despite the fact that GE is one of the world's biggest companies, Angbazo says it is fairly small in Africa. 'The Africa operations have less than two per cent of the company's global revenues and fewer than 0.5 per cent of its total number of employees.'

Angbazo, who is also GE's Commercial Growth Leader for the Africa region, believes the continent's infrastructure deficit is a major opportunity for a company with capability in this area. 'Africa is a key region for both GE and the world; resources are abundant and potential is boundless. The company is focusing on oil and gas, power, healthcare, water treatment, transportation, aviation and financial services.

'Obviously a lot of the existing business is in the oil and gas sector because the continent has a number of large international oil and gas companies in Angola and Nigeria, and there are many new discoveries across the continent that will further open up this sector. Power is also an obvious opportunity because the shortages across the continent are so huge and we believe the pipeline is going to get much bigger.'

Nigeria is a priority market for GE in general, and particularly in the power sector, where a major reform and privatisation programme is under way. This country of an estimated 167 million people has installed capacity of 10,000 megawatts (MW) but generates a mere 4,000MW. Less than half of Nigerians are connected to the grid and most people rely on their own sources of power generation.

The ailing state power holding company has been unbundled into 18 entities. Of these, six power generation plants and 11 distribution companies are earmarked for privatisation. The government aims to generate 40,000MW by 2030. The privatisation process has attracted considerable investor interest although delays in the reform timetable have raised concerns.

Angbazo believes there is no turning back on the reform process. GE signed a five-year power development memorandum of understanding with the Nigerian government in 2012 to invest in the sector. 'We see the power sector as a major growth catalyst in this country,' he says. The deal raises the possibility of GE and the government taking minority equity positions in viable projects, where GE would supply power generation technology and services. GE's 'company-to-country' agreement with Nigeria is the first of its kind in Africa and also covers other critical infrastructure in sectors such as healthcare and rail transportation.

Angbazo says the tendency of African power utilities to operate as monopolies is a deterrent to investment. 'Nigeria had created its power sector structures in such a way that no investor came near it for decades.' He adds that South Africa's Eskom is also a monopoly. 'It is an operator, generator of last resort and a regulator. This makes it difficult to reform the system.' It was only in 2011 that South Africa allowed in independent power producers.

Other African countries are also reforming their power sectors, with varying degrees of success. The Ghana Power Sector Reform Programme was initiated in the late 1990s and has yet to be completed. Kenya, on the other hand, has made great strides into new areas of generation such as wind energy (in which GE has an investment) and geothermal energy. The country plans to get half of its electricity from geothermal sources by 2018.

Things are not happening as quickly as they could, but, says Angbazo, governments in Africa are stretched. 'As countries reform, governments are being asked to do things they are not structured to do well. As well as trying to address poverty and provide employment, they have to manage their fiscal position and many other issues. On top of that you have the challenges from the global financial crisis. All this is a big stress on governments.'

He maintains that the main political risks in Africa are not so much conflict but bureaucratic stagnation and a lack of policy continuity. Security is also an issue – security of people, assets and payments. 'We fly in, sell equipment and hope to get money out at the end of it but there is always payment risk. Governments do eventually pay – the risk is not one of default, it is a timing risk.

'The risk and opportunity equation has always been a factor in investing in Africa. But we are finding ways to manage all these risks intelligently. As risk becomes more complex, it forces us to change our models. In doing so we need to strike a balance and make sure we are not, in the process of addressing risk, actually stifling business growth. But the perception of risk in Africa is much higher than the reality.'

He says the way business is conducted in Africa is changing and there are real moves towards partnerships and increased demand for localisation of businesses. 'You have to put down proper roots in a country and you also have to develop local partners. A local partner will help you to manage the risk but you have to be extremely selective. But that is also getting easier as African companies are becoming more sophisticated. We are certainly seeing this in Nigeria, for example, where you have probably the largest group of local indigenous entrepreneurs outside South Africa. The country is becoming world class in terms of the capacity and talent it is building.'

Angbazo says countries such as Nigeria and South Africa are self-sufficient, but a lingering socialist legacy in some countries still holds back private sector development.

CORPORATE FOOTPRINT

GE has had a presence in Africa for more than a century, signalling a commitment to a market that many global multinationals are only now starting to pay attention to. It has seven offices around the continent, including two in North Africa, in Egypt and Algeria. Its oldest presence is in South Africa where it established itself alongside other American multinationals such as Coca-Cola, General Motors and IBM many decades ago and where it now has an operation with about 300 employees.

It has been in Angola since 1967 and has a long-standing presence in Nigeria and Kenya. By 2011 GE had more than 1,500 employees in Africa and $3.6 billion in revenues.

All of GE's business segments, including energy, healthcare, aviation and transportation, have operations on the continent. Its key facilities in Africa are:

- GE Oil & Gas workshop in Cabinda and Luanda, Angola
- GE Oil & Gas workshop in Malabo, Equatorial Guinea
- GE Energy and GE Oil & Gas facilities in Lagos and Onne, Nigeria
- GE Oil & Gas Repair, Training & Global Service Sales Centre, Port Harcourt, Nigeria
- GE Energy Africa headquarters and GE Energy Management-Switchgear Manufacturing and Assembly, Johannesburg, South Africa.

The company has a $30 million corporate citizenship initiative, Developing Health Globally, to improve hospitals and clinics in ten countries on the continent – Ghana, Ethiopia, Kenya, Malawi, Mali, Nigeria, Rwanda, Senegal, Tanzania and Uganda. The project has been running for nearly a decade and has built goodwill and profile for the company even in countries in which it does not operate. It is also gaining knowledge that it hopes will help it to design products for African markets, something it has already done in Asia.

'The solutions for Africa's problems, challenges and issues must originate from the people living on its continent. That does not mean discounting the technological strides made outside the continent, but rather incorporating the global experience with local innovation,' says Angbazo.

GE focuses its healthcare efforts in countries that are politically stable, transparent, committed to improving healthcare and willing to invest their own money. It has made interventions in more than 150 healthcare facilities and its Africa programme has been so successful that it has been expanded to Southeast Asia and Latin America.

In 2008 senior executives from GE's Business Management Course visited Africa and spent time in Kenya, Nigeria and Mozambique meeting industry leaders, governments, academics and others in an effort to better understand challenges and opportunities on the continent. This month-long 'field study' resulted in GE stepping up its African investments.

Angbazo says the company has adopted a partnership approach for projects. 'We are working with many governments in Africa and taking a degree of commercial risk in projects in which we get involved.'

He cites the example of the evolving relationship with Nigeria through the company-to-country agreement and a $250 million seawater desalination plant in Algeria where ownership is shared between GE and the government of Algeria. But partnerships are increasingly with private sector indigenous African companies. Both approaches are helping GE to localise operations and become a local African company.

PROJECT CHALLENGES

Angbazo says governments in Africa see PPPs as a solution to the challenges of getting projects off the ground, but the concept is still at an evolutionary stage.

'The PPP model is mostly still academic. Laws to facilitate PPPs are just being developed in many countries and the institutional capacity for the relevant ministries to create PPP projects that are attractive to the private sector is not really there. Even in a rapidly developing country such as Nigeria, there are still just guidelines in place in this regard. South Africa is an exception as it is much further developed but, even there, we have seen delays in terms of getting healthcare PPPs off the ground.

'We tend to invest a lot in capacity building within governments to enable them to move from the concept stage of projects to the development phase. They have the budgets and good ideas but the process of translating the ideas into bankable projects is where things sometimes break down.

'So our focus is to expand our scope and co-develop these projects with governments and private investors to the point where we can take them to market. The advantage of having GE on board is the technical pull-through of projects for our business.'

Political will to get projects off the ground is another constraint to development. 'We always hope regional economic communities will be a catalyst and conduit for regional mega projects. But they have long pipelines and the discussions about projects can go on for decades in some cases. There are huge needs for power projects, rail and other infrastructure and some of it needs to go across borders. Different countries are not at the same level of preparedness or capability and the political will is difficult to get.'

Angbazo says GE is committed to steering clear of any corrupt business practices. 'We are in an era where we have an emerging class of political and corporate leadership that is insisting on ethical business models.' Though companies themselves can be a corrupting influence, if governments are serious they will look for companies to do business with that operate with integrity.

SILVER LININGS

The return of skilled Africans from the Diaspora has been a silver lining of the global financial crisis. 'In the hunt for talent, global companies are focusing on the main Diaspora markets to fulfil their own talent requirements and localisation needs. It is not easy to bring expatriate talent into African countries anymore and governments are implementing quotas using work permits and visas. Getting the right human resources is one of the challenges of putting down roots in new markets.

'In almost every country there is huge interest in upgrading and modernising the infrastructure that is already there. There is a clear rationale in this – connecting the hinterland to the ports and the sea, which is compelling, and this offers GE many opportunities.'

On the infrastructure front, Angbazo is particularly upbeat about the future of rail, which has assumed a new importance in the investment landscape. The resources boom has provided new impetus to the rehabilitation of rail networks such as the Tanzania-Zambia Railway (Tanzam) from Dar es Salaam port to the mining region of Zambia and the line from Lobito in Angola into the hinterland, connecting to the commodity rich regions of the DRC and Zambia. In countries such as Mozambique and Guinea, resources companies Vale and Rio Tinto are building new railways to get goods to port. South Africa started a major rail rehabilitation project in 2012 and the government plans to spend $25.9 billion on rail by 2019.

'Our focus at the moment is on providing rolling stock because even if the railway lines are rehabilitated there is a major shortage of locomotives and trucks. GE is modernising 18 locomotives for the Tanzania-Zambia Railway Authority and will install the Bright Star Control System, which will lead to better fuel consumption and fault detection. In 2010 GE supplied 25 of its latest and most fuel-efficient diesel locomotives to Nigeria, which increased rail freight tonnage by 30 per cent and helped launch systems-wide modernisation of the rail logistics infrastructure.

South Africa's Transnet bought 43 diesel-electric locomotives, the first of their kind in sub-Saharan Africa, from GE South Africa Technologies in 2012.

These were in addition to another 100 locomotives bought by Transnet from GE, 90 of which were to be built in South Africa as part of the government's competitive supplier development programme, which requires suppliers to commit to stringent local requirements of industrialisation, skills development, job creation and preservation of technology and intellectual property.

'There is pressure for the private sector to assist with developing the healthcare sector, which has been largely left to local government. We are probably three to five years away from real commitment to and investment in the sector. Increased per capita incomes and demand for better living standards will drive investment in healthcare infrastructure.

'Power is also a big factor because it is a key catalyst for growth and countries need to keep up the growth momentum, not least because there is a rapidly growing young population that needs opportunities. In general, improving infrastructure is key not just to growth but also to sustainable development.'

He says multinationals are helping to drive the development of the continent, bringing significant capability to Africa. 'Their presence here speaks for itself about the kind of opportunities that exist on the continent. GE itself has been here for more than a hundred years and there are many others with deep roots in Africa. They are all playing a significant role in bringing benefits such as technology and capacity development and they are emphasising the benefits of good corporate governance. Multinational companies put the same emphasis on these issues in Africa as they do in advanced economies.

'And it is now imperative to reinvest profits in markets in which you operate. The days are gone when companies went into markets and just took profits out. There is much longer term thinking now and Africa is not just a sales market for international companies. There are high expectations for genuine partnerships. Consumers also want value for money and will look for quality of products and services.'

Angbazo says the debate about Chinese versus Western products is a non-issue. 'Under the right circumstances, Africans will go for quality over cost. The African customer now has the best of both worlds. Everyone has to compete for a rising customer base in new emerging markets. But there is also room for co-operation between Western companies and between Western companies and emerging market companies, providing new opportunities for smart partnerships.

'GE is effectively competing and collaborating simultaneously with Chinese, Korean and Brazilian companies. The company's Global Growth and Operation division focuses on these emerging markets and partnerships with leading entities from these regions.'

Established in 1975, Imperial Logistics is a division of South Africa's Imperial Group, a listed globally diversified industrial services and retail conglomerate with activities in car rental, tourism, financial services, vehicle distribution and retail as well as logistics in Southern Africa and Europe (Germany). Imperial Logistics in Southern Africa has five key divisions – Transport and Warehousing, Consumer Products, Specialised Freight, Integration Services and Africa, which covers Southern Africa and is expanding into East and West Africa. The Africa division subsidiaries include CIC Holdings, Colbro Transport, Etosha Transport, Interchain Logistics, IJ Snyman Transport, Namibië Multi Loads, Transport Holdings, Express Cartage, Petrologistics, Truckafrica Group, WP Transport and Zimbulk Tankers. In 2013, the company expanded to West Africa, acquiring a significant stake in MDS Logistics, a division of UAC Nigeria.

LOGISTICS AND SUPPLY CHAIN

IMPERIAL LOGISTICS

'With the new interest in African markets, the continent's strategic importance within the global supply chain is on the increase and that's a substantial opportunity for Imperial,' says George de Beer, Financial Director of Imperial Logistics Africa.

'Circumstances are improving on the African continent all the time, but the hype about the continent as the next emerging market investment opportunity is a perhaps little overheated. There is a sense that all businesses have to do is to invest and set up shop and they will rake in the millions and walk away. In Africa it's not that simple. It's not cheap to invest and it's not easy to do business. The further north you go from where we are in South Africa, the harder and more expensive it gets,' says De Beer.

Some of the highest growth markets on the continent have the weakest infrastructure, such as the DRC and Angola. Companies such as Imperial are urging government and industry bodies to promote infrastructure development by whatever means possible, whether through PPPs or by other means.

'We need more regional infrastructure but this requires countries to collaborate and the political will is not always there,' notes De Beer. 'Even though regional organisations are doing a lot of work on cross-border projects, they have to get these signed off by heads of state and this is where the problem lies. If leaders and governments are too nationally focused and can't see the benefits for the region, that is a big stumbling block to getting projects off the ground.'

The logistics business is very sensitive to national politics, De Beer explains. He cites the case of Malawi, where the economy ran into trouble after Britain, the biggest donor to the aid-dependent country, withdrew its budget support because of economic mismanagement and poor governance by the previous government and was followed by other donors. Cargo flows from South Africa dried up shortly afterwards.

In Zimbabwe, where logistics companies endured tough times during the decade of economic decline, business is on the rise again following the political settlement of 2009. 'Zimbabwe is a strategically important country because it will always be a transit hub for goods into the rest of the region.'

With Angola's economy opening up, business has generally been brisk of late with notable increases in consumer goods being trucked in from South Africa. But, during the global financial crisis, which hit commodity-dependent Angola hard, business dropped right off. Although it has picked up again, road volumes have fallen as a result of increased efficiencies at the port in Luanda.

There are other kinds of political problems. In Zambia, during the 2011 election, vehicles were being stoned by protesters and the company had to park its trucks in a protected location for nearly a week. 'At a cost of R3,000 (about $375) per day over the period for each truck, it was quite pricey. And that was a peaceful election,' observed De Beer.

'Political risk is very high on our agenda. We have to follow events closely. We get a lot of overseas consultants who want to sell us country reports and sometimes we have to ask if they have ever travelled in Africa. Macro-economics is one thing but it is crucial to understand what is happening on ground level and it is difficult to do that from behind a desk. There is no rule book for Africa. You have to adapt quickly to situations, you must be entrepreneurial and think on your feet.'

He believes the easiest way to sell the continent to company executives elsewhere who are unsure about investing is to get them to travel in Africa. They are usually impressed with what they see and come back with a different view of the potential. They see good businesses, properly functioning cities and many other things that they did not expect to find.

'Many people no longer view the continent as "darkest Africa". Most countries have been stable for a long time and their economies are opening up. Urbanisation is happening rapidly; people are becoming Westernised and they want Western goods, such as mobile phones. Improved communication has benefited everyone in Africa, including us. It has made it a lot easier to do business,' says De Beer.

THE CORPORATE FOOTPRINT

Imperial Logistics, one of three divisions of the Imperial Group, is a global logistics and supply chain provider. It has five key divisions, namely transport and warehousing, consumer products, specialised freight, integration services and Africa. Operations span 14 African countries and, through Imperial Logistics International, its reach is extended to Europe, the US, India and the Far East.

The Africa division operates throughout the Southern African market, from Launda in the west to Tanzania in the east, with the mining areas of Katanga province in south-eastern DRC included. Being a South African company, Imperial Logistics' first regional expansion was into neighbouring countries, but it went further afield as its clients spread into other markets. By 2012 it operated in 14 countries and was looking at East and West African expansion.

Growth in Africa has been pursued through acquisitions. 'But it can be an expensive exercise. Good local companies have been through the hard times and built up brilliant businesses despite the challenges. You are not going to acquire them at bargain prices, particularly because there are not always a lot of choices. But, as economies are improving, so the pool of potential partners is growing.

'We find that our local partners don't want our funding; they want our global systems and management expertise. We bring to the table world-class IT systems, transport and warehouse management systems, staff training and new ideas based on our global experience. It is important to find partners with good corporate governance principles – it saves a lot of time and is important because of our zero tolerance for corruption.'

THE RESOURCES CHALLENGE

The resources boom in Africa has highlighted the continent's rail deficits. Railway infrastructure built several decades ago has suffered from neglect and is barely functioning in most places. This is a particular challenge for resources companies.

In northern Mozambique, international coal mining companies have had to invest heavily in infrastructure to meet demand. A major coal terminal has been built at Beira, the nearest port to the Moatize coal fields, and the shallow port has been dredged to accommodate large Panamax vessels. Further investment in rail capacity is being planned. The existing railway line in the area, the rehabilitated Sena line, only has a capacity of six million tonnes, yet Brazilian miner Vale alone expects to produce more than 20 million tonnes of coal a year from 2014.

By 2020 more than 50 million tonnes of coal will need to be moved, making alternative transport options imperative. Moving the coal by road is not an option as that would require vast numbers of tipper trucks, which would destroy the existing infrastructure. Barging coal down the Zambezi River is also not an ideal solution as continual dredging of sandbanks would be needed.

De Beer says the Chinese have seen the opportunity in rail and are rehabilitating the 1,860km Tanzania-Zambia Railway, built in the 1970s, from the mining area of Kapiri Mposhi in Zambia to Dar es Salaam in Tanzania. Chinese interests have also rebuilt the 1,344km Benguela railway line from Lobito port across Angola with the aim of linking it to the mines in Congo and Zambia.

'There are a lot of rail plans on the table. It will take a long time to get these up and running but improving rail links will change the whole pattern of trade and movement of goods across Southern Africa. While this is good for producers, it will present problems for logistics companies,' he observes.

Despite the high volumes of consumer and capital goods moving from South Africa to regional markets, transporters try to find business on the return leg of a journey to keep costs down. 'Currently we carry copper and iron ore, as well as tobacco, cotton, sugar and other commodities, to Durban and the back hauls are about 70 per cent full on average.'

If companies start to ship their goods by rail through regional ports other than Durban, the back haul loads will be much smaller, making each journey more costly.

'But it makes sense for companies to use the ports closest to them. And as regional ports are being upgraded customers have multiple options. Distance equals cost so the shortest route will always be cheaper, even though it is not the only cost factor. You just have to look at a map to see the business case for using Mombasa (Kenya), Dar es Salaam (Tanzania), Lobito (Angola), Beira (Mozambique) and Walvis Bay (Namibia).'

It is 1,675km from Harare to Durban and less than 600km from Harare to Beira in Mozambique. Similarly, it is more than 2,400kms from Lilongwe in Malawi to Durban, but just 950kms to Beira; 2,000km from Lubumbashi in DRC to Dar es Salaam, but more than 2,700km to Durban.

But, for all the improvements under way, ports are seeing vastly increased volumes and are therefore still experiencing capacity constraints. 'Port dwell times are one of the biggest cost drivers in the supply chain and there are still major inefficiencies in regional ports,' explains De Beer.

'For example, in Mombasa, bulk time – the time taken to get a ship to shore and goods unloaded – is several weeks. Dar es Salaam is also slow. But Maputo is improving and Walvis Bay is very well managed and provides easy transit of goods into Angola, Botswana, Zambia and the DRC. Beira is also improving with all the new investments there. There has been a decision to take logistics operations out of the harbour to create more capacity for stevedore operations.'

BORDER ISSUES

Another major cost factor is delays at road border crossings. These persist despite trade facilitation efforts by governments, donors and private organisations. 'Delay is our biggest enemy. Long waits at border posts cost us money and have a knock-on effect that goes right to the consumer. If free trade zones work well, the cost of logistics will really come down. But we are not seeing that yet.

'There are also many other expenses that push up the cost of moving goods across the region – toll fees, road insurance funds, permits and other ad hoc fees. Governments are always looking for ways to raise revenue and this all adds up.'

De Beer cites Kasembulesa, the crossing from Zambia's Copperbelt into the DRC mining province of Katanga, as a case of a poorly run and expensive border. It costs about $1,000 each way to get a truck across because of fees, delays and other factors. 'A new border post has been built, but it is only on the Zambian side. The DRC side remains chaotic and expensive. It is a classic case of ad hoc planning that serves national interests but not regional interests. If heads of state are not willing to sign collaborative agreements for infrastructure we will continue to have this problem.'

De Beer says one-stop border posts are a good solution for congested border posts. The first of these, at Chirundi, between Zimbabwe and Zambia, has been relatively successful. But a roll-out of similar posts has been slow, with other transport bottlenecks such as Ressano Garcia, between South Africa and Mozambique, and Beit Bridge, between South Africa and its hinterland, sorely in need of improvement. 'About 13,000 people move through Beit Bridge every day and there are often long delays. The border post has good infrastructure but it is poorly managed.'

More than $1 billion has been pledged by funders to improve the North–South Corridor from South Africa to regional markets but De Beer says this is not the most cost-efficient route for moving goods to other African countries.

'We always point out to our customers that there are cheaper and faster alternatives than using the traditional North-South Corridor. Some believe it is safer and more efficient to use South Africa but, as the continent opens up, people will be more aware of the other options.'

OTHER CHALLENGES

The ban on importing second-hand vehicles into South Africa has affected the competitiveness of hauliers based in the country. 'Countries such as Zambia and Tanzania don't have this restriction and they are able to cut their operational costs by up to 15 per cent by importing cheaper used vehicles to use in their fleets,' says De Beer. 'That is why it is important for us to have operations in other countries – we can compete on a level playing field with operators there.'

Security is a growing issue in transportation of valuable commodities. 'Copper theft is big business, particularly in South Africa because there is a market for it here. And the scale is big. It is not just theft of goods off the truck but sometimes the whole truck and its cargo disappear. One truckload of copper is worth about R2.6 million (about $350,000) and this doesn't include the truck or trailer. It is safer to take these loads to Beira or Walvis Bay. We have all the safety and satellite tracking devices necessary to track loads, however syndicate operations can circumvent these.'

Tyre costs are much higher in countries outside South Africa due to poor road conditions. De Beer mentions a 40km stretch in Angola that takes eight hours to navigate during the rainy season. 'Where you are able to do an average of 15,000kms a month in South Africa, in the region it is more like 6,500kms because of the condition of the roads.

'Labour is also an issue. It can be your biggest asset but also your biggest problem. A service industry is really about people and you have to make sure you treat your staff well. But, if there is a problem, you will find that most governments are on the side of employees.

'You cannot close a business in an African country and think you can just walk away. In countries such as Zambia and Zimbabwe, if you want to retrench someone you have to pay them up to three years' salary. While this may be good for the employee in one way, it is bad for employment. Businesses don't want to hire if they can't fire.

'Beware of regulatory bodies,' he warns. 'You can't wish them away so get close to them, understand their role and function and operate accordingly.'

He cites indigenisation and competition policy as other issues that need to be flagged.

'No matter where you come from, if you want to play in someone's sandbox, you have to play by the rules in that sandbox. Each country is very different, even from their neighbours, and you need to respect the way things are done and listen to the locals.'

NEW DIRECTIONS

De Beer sees patterns of trade changing as countries in East and Southern Africa improve their facilities and infrastructure. 'We are going to see shifts in trade routes as clients are able to make use of other ports in the region and the shipping lines will have to adapt. The port of choice won't always be Durban. As facilities improve in the region, South Africa is going to become less important as a transport hub. We are already seeing cargo flows changing.'

He also predicts that increasing competition over the next five years will bring down margins. 'Competition in the logistics business is rapidly growing in Southern Africa, much of it from South Africa but also from other parts of the world and from within African countries themselves. Some international logistics companies already have a growing footprint in Africa.

'Currently margins are high in other African countries – more than double what they are in South Africa. As the message spreads that this is the place to invest, the environment will become more competitive and these margins will go down.'

Liberty Properties, established in South Africa in the 1960s, is part of the Standard Bank Group. It is a wholly owned subsidiary of Liberty Holdings. Its asset management business was recently migrated to STANLIB, its sister company within Liberty Holdings. One of South Africa's top property investment, development and management companies, by 2012 it managed property assets worth more than $3,2 billion. These included several of South Africa's most prestigious shopping precincts in Johannesburg, such as Sandton City, Nelson Mandela Square and Eastgate, as well as 13 hotels around the country. In 2011 Liberty completed its first shopping mall development outside South Africa and it is expanding its footprint in Africa with investments in commercial property and financial services.

PROPERTY

LIBERTY PROPERTIES

African real estate presents an obvious business opportunity, given the high growth rates being experienced in many countries. 'Wherever there is economic growth, property investments tend to thrive. Urbanisation and the related growth of consumerism, and the rise of a middle class, are creating demand for offices, retail outlets and residential units across the continent,' says Samuel Ogbu, former CEO of South Africa's Liberty Properties, who was appointed Group Executive for West Africa Business Development for Liberty Holdings during 2013 to spearhead expansion in this rapidly growing region.

'Property is both an enabler of and a beneficiary of economic development and investors looking at African markets are finally waking up to the fact that this is just as true in Africa as anywhere else. It is a good hedge against inflation and a tangible asset, and although it is management intensive it has social and economic benefits beyond the funds allocated to it.'

Private equity has played a role in property development and institutions are well positioned to invest in the sector, but there is still a way to go before the opportunity is fully realised.

Ogbu says there is a severe shortage of commercial and residential space across the board which means that, given the insatiable demand, many developments are profitable from inception, offering premium returns to investors. This is not the case in developed markets where supply and demand are in better balance and developments can take many years to become viable at relatively unexciting yields.

Retailers with an appetite for African markets are finding the lack of suitable property stock a constraint to their expansion plans. There is also a significant shortage of premium grade office property in urban areas, which can mean very high rentals and, in countries such as Nigeria, rentals payable several years in advance in hard currency. Another area of opportunity is in hotels, where the need for quality accommodation is increasing, spurred by economic growth and foreign investment.

THE ZAMBIA DEAL

'In our first development on the continent outside South Africa we learned a lot of lessons and paid some "school fees",' notes Ogbu. The development in question is the $200 million Levy Centre in Lusaka, Zambia – the country's first mixed-use shopping centre, which combines 30,000m² of retail with 10,000m² of office space and a 104–bed hotel. The centre, with 72 stores, was financed by the National Pension Scheme Authority of Zambia.

'We came up with the concept, which the client liked, and we signed up for a turnkey arrangement in terms of which we managed the development including engaging the professionals (both Zambian and South African), dealt with the contractors and found the tenants. It has been very challenging but also very rewarding.

'There were many steps along the way that would not arise in a South African project, for example having to work with the authorities to update their legislative framework for public-private partnerships. The legislation was in place but the rules and processes that underpinned it were in need of modification for the intended objectives to be realised in practice.

'We also had to work with certain stipulations in terms of empowering people and building capacity locally. We were very happy to do so as that is the philosophy under which we and Liberty Africa operate since we plan to be in our target countries for the long term. However, making it happen was not easy as we had to convince seasoned South African professionals to take on local partners who did not always have the same skills in terms of construction, architecture and professional management.

'But it worked well because it was a genuine partnership and not just a question of getting a local face in place in order to win the tender. There was a lot of training and hand-holding and it did take longer, but the end result was greater sustainability. It was also delivered on time and it came in under budget.'

At its opening in November 2011, the centre was fully let. Tenants were mostly South African retailers with South African supermarket chain Pick n Pay as the anchor tenant.

THE CASE FOR AFRICA

Liberty Properties' decision to expand its operations into the rest of the continent was driven by several factors, explains Ogbu. 'One was the evidence of rising growth rates, fuelled partly by resources and the influx of money from Asia and other regions. Another was improving legislative environments and an increasing democratic deepening. Even where democracy is not really following a Western model, there is greater economic freedom.

'There is also the communication explosion and the development of ICT as an industry in itself that is fuelling economic growth. This keeps money flowing in the economy which creates disposable income and that is what we look for in order to build shops and offices.

'We are also seeing increasing investment in infrastructure which means people can live further from the office and can afford to build homes. Then they need places to get their daily requirements, which increases demand for shopping nodes. And, as more companies emerge, they need offices. All of this is good for the property sector.

'There is a bit of a beneficial circle under way in Africa. I wouldn't go so far as to call it the dawn of an African Renaissance, but a positive economic growth story is emerging. It is patchy and some countries are growing off a very low base, but there are states with very attractive growth rates such as Mozambique and Angola and East African economies such as Ethiopia. The growth story is replicated to one degree or another across the continent.'

MOVING NORTH

Liberty Properties operates in three main areas: the development of property, the day-to-day management of property and the management of capital. It has grown a large portfolio within South Africa, from the high end of the market in Sandton, Johannesburg, to the previously disadvantaged area of Mitchell's Plain near Cape Town where it completed the extension to its Liberty Promenade shopping centre in 2011, making it the second largest shopping centre in the Western Cape province.

'We want to replicate our experience in South Africa in other countries by building a portfolio of quality assets. Changing growth conditions in Africa are attracting South African companies on a big scale, which is creating opportunities in shopping centres, offices and residential segments.'

Liberty's move from South Africa into the rest of the continent started in 2008 when the company decided it would grow into the African footprint of its parent company, the Standard Bank Group, which has a presence in 22 countries.

'Zambia was our first project north of the border. The project came about after we made contact with the Zambia pension fund at a conference held by our sister company Stanlib. The event aimed to increase awareness among African sovereign wealth funds, social security schemes and pension funds of the investment value of real estate.

'At that time, and even now, funds were underweight in property. They were investing in government fixed interest securities and local stock exchanges, which invariably were limited and lacked depth. Our case was that real estate was an asset class to consider, especially if the nature of their liabilities was long term. The Zambians came to us afterwards and asked us to put our money where our mouth was. So we did.

'We've chosen to focus on seven countries outside South Africa – Ghana and Nigeria in the west, Kenya, Uganda and Tanzania in the east, and Zambia and Botswana in the south. A number of things have informed that decision. We have looked at the size of the economies and the size and organisation of the real estate market.

'But we have also looked at the nature of the risks and our ability to understand and manage them sufficiently to be able to deliver projects and manage assets in a way that generates adequate returns to investors,' says Ogbu.

LEARNING CURVE

'There are a number of things you need to consider to be successful in an African market. There is no substitute for doing your homework and delivering what you have promised – this reduces the possibility of difficulties later on,' says Ogbu.

'Part of risk mitigation is ensuring you have the right clearances and certificates. The biggest risk is that you will not deliver your project on cost and on budget. Agreements also have to be robust and clear – people need to know what roles they will play and who pays for what and how.

'You must choose your local partner very carefully. You need to do deep due diligence and spend time in the market. There is no short cut. Relationships are critical. You need to understand who you are working with and what makes them tick.

'It can be difficult at times. Property is a very emotive thing. Everyone wants a five-star hotel but it is difficult to make money out of one and often the better prospect is the mid-class hotel. If it is the client's dream to have a luxury hotel it can be a challenge to take the emotion out of the situation.'

CHALLENGES

There are many challenges for South African operators going into the rest of the continent. They include operating in unfamiliar territory, understanding the political environment and finding local partners. There is also limited information in terms of property market trends – rentals, vacancies, indices and other indicators that are very easy to come by in South Africa.

'Security of tenure is a big issue, especially for the property sector. Given that we are often managing money for financial institutions that manage other people's money, the tenure issue is crucial. A project cannot proceed if there are any uncertainties about the land ownership. These assets take a long time to pay back.'

South Africa is one of the few countries in Africa with freehold ownership and a fully functioning deeds registry. Its property tenure system is sophisticated and easy to understand. Further north, tenure tends to be leasehold but the length of leases – typically 50 years – makes it viable for property developments only if there is a real possibility of extending the leases.

There are still many problems in intra-African trade, including non-tariff barriers. For example, shipments for Zambian-based retailers were held up at the Zimbabwe border for weeks because of computer problems at the crossing. The ferry across the Zambezi River at another Zambian border crossing was broken and goods could not go that way either. These problems make life more difficult and more costly for business.

'The further you go the greater the problems. Delays at Apapa port in Nigeria's commercial capital Lagos are legendary. Companies have to be very resourceful and create new areas of local sourcing, but unfortunately the local industry is not yet robust enough to support the needs of big retailers on an ongoing basis.

'Currency risk is an issue, but we mitigate this by denominating our income in US dollars. We try to match the income stream to the currency of the major costs. The improving state of the African financial system allows us to do this,' says Ogbu.

One of the biggest challenges is the availability and cost of funds. It is very expensive to borrow in many countries, which is why a lot of buildings do not get finished. The tendency of African banking institutions to provide only short-term funding – about seven years – is a problem for the commercial property sector. And there is also a comparatively low loan-to-value ratio – in the order of ten per cent of total requirements.

The lack of mortgage credit in Africa is a major constraint for the real estate industry. Despite this, the residential sector is surprisingly buoyant, which means there is money in these economies. But high ownership costs mean a growing trend in the rental of good quality properties. Remittances are funding residential development, but mostly private dwellings rather than commercial properties.

The need to provide municipal services such as power and water adds new dimensions to the cost and complexity of projects. 'There is no question of writing to the local authority to switch on the power once the project is completed. You have to provide the power yourself and water to the site for construction.

'The lack of a maintenance culture to support sustainability and value preservation of property developments is a challenge and it is important to ensure that professional property managers are part of any development. The shiny glass and marble edifices that everyone wants can degrade very quickly if there is not a procedure in place to look after them.'

Legislative issues must be considered. For example, in Nigeria a ban on the import of textiles and clothing has been a constraint on shopping developments. 'We tried for three years to strike a deal to build a shopping centre there but, without a good old-fashioned anchor, it is difficult to have a sizeable centre of any scale.'

Although supermarkets demand space, grocery margins do not support high rentals. Nonetheless, they are good to have as they attract customers to centres. However, the size of a shopping centre is restricted without a fashion store anchor tenant that has high margins.

'Unfortunately the clothing ban failed to protect Nigeria's textile sector, which is smaller today than it was when the ban was imposed in 2003. And it only encouraged smuggling.' The ban was lifted in 2011 and large South African clothing retailers such as Pep Stores, Woolworths and Mr Price are setting up in that market.

LOOKING TO THE FUTURE

Ogbu foresees significant opportunities in property in various countries. 'In the west this includes Ghana, now that it is gearing up for oil production, and Nigeria. Lagos is still the biggest opportunity. Although the residential property bubble that was driving prices sky high up to 2008 has burst, prices have not plummeted even though the rate of increase has slowed significantly. There are also good opportunities in the capital, Abuja, and some of the cities in the east of the country such as Enugu, Aba, Port Harcourt and Warri.

'Kenya is a good prospect if it can maintain political stability, and Uganda as it enters an era of oil production. Tanzania is also growing nicely. It is too early to tell how the Zimbabwe market will develop, given its slow recovery. We have potential projects in Democratic Republic of Congo but otherwise we have no ambition to grow our business in Francophone countries right now. It is easier to be in Anglophone Africa.

'However, property development is opportunistic by nature and, where it makes sense and we can manage the risks, we will take on development management work in countries outside our ideal target set.

'We do see future engagement with Chinese developers given the increased interest in Africa from this region, although we have not done anything with them yet.

'There is not enough investment grade property across the continent. Through our development business we are helping to create it, either on our balance sheet or someone else's. We are also good at managing funds related to real estate so can we get capital from investors and manage those funds for them.

'We are optimistic about the future growth of the sector. Governments in Africa are becoming more enlightened and they are starting to understand that they are also part of the value creation process and it is not in their interests to have procedures in place that hinder investment.'

Pay television company MultiChoice is a subsidiary of South African-based international media and entertainment company Naspers and offers 24-hour multichannel digital satellite television services across Africa on the DStv platform. In addition to DStv, MultiChoice's key brands include DStv Online; M-Net, which provides exclusive local and international content; SuperSport, with seven channels dedicated to global and local sport; DStv Mobile, and MWEB, an internet service provider in South Africa. In 2012 MultiChoice had 5.2 million subscribers across 47 markets in sub-Saharan Africa.

TELECOMMUNICATIONS AND ENTERTAINMENT

MULTICHOICE

'We believe there will be continued growth in the market due to continued economic growth in Africa. The continent has remained resilient in terms of GDP growth as compared with developed markets, although it's a tough economic environment for consumers due to inflationary pressures in many economies,' says Nico Meyer, CEO of MultiChoice Africa, a multichannel digital satellite television services provider.

'New market segments have been created through the growth of the middle class as well as the introduction of a number of new technologies, such as the migration from analogue to digital television services. The business continues to drive innovation in terms of new technology and local content investments.'

Collins Khumalo, the previous CEO of MultiChoice Africa, who now heads up MultiChoice South Africa, says, for the industry to grow, governments need to put in place sound telecommunications policies and predictable regulation, as well as ensure access to adequate bandwidth. 'A lack of bandwidth has been a constraint to developing new products and increasing it would allow the new generation to leapfrog over many of our current challenges.

'Obviously, being pioneers of expanding into the rest of Africa, we had limited knowledge and while we initially used expatriates to run the Africa operations, as they understood the business, we also created partnerships with local entrepreneurs and national broadcasters who were able to bring to the table the much-needed local knowledge and understanding of these markets,' says Khumalo.

'Nearly 20 years later we have evolved to a point where we have almost 100 per cent local management. Local management have a deeper understanding of what is happening on the ground and hence our ability to respond to issues and problems is much quicker. This also fits in with the growing pressure for local people to benefit from foreign investments and it gives our employees in Africa operations a sense that there is a career path for them in the company and they could possibly run it one day.'

Khumalo, who was the General Manager of MultiChoice Nigeria for five years, says people often ask which are the really difficult countries in which to do business in Africa. There is no obvious answer. 'People think Nigeria would be much more difficult than Botswana, for example.

'However, I found Botswana to be a complex and difficult place to operate in and made an easier transition in Nigeria. Perhaps it is because I anticipated Nigeria to be different and primed myself to adapt.

'You need to view and respect each market as a unique environment because they are all very different. Allow yourself an opportunity to learn from people in them. If you move from South Africa, for example, and take your way of operating here with you, and judge the market according to how you think it behaves, it could compromise your success.'

BUILDING THE BUSINESS

MultiChoice Africa was among the first South African companies to move into African countries beyond its immediate neighbours and it was the first company globally to bring pay television to Africans.

The company has its roots in South Africa's first pay television station, M-Net, which was established in the mid-1980s. The decision to expand M-Net beyond South Africa's borders was taken in the late 1980s by veteran businessman Koos Bekker, CEO of M-Net's parent company, Naspers. He wanted to position the company as a modern pan-African player despite the then stigma of apartheid in South Africa. At the time, African countries were in the starting blocks of economic and political reform and new investment was in short supply.

In 1991 M-Net formed a joint partnership with a Namibian company and was awarded a licence in that country – its first outside South Africa. The following year it launched an analogue service to more than 20 countries in Africa, starting a journey that is continuing 20 years later.

In 1993 MultiChoice Africa was formed and split off from M-Net to drive the company's rapid expansion plan across sub-Saharan Africa. By the end of 1995, MultiChoice Africa had established the backbone of its operation with offices in Namibia, Botswana, Ghana, Nigeria, Tanzania, Uganda, Kenya and Zambia, and franchises in half a dozen countries.

In 1995 the company moved from analogue to digital technology with the launch of the DStv bouquet. Television viewing in Africa changed forever with the launch of the dual view decoder in 2003 – a world first, allowing viewers to watch two different channels on separate television sets using one satellite link. Further progress came with the PVR in 2005, enabling subscribers to record, rewind, forward and pause broadcasts.

In 2012 MultiChoice Africa had 1.5 million subscribers in Africa outside South Africa. The penetration level is still low outside South Africa and the company is still virtually in virgin territory. Nowhere is it anywhere near saturation point and is expecting major growth in the next two decades as incomes grow and people seek more quality television viewing.

South Africa remains the company's biggest market, accounting for 70 per cent of its total pay television subscribers. For 12 years it was the sole pay television provider in the South African market, which provided a strong platform for growth into Africa. This monopoly ended in 2007 with the entry of several new market players.

The PricewaterhouseCoopers *South African Entertainment and Media Outlook 2011-2015* says that in 2010 South African pay television subscriptions grew by 600,000 – the highest in a single year thus far – and predicted that pay television would reach 66 per cent of households in the country by 2015, from 43.2 per cent in 2010.

Nigeria is the next fastest growing market, although penetration is still low relative to the size of the population, with only a small percentage of the 160 million Nigerians being DStv subscribers. Kenya and Angola are the next two fastest growing markets.

MultiChoice's entry strategy into African markets has been three pronged.

In some countries, such as Liberia and Sierra Leone, it has agreements in place with local agents. Operations in states such as Zimbabwe, Malawi, Mozambique, Ethiopia and Mauritius are franchises that run the whole operation and pay a fee to the company. In Nigeria, Ghana, Tanzania, Uganda, Namibia and Zambia the company has joint ventures with local partners.

Says Meyer, 'My experience in working in sub-Saharan Africa, rather than just the South African market, has been that the African business environment is a far more complex one which requires multiple solutions that cater for the very diverse countries in which we operate. This is not only in terms of the language requirements, but also in terms of cultural and infrastructure issues.'

CHALLENGES

Khumalo, in his previous job of running Africa operations, is a man who has spent a lot of time in the air travelling across the continent. It is no surprise, then, that he rates improvements in air links as one of the biggest changes he has seen on the continent over a decade.

'Doing business in Africa has definitely become a lot easier now that you don't have to fly via Europe to get to countries on your own continent. There has also been a huge improvement in the availability and quality of hotels on the continent. In general, there have been a lot of changes over the years I have been travelling around Africa.'

But, he adds, there are still many challenges. 'People often underestimate the difficulty of launching a pay television service. They just see the end result and it looks easy.

'Africans are used to the state providing television for free and we have had to undertake a long process of educating people about the benefits of paying for additional channels. Pay television was a totally unheard of concept, which made an education process necessary. Hence growth was slow. The fact that the technology is intangible makes it even more difficult to do this. But once people have it in their homes and see the benefits, it is easier to make a business case.'

Payment systems are a challenge in some markets, particularly in the cash-based economies of West Africa where banking penetration was, until recently particularly low and banking products hardly used. Innovative payment solutions had to be found.

'In South Africa, up to 70 per cent of our business is conducted by way of debit orders. But, in the rest of the continent, people pay cash upfront every month. Managing that has been a big learning curve.'

Nigeria presented another kind of challenge. 'People negotiate for everything there and customers wanted to negotiate the fee for the service. It was difficult to convince them it was a fixed fee. That was a big stumbling block for us in the beginning.'

A major challenge for MultiChoice Africa is infrastructure. 'It is easy to go into a market with big ideas but without understanding the infrastructure challenges. These challenges can completely change the way you do things. Once we were in a market we had to quickly adapt and make the best of it.'

For example, in Nigeria, most people rely on generators for power due to intermittent and unreliable supply from government agencies. The fuel to run generators is an extra cost on top of the expense of decoders and the upfront set-up. 'In East African countries, where there is frequent load shedding because of power shortages, people often cannot get the signal and then ask us why they must pay for the service.

'Decoder costs are coming down and we are continually working to make the service cheaper for subscribers. The introduction of digital terrestrial technology will help to lower set-up costs and encourage more usage at the bottom end of the market. Users won't need to buy a satellite dish or pay professional installation fees. That will remove a big chunk of the cost.'

Intellectual property rights have been, and continue to be, a challenge. 'Borrowed' MultiChoice programming, albeit often grainy, is commonly found on the proliferation of small independent channels in Africa.

'People don't always know it's illegal to take content. They feel they are entitled to take something that is in the public domain and don't see it as theft. We have been involved in educating, not just the public but also the regulatory authorities, about the serious effect the violation of intellectual property can have on the success of an industry. It is a real constraint on growth. Most countries are signatories to international conventions on intellectual property but don't enforce them.'

Being a pioneer in Africa had its challenges in terms of human resources. 'In many countries we went into, there were no big companies at the time. People tended to work in small enterprises and there was no services market. We had to train people in the culture of working for a big corporation and develop that talent. That really changed the way people did things in the workplace.

'But other big companies coming also had staff challenges and they tended to poach our employees, who were already trained, and we had to keep starting again.'

Availability of statistics has also been an issue for a company relying on consumer markets for its success. 'There was nothing available to assess markets. We just had to go into the markets and then assess them from inside as we went along. That is changing and now there is a lot more reliable market information available.'

A big concern is the tendency of governments to use multinationals, particularly highly visible companies operating at the top end of the market, as a cash cow for the state by imposing multiple levies, duties and tariffs on the industry and on imported equipment. 'It has been easier for them to do this to us because the pay television industry is unique,' says Khumalo.

It is not just the company that has been targeted. One local government in Nigeria saw a revenue opportunity with the proliferation of satellite dishes on the rooftops in upmarket areas. It imposed an arbitrary satellite tax on each household with a visible unit.

Duties on set-up boxes can be up to 45 per cent, which adds another layer of cost to the operation. 'We don't get a sympathetic hearing because of the nature of the service. But we could increase employment if some of the taxes were waived as we could have a more vibrant industry.'

LOOKING TO THE FUTURE

The company's objective has been to give African viewers the same quality of viewing as they would find anywhere in the world. But this comes at a price.

Margins are under pressure with the cost of buying additional satellite capacity, increasing decoder subsidies to lower entry costs and paying large, and growing, sums of money to acquire international sports rights. Added to this is increasing competition from other pay television operators fighting for a piece of the advertising pie.

Keeping ahead of the game has meant using some of the most advanced technologies in the broadcast industry, combined with sophisticated back-end hardware and software. The complex signal is delivered to subscribers by several satellites, each of which serves a different part of Africa, all of which must be constantly upgraded.

'MultiChoice has set itself the objective of delivering the most exciting channels to Africa on a highly sophisticated technology platform,' says Meyer. For example, it launched a new digital terrestrial television (DTT) service called GOtv in four markets last year – Nigeria, Uganda, Zambia and Kenya – specifically for mass-market audiences.

'At the moment our channels can be delivered in some markets to multiple devices including a television (either through satellite or DTT) via a set-top box as well as on a mobile phone, i-Pad or computer through either a Walka or Drifta devise. This enables subscribers to access our programming on DStv or GOtv through multiple devices.'

The company enthusiastically supports local content. Although that, too, comes at a price, the company sees it as being integral to building subscribers for the future.

'MultiChoice works closely with its sister companies M-Net and SuperSport to enable the production of local content in Africa. Localised programming and channels remain a key focus for the business, with the launch of specialist channels, including Bukedde in Uganda and Africa Magic Swahili and SuperSport 9 East in East Africa,' says Meyer.

A number of original local productions have been broadcast on the M-Net channels, including Mashariki Mix (an East African lifestyle show), 53 Extra (another lifestyle programme), Jara (a magazine programme focused on the Nollywood movie industry), Big Brother Amplified (season six), a new season of prime time drama Jacob's Cross, Tinsel (a soap opera filmed in Lagos), Comedy Club (produced live in Lagos and Kampala), a new season of Changes (an East African drama) and season three of Glo Naija Sings.

MultiChoice has invested heavily in local sporting content, particularly football, which is aired on SuperSport. The football coverage includes games in Angola, Ghana, Nigeria, Kenya, Zambia and Uganda. Football tournaments, in particular, are big drawcards – as shown by nearly a million subscribers signing up during the 2010 Fifa World Cup.

The company is increasing its focus on regional peculiarities. In East Africa it has launched a channel in Kiswahili, the dominant regional language, and has introduced content in Nigerian languages Hausa and Yoruba. There are several local content channels, including the reality show Big Brother Africa, local music on Channel O and movies on African Magic. The latter has been well served by Nigeria's prolific Nollywood output. Despite the sometimes indifferent quality of the movies, with many being made with rudimentary equipment, they are extremely popular.

'We have invested a lot of money training cameramen, sound technicians and developing many other technical skills in the industry. Our role in developing Africa's entertainment industry is underplayed – we have created a platform and a market for the entertainment industry and trained people to work in it. That is a big contribution,' says Meyer.

While the premium end of the market continues to see new products emerging such as high-definition television, future growth hinges on growing the mass market. Already, 20-channel, low-cost bouquets account for nearly half of the market outside South Africa and the company is looking for ways to further reduce entry costs and compete with other entertainment, including the internet.

'The focus right now is the roll-out of DVB-T2 (DTT) technology which provides low cost access to digital television. We are currently rolling out one of the most sophisticated DVB-T2 networks worldwide. Innovations in DStv Mobile also allow television consumers to access their content on multiple screens through devices such as the Drifta and the Walka.'

Meyer says the pay television landscape continues to become more competitive with the entry of new operators into the various markets. 'Technology is constantly transforming the way in which consumers watch television and new platforms of delivery such as the internet and broadband in Africa offer alternative ways for consumers to access programming. While growth in this area is still relatively slow due to the lack of bandwidth, it is likely to increase as broadband becomes more available.'

The increasing capacity of broadband as a result of sea cables landing at strategic points along the coast of Africa will remove a significant constraint to the development of interlinked technologies and devices, with viewers being able to connect to the internet from their decoders and link up with online content such as social networking and YouTube.

Says Khumalo, 'We have to innovate to keep up with the ever-changing technological environment. Technology is the future. It is the enabler and catalyst for opportunity and development and it allows us to look for multiple ways to deliver content.'

Nando's is an international chain of restaurants that originated in South Africa. The company started out in 1987 as Chickenland, selling Portuguese-style chicken in Johannesburg, before changing its name. By 2012 it had about 1,000 stores in 26 countries on five continents. It has operations in several African countries as well as in the US, the UK, Australia, the Middle East and Asia. It specialises in spicy peri-peri chicken and sauces and operates both corporate stores and franchises. It listed on the Johannesburg Stock Exchange (JSE) in 1997 and delisted in 2003.

FRANCHISING AND RETAIL

NANDO'S

'Our vision for Nando's has always been very clear and simple – to have fun and make money. To achieve both of these means getting the culture of the business right,' says Robbie Brozin, co-founder of Nando's, the global restaurant business. 'Our mission is to change the way the world thinks about chicken and to change people's lives one chicken at a time.'

In 2012 the company celebrated 25 years of serving customers its 'fast casual' peri-peri chicken, both in Africa and globally, where it has taken on established brands in developed countries. But success has not come easily in Africa, with Nando's pulling back from a number of key markets such as Mozambique, Angola, Kenya and Nigeria because of a misalignment with local partners on a number of issues, including the way the brand was interpreted.

'It's all about having the right partners and also the right entry strategy. It's also about being the right partner to your local partners. It's a two-way street. Your values must be aligned,' explains Brozin.

'We went backwards a bit in the rest of Africa in order to go forward. We were in a lot more markets than we are now. But we need partners who can focus on our brand and give it the care it needs rather than having it as part of a bigger company with multiple focus areas. We will definitely go back into the markets we were in and do things differently.'

Nando's went into a number of East and Southern African markets in a joint venture with Zimbabwean conglomerate Innscor, which owned the Nando's franchise in Zimbabwe, and Exxon Mobil, to include Nando's franchises in the rollout of Innscor's franchises such as Pizza Inn and Chicken Inn, some of which were in filling station forecourts. In 2007 Nando's terminated the agreement with a view to re-entering those markets directly. In Nigeria, it had a joint venture with a local company involved in the food business, which seemed like a good fit. However, in late 2011, they agreed to part ways.

'We have found that working through a third party is difficult. We want to build the relationship directly. Previously we were in arrangements in some of these countries where we were just one brand among many. That meant ours didn't get the love and care and, importantly, the focus it should have. We needed a greater commitment to the company ethos by franchise holders.

'We don't like doing regional deals. We've learned that the best way for Nando's to work is to go with a direct line of sight into the country and work with the locals.'

SMALL BEGINNINGS

The story of Nando's beginnings appears on many websites around the world. It tells of how 27-year-old Robert Brozin and his friend Fernando Duarte were eating at a restaurant in Johannesburg by the name of Chickenland and liked the food so much they bought the place. Chickenland was in the suburb of Rosettenville, the base for many Portuguese migrants from Mozambique after its independence in 1975.

They changed the name of the business, using Duarte's name, but continued to cook Portuguese themed spicy food, making it the trademark product that they would later take to the rest of the world. 'The taste of the food was fantastic. Fernando and I discussed it and felt there was an opportunity for another great offering in the world. That was the origin of the business. I am very passionate about the fact that Nando's came from Africa. You could say the heritage of the brand is African Portuguese, with its roots in Mozambique.'

The company has developed a range of spices and sauces based on peri-peri flavours gleaned from African bird's-eye chilli and has made the Rooster of Barcelos, part of Portuguese legend, its logo.

After rapid success in South Africa, Nando's quickly embarked on an international expansion strategy, starting with Australia in 1990 and then Zimbabwe and Botswana in 1993. The Nigerian launch was in 2005. By then the company was well established in the UK, where it now has more than 50 stores in London alone, as well as in Southeast Asia and the Middle East. In 2008, it opened its first store in the US, taking on well established chicken franchises such as KFC. It opened three more stores there in 2012 and Euromonitor, the international research group, nominated it as the food service chain to watch.

'We have franchises in each country and a master franchise per country. We encourage the master franchisee to own all the stores in their country rather than having multiple franchisees.

'But there are different models. For example, the UK Nando's are all fully owned company operations, while in Australia it is franchises. In Malaysia, the master franchisee owns all the stores; in Zimbabwe our franchisee is local company Innscor and all the restaurants around the country are owned by Innscor. Our franchisee in Zambia also runs all the stores there. The model depends on the culture of the country you are operating in. We believe the best model for Africa is for one franchisee to run all the stores in that country.'

The company has remained true to its peri-peri roots no matter where it operates, although it is open to its franchisees adapting parts of the menu to cater for local tastes. In some regions it offers halaal and kosher meals. 'Our sauces come out of our factory in South Africa so that it is standard, but we allow our franchisees to localise some of the side items. We will always have chips but we might add mealie meal or yam or local flavours in different markets. Franchisees are allowed to experiment with the sides, although we keep the core product as standard as possible.'

THE CREATIVE QUESTION

Nando's marketing and advertising campaigns have become famous for being creative but also for pushing the boundaries and creating controversy. The company made the headlines in 2012 with its advertisement for a new six-pack meal that poked fun at Zimbabwean president Robert Mugabe.

It showed a lookalike character reminiscing about happy times with other autocratic rulers such as former Libyan dictator Muammar Gaddafi, but eating his chicken alone at a table set for the now departed dictators. The commercial went viral on YouTube but was withdrawn when the Zimbabwean franchisee's staff and management received threats from Mugabe loyalists after it aired on satellite television. Under Zimbabwean law it is an offence to insult the president or undermine the authority of the office. The advertisement was also banned in the UK.

The company also ran foul of South African political firebrand, Julius Malema, by running an advertisement using a lookalike puppet that talked about change. The clip hinted at political change but in the end it referred to the plentiful change one gets after paying for an inexpensive Nando's meal. The African National Congress (ANC) Youth League, over which Malema then presided, threatened mass action in protest against the advertisement and it was withdrawn. However, it was replaced with an altered version in which the puppet's face was pixellated and the voice changed. The puppet was later sold at auction for R100,000 (about $12,500), which was donated to charity.

There have been other humorous campaigns that have skirted close to what many deemed to be limits of public acceptability. Some were withdrawn after complaints but many survived. The company's website is unapologetic: 'Needless to say Nando's ads have been the centre of some heated topics of conversation. We've also won a lot of advertising awards along the way and they've been fantastic!'

Says Brozin, 'We have a team that drives the advertising out of South Africa and it uses local agencies. We provide manuals to master franchisees that come with a complete operating system of how to operate a Nando's franchise, including a marketing module. We advise them to take some of the ideas we have had and adapt campaigns to suit the local market.

'Whether to do political campaigns depends on the sophistication of the market and the political dynamics. In some countries you can push the boundaries a bit but in others you might want to be more careful. It's the same in other regions. For example you would do a different campaign in Saudi Arabia from what you would do in Dubai. We can be cheeky here but it doesn't always work in other markets.'

OPERATING IN AFRICA

'We are aware that operating in many African countries can be challenging and franchisees can struggle,' says Brozin. 'It is important to have a deep understanding of what their problems are without compromising your brand.'

The Zimbabwe operation run by Innscor went through tough times during the decade of economic decline in the country, when foreign currency and local supplies were scarce. 'We let them get on with what they needed to do to survive without insisting that they stick to a lot of global standards that were impossible to meet in that business environment and we had to scale the menu right down. Things are now back to normal in the country and the business is really bouncing back. It shows the importance of having entrepreneurial people on board who can make a plan. Our biggest African operation now outside South Africa is in Zimbabwe – we have a dozen stores there.

'In tough markets, it's important to have our partners focused on our brand. If a company takes on a Nando's franchise in addition to others and they have problems, they have to manage those problems across all their businesses and that might compromise your brand. Although Innscor in Zimbabwe has other brands and businesses, they have appointed an executive specifically to look after the Nando's brand.'

Brozin says the company hasn't had a problem with franchisees not fully understanding the concept or with people paying franchise fees. However, there has been a tendency to take shortcuts with the brand to solve internal problems. 'In Angola, for example, they ran out of branded packets and started using their own packets to serve the chicken in. If there is a problem at the port and they can't get stock in, they start using unbranded bags or unbranded serviettes. They do it for a week, then a month and, before you know it, this becomes standard.

'The brand is sacrosanct so it is a problem if partners don't understand the brand management and start compromising on it. Unless you have the right kind of operating procedures from a head office point of view this can happen. But you don't want to be slapping them with breaches every two minutes. It can be quite a balancing act. Even if the franchisees are committed to your product and share the vision and values, you sometimes still have to educate them about what it means to be part of a global brand.'

Finding a suitable master franchisee can be a challenge. 'Once you've targeted an area, you have to investigate all inquiries, using experienced people in the market for referrals or auditors to do due diligence. You really hope that, once you've chosen, it's going to work. You don't always know until you are already involved.

'If we've done it properly, it hasn't been an issue. The problem has been where we haven't done it properly. There have been times when one or the other party has messed up and sometimes it has been a joint problem where, for example, we haven't used the right design for the restaurant or we have chosen a poor location. But where you have joint commitment to drive the brand, you won't have issues. We have never felt the brand itself has not been suitable in a market but we may not have always delivered it properly.'

Brozin says supply chain issues in Africa are 'night and day' when compared with developed country markets such as the UK. 'In African markets we don't have great supplier choice but in developed markets we have a big choice and there is a great supply chain.'

In Africa, the logistics are very different and there are very few countries where you can get critical mass in the same way you can even in other emerging markets. 'For example, we have 40 restaurants in Malaysia. In Africa you are not looking at more than 15 in any one place outside South Africa.

'You also have issues here that you don't really have in other parts of the world. For example, we were in Maputo one day when there were riots over bread prices. The previous day we had felt no tension at all and then suddenly this erupted. We could have been stuck there for days – there were tyres burning in the roads and the airport was blocked. It is unpredictable and that unpredictability comes at a cost.

'Malaysia is much more predictable and this allows you to do more long-term planning. But in Africa it also depends on the country. You can't compare Malaysia and Africa. Botswana has been great for us – stable, steady and we have great partners there. But we have had many challenges in Zimbabwe. Ghana is steady and stable but Nigeria has ups and downs. It is very hard to predict how things will turn out. You just have to go in and trade and take it from there.

'You've got to have very strong business principles and disciplines and, if you arrive with a blueprint for your business, you must be able to adapt it if necessary.

'It can be very difficult to keep a handle on all our diverse operations. We have had to change the way we run things. Once a business gets to a certain size, you need to put in place more processes, fill in more forms and rely more on consistent, rather than subjective, measurement and analysis of the business. After 25 years in the business, we finally have global matrixes in place!'

THE FIGHT AGAINST MALARIA

Brozin and his executive team have enthusiastically embraced the fight against malaria in Africa, bringing the typical Nando's passion to the campaign. 'We've taken a view that malaria is an African issue, even though it exists elsewhere, and it is an issue that needs to be dealt with by Africans. We are looking for funding and strategic partnerships outside Africa but the energy and drive to sort out a sustainable solution to the problem must come from within the continent.

'Governments that have made progress in fighting malaria tend to be good governance governments because they know how to tackle issues. And it makes sense to address it because illness from malaria comes at a high cost to governments and business.

'There is no direct link to the Nando's business except that we are an African brand based in Africa, where the problem is enormous. As South Africans, we have a huge obligation to help with African problems even though malaria is not a big issue in this country.

'Although we are doing the malaria work in some markets where we don't have a presence at the moment, we do believe this will ultimately be good for our business as well. If we can change the world of chicken, we can change the world of malaria. We want to add some impetus to this fight. For us it is like giving Africa a hug. It brings the Nando's philosophy of changing lives into another arena and it is hugely gratifying.'

Nando's came to the malaria project through well-known African explorer, Kingsley Holgate, who has linked the fight against malaria to his travels to remote parts of the continent.

'Kingsley and I met many years ago when we were looking at putting a trip together to other African countries. We didn't know anything about exploring Africa so I told one of my guys, Eugene le Roux, to go and find Kingsley. It took him about a year to track him down but eventually in the early 2000s he found him. He was putting together his Outside Edge expedition to travel around the edge of the continent and hand out mosquito nets along the way. He invited me along and we did the Namibia leg and Nigeria together.

'Almost a year later I joined him in Mozambique where we did it again. I just loved what he did – improving lives through adventure. It was the first time I saw how much it meant to hand out nets and give something to people in remote places who were never going to eat a Nando's chicken in their lives. Often when you give, you hope for something back. There's no greater giving than knowing you aren't going to get anything back.

'I invited guys in our South African restaurants to come and hand out nets. We gave them the opportunity to travel around Mozambique and it created a major spark among many of our people.'

The Bill Gates Foundation in the US ran the programme United Against Malaria at the time of the 2010 Fifa World Cup in South Africa. 'We helped to put together a partnership with other companies operating in the rest of Africa to work with them in highlighting the plight of people with malaria. But, after the tournament, they all went back home and we were very disappointed because we were in it for the long haul.

'But we have continued with our work. We have developed a programme in South Africa to make bead bracelets for sale in our outlets in Australia and a few other markets and we have been able to raise a lot of money. In South Africa we have linked the programme to HIV/AIDS because malaria is not a big issue here and it is difficult to get people to support a cause that is not affecting them. We are looking at ways to galvanise African creativity to raise awareness and money for malaria using artists, musicians or even some cheeky adverts.'

Brozin and his team are doing the rebranding for the United Against

Malaria programme. 'We are the creative energy behind developing malaria awareness programmes. 'But, at the end of the day, governments also need to contribute to reducing the incidence of malaria. It shouldn't be up to global leaders and organisations to get African governments to do what they should be doing anyway.'

LOOKING FORWARD

In addition to re-entering markets it pulled out of, Nando's is eyeing the opportunities in Tanzania, Kenya, Uganda and other areas of West Africa where it has no presence yet.

'We are seeing more competition. KFC is growing quite strongly now in Africa, particularly in Kenya and Nigeria. We don't really see it as a competitor just because they also sell chicken. Our products are very different. If KFC is in a market, we would view that market as being a bit more sophisticated as it would indicate there would already be local suppliers and some capacity in the supply chain. We are very comfortable to sit alongside them.'

Does Brozin have any tips for companies planning on expanding their operations into Africa?

'The attitude of trying to colonise Africa can never work. South Africans must be careful not to be arrogant. We also tend to hunt in packs and have South African centres. If you travel in the rest of Africa with a view that whatever is good comes out of South Africa you will not do well.

'Humility is a big factor in operating in Africa. You need to be humble and listen a lot. Companies also need to have strict compliance and monitor it carefully – this is critical. It is also important to treat all countries in Africa as individual markets – you cannot think of the continent as one country with slight variations. But, most important, is to be adventurous. Go in and make a difference in any way you can. Get involved.'

Mobile Telephone Networks (MTN) was incorporated in South Africa in 1994. In 1998 it began expanding into other African markets and by 2006 had operations in ten countries. During that year it added ten more countries to its stable with the acquisition of Lebanese company, Investcom. By 2013, MTN had operations in 22 countries in Africa and the Middle East and comprised three wholly owned companies: the MTN Group; MTN International, which houses the non-South African operations, and MTN Mauritius, an investment holding company. By mid-2013, it had 197 million subscribers.

TELECOMMUNICATIONS

MTN

Nigeria was a game changer for MTN in its international expansion, says the company's Group President and CEO, Sifiso Dabengwa.

'With a population of 150 million people and less than 400,000 landline telephones at the time we entered that market, Nigeria presented a massive opportunity and shifted our scale of doing everything by two or three times. It also positioned us to take on other big and complex markets outside Africa.'

By 2013 MTN was the largest primary listing on the JSE, with a market capitalisation of more than $36 billion and had operations in Iran, Yemen, Syria and Afghanistan, positioning it as an emerging market player beyond Africa.

Nigeria was the fifth African market outside South Africa that MTN invested in – after Swaziland, Uganda and Rwanda in 1998 and Cameroon in 2000. The company won one of four GSM licences put up for auction in Nigeria in 2001. In the space of ten years it had signed up more than 40 million subscribers in the country – more than it had in its home base of South Africa.

The 2001 licence auction process marked the company's third attempt to gain a foothold in Nigeria. It had been approached to join a locally based consortium in the mid-1990s to bid for one of four licences put up for sale by the military regime of Sani Abacha. The proposition did not look attractive enough and MTN walked away. In 1999 it went further, signing an agreement with another local company for a 70 per cent stake in a GSM licence.

However, before this could become a reality, the new, democratically elected president, Olusegun Obasanjo, cancelled all prior deals and in 2001 put four GSM licences up for sale in Africa's first telecommunications auction.

The market in South Africa reacted negatively to the $285 million eventually paid by MTN to secure one of the licences in what was considered to be an unknown and risky market. The company's share price plummeted. 'Nigeria was literally virgin territory,' says Dabenqwa. 'Because of decades of mostly military rule it had not been an attractive destination for investment and it was considered to be a very high risk market. Many people saw the price as idiotic but we viewed Nigeria as a high-return market that held great future value.'

He adds that the mobile phone industry itself was still relatively new at that time and people did not see the growth potential in African countries with low disposable incomes. Just five years later, GSM licences in the Middle East for which MTN bid – in Iran and Saudi Arabia – were in the $2 billion to $3 billion range, reflecting the perceived growth value of a maturing industry.

'Building the industry in Africa was a major learning curve for MTN. We played a big role in shaping the regulatory framework for telecommunications on the continent. Before the mobile phone industry came along, there was not much in the way of regulation because most countries had state-owned fixed-line monopolies. Sometimes an official in the department of telecommunications acted as a regulator. Without multiple players, there was no need for the kind of regulation you see today,' explains Dabengwa.

'When we started our expansion, the opportunity for mobile communications was huge because there was hardly any landline penetration. But no one predicted the levels of growth that we saw later. Our early assumptions were that mobile phones would be used by only ten per cent of the population and mostly for business. They were not perceived to be a mass market product.'

But penetration levels have risen sharply from three per cent in 2001 to 65 per cent in 2011, according to the GSM Association, which says Africa is the world's second largest mobile phone market by connections. The number of mobile phone users in Africa has increased by 20 per cent every year since

2006, reaching nearly 700 subscribers by 2013.

'Just being able to communicate has changed the way things are done in Africa and it has definitely improved efficiency. Although it is difficult to quantify, the percentage of GDP that can be directly related to telecommunications in a country like Nigeria must be about five per cent.'

MTN also benefited from limited competition in the early days. The industry was dominated by state monopolies with a sprinkling of small local companies and international operators such as France Telecoms, Celtel (now Airtel) and Orascom (now Etisalat).

'It took a lot of courage and foresight for companies to invest in some of these places in the early days. Now it makes perfect sense to do so. The improving economic and political climate has significantly reduced risk and made it easier for companies to get approval for investments.'

EXPANDING THE FOOTPRINT

Once MTN decided to expand beyond South Africa in 1997, its growth was rapid. In Uganda, for example, it doubled 'teledensity' in a year. In Cameroon, Africa's first GSM operator, Camtel Mobile, was able to triple capacity and double its customer base after MTN bought a stake in the company.

A big driver of growth was the pay-as-you-go package MTN had pioneered in South Africa and which resonated with cash-driven markets to the north.

Entry strategies have been opportunistic. Where licences were for sale, MTN bought them. Where existing companies had stakes up for grabs, the company went after them. Rwanda was an exception, where the company went in as a minority shareholder, with the government holding the majority stake. But by 2012 it held 80 per cent of MTN Rwanda.

After Nigeria, MTN held back on further expansion for two years – the size, difficulty and cost of setting up that operation forced the company to pause for breath. But the African footprint was soon growing again, with licences in Côte d'Ivoire, Congo-Brazzaville and Zambia. It also took its operations beyond Africa for the first time, securing a licence in Iran.

The next big turning point was the purchase of family-owned Lebanese company Investcom in 2006, a deal which the CEO at the time, Phutuma Nhleko, describes as being very difficult and a steep learning curve for him. This transaction brought in ten new, geographically and culturally diverse, markets, which had to be assimilated into the group's operating structures.

Ghana was the market in Investcom that initially piqued MTN's interest, but it came in a package with nine other countries, including Yemen, Syria, Afghanistan and Cyprus, as well as several small African states such as Guinea, Liberia and Guinea Bissau.

As with Nigeria, the company was criticised for paying above the odds for Investcom – $5.3 billion. Its original offer for the company, $2.9 billion, was below the asking price of $3.2 billion and was rejected. Investcom then listed in Dubai and London and when MTN returned to negotiate the deal a second time the price had jumped. But, believing the gamble would pay off, MTN paid the premium.

Dabengwa says many of the challenges in the Middle East have been different from those in Africa.

'You have to be prepared to accept the rules and cultures of these countries. The fact that we already had experience in other challenging countries by the time we went into the Middle East enabled us to adapt more easily.'

One of MTN's key survival strategies in a diverse range of markets has been its strict adherence to corporate governance rules as they are laid down in South Africa's governance bible, the King Code on Corporate Governance Principles. 'It is more challenging in some places than others to keep to those principles because corporate governance is not always well understood or practised in many African markets. But for us it is non-negotiable no matter where we are.

'The reality is that if you want to move into markets outside your own country there will be challenges. The differentiator is your level of preparedness to deal with them. MTN has been fortunate in having a strong team that has been able to manage difficult markets in Africa and beyond. Being from South Africa has positioned us well to deal with diversity.'

GROWTH CHALLENGES

A major challenge has been trying to estimate the size of markets and build capacity accordingly. The growth of the South African market was a surprise. MTN's first business plan, in the early 1990s, estimated that the company would have 350,000 subscribers by 2010. Instead, it had 129 million customers in 22 countries. By mid-2013 this had risen to more than 195 million.

The same phenomenon was experienced in other African markets. Says Dabengwa: 'We had very little real information to work from. Available data on population numbers, economic statistics, disposable incomes and other indicators were poor and often inaccurate. The structure of African economies, particularly the size of the informal sector, made it difficult to gather reliable information. It is difficult to estimate the size of a market if you cannot easily see how it works.'

In Nigeria, despite billions of dollars of investment, the market still defies operators' efforts to match capacity to demand. In 2011 the Nigerian state telecommunications commission gave mobile phone companies a deadline to improve capacity or face penalties.

'When we went into Nigeria we would put in base stations and they would be at full capacity within 24 hours. There was no indication of what the demand was going to be,' says Dabengwa, who ran MTN's Nigeria operation for more than six years.

'In Nigeria it is sometimes difficult to see what you are dealing with because of the structure of the market. For example, in a town like Onitsha in the east, it looks like chaos and you wonder how anyone does business there.

'But most of the containers you see in the harbour in Lagos come from Onitsha. Traders are doing everything on their mobile phones – they are talking to their customers and suppliers and moving money on the phone. They may not be operating from a five-storey building but that doesn't mean business isn't happening. The mobile phone has become an integral business tool.

'We also tended to underestimate peoples' aspirations. We would go into a country with equipment aimed at the lower segment of the market. But customers insisted they wanted the best. The aspirations of African consumers have been overlooked in projections, not just in telecommunications but in other sectors too.'

He says local business partners are often impatient to see quick returns from the business, which is not always possible. 'Building the business is a long game. Getting to the point of paying dividends can be the result of six to seven years of continuous investment.'

The company's high profile makes it an easy target for accusations that it is exploiting foreign markets by making hefty profits and repatriating the money back to South Africa rather than re-investing it. However, MTN has been one of the biggest investors on the continent and has reinvested significant amounts of money into the fast-growing markets. In 2011 alone it invested $1 billion into Nigeria and earmarked the same investment for 2012.

'There is unfortunately little recognition in Africa of the sizeable contribution foreign investors make and the multiplier effect of large investments. For example, the number of people involved in our distribution network in a country like Nigeria is huge and in most countries we are one of the biggest taxpayers.'

The company's large appetite for risky markets has several downsides, one of them being the effect of political and economic problems on the company's share price. In early 2012, political headwinds in its two biggest markets – Iran and Nigeria – had an instant negative impact on the share price. It has faced security challenges in Nigeria and war-torn Syria but Dabengwa says MTN has few regrets about its choice of markets. 'The starting point for entering frontier markets is the business case. The other risks we can manage,' he says. The company has shown its resilience in markets that other companies have shied away from and continues to rely on this appetite for risk to keep the business growing.

Inevitably, logistics have been a problem. Moving equipment around is difficult and costly and supply chains are a nightmare, particularly in landlocked countries. In many cases the company has to supply its own power and import equipment, specialised skills and many other requirements that are not available locally.

Working in states where conflict can break out at any time is a further challenge. 'No one willingly goes into a conflict zone, but what we've learned is that people need communications during conflict – mobile phones become a critical, even life saving, device although in Afghanistan the rebels have caused significant damage to the infrastructure. However, we would never put our staff at risk. In Côte d'Ivoire, for instance, staff stayed at home when fighting broke out and we assisted people to get out of dangerous areas,' says Dabengwa.

INSIGHTS INTO MTN'S SUCCESS

'One of the cornerstones of our success has been working with local partners in all our markets,' notes Dabengwa. While MTN's model is to have a majority stake and management control, it values its partners, who tend to be influential people in the respective markets.

'We are also very focused on rolling out the network and creating distribution, which is the basis of our business. You have to get these two things right to succeed. And, to do this, you need to be willing to invest faster than your competitors.

'It helped that we were able to fund our African operations mostly from South Africa in the beginning because it was not easy to get funding in the early days. We have focused on repaying debt and getting our businesses to become self-funding.'

Staffing for international operations has been another challenge. 'You have to pick staff carefully for operations inside and outside Africa and make sure they respect different cultures. We have learned over the years what works and what doesn't.'

The company does detailed assessments of staff earmarked for international operations, including psychometric testing. 'We also like to meet the spouse to ensure there is a realistic understanding of what families should anticipate from such a relocation.'

The company has built a cadre of managers from different African countries who are not confined to operating in the country they hail from but are moved around the group as needs arise. The new opportunities in Africa created by companies such as MTN have also attracted expatriate

African skills from outside the continent.

The 'South African factor' is identified as a key part of the company's success. 'There were many companies that had opportunities as good as we had, or even better, but they didn't always succeed, despite this. South Africans are resilient and are willing to work hard, face the challenges and stay the distance. The political situation at home also contributes to the company being sensitive to diversity and politics in other countries.'

NEXT STEPS

The next step for the company is to change the business model to gear up for a new era, focusing on technology rather than geographical expansion. Although the footprint may continue to grow opportunistically, the next phase is acquisitions focused on technology.

'We have successfully gone through an industry phase in which acquiring new licences, building market share and rolling out networks have been key drivers of the business. Whilst these remain important, it is clear that we have to focus more on new services that generate data revenue, improve efficiency in all aspects of the business and deliver superior customer experience.'

Dabengwa expects some consolidation in Africa in the voice market as more operators come on board. But he sees value share, as opposed to merely subscriber market share, as being a key consideration for the future.

'In many of our markets, basic internet penetration is still very low, so the data opportunity is significant. Affordability of laptops has been a limiting factor, but if you bring down the cost of devices that can provide internet access it will increase data usage significantly – and that is a very important part of our future.'

At a broader level, he believes the private sector should have more opportunity to develop the key building blocks for the continent to grow. 'The telecommunications industry shows how the private sector can succeed if governments put the enabling structures in place and let companies get on with their business. It is clear the role of business in development has not been exploited sufficiently and, for Africa to really move forward, it needs to be encouraged to participate in more areas of the economy.'

SacOil Holdings is an AIM and Johannesburg stock exchange listed independent African upstream exploration and production company based in South Africa. It has equity investors such as Encha and South African institutions, including the Public Investment Corporation, Metropolitan Asset Managers and Investec Bank. SacOil has two licences in Nigeria (OPL 281 and OPL 233) alongside an indigenous company, Energy Equity Resources, and equity in a key exploration block, Block III, in the DRC in which Total is operator at a 60 per cent stake, as well as Block 1 in Malawi. In 2013, it was given the right to explore for oil in Botswana. Other opportunities in the deal pipeline are being looked at. Following board and management changes in mid-2013, the company is being restructured.

OIL AND GAS

SACOIL HOLDINGS

Negative perceptions about oil being a 'curse' in Africa still linger in some investors' minds, says Robin Vela, founder and former CEO of SacOil Holdings, an independent African oil and gas company. 'But it is not about oil, it's about governance. The same could apply to any resource – copper, gold, platinum and others. The basic issue is that governments must be transparent about revenues. They need to put more of the value that is realised from the resource back into the economy and into the communities where the resource came from. The whole value chain should create opportunities for Africans,' says the Zimbabwean-born Vela who resigned from the company on 31 May 2013.

The opportunities in Africa's oil and gas industry are significant and growing. About ten per cent of the world's proven oil reserves are in Africa and, in 2012, around 13 per cent of global output came from the continent. Oil and gas output is expected to rise significantly over the coming decade, with increased oil production from discoveries and new field developments, and fast-opening exploration frontiers in East and West Africa.

'With improving governance, Africa is becoming a lot more attractive as an oil and gas destination simply because there is a lot more proven potential and "prospectivity" is high here,' notes Vela. 'Africa is immature, which provides a great frontier opportunity, and corporate players from all over the world are upgrading their African portfolios.'

Vela adds that the operating environment in Africa is definitely improving, driven, in part, by the fact that more companies have entered the environment and young African business leaders are returning to the continent and doing things differently. 'They have worked for global companies and institutions and they are less inclined to want to get a $500,000 envelope through the back door when they know they can create $5 billion by doing things properly. This evolution of corporate leadership is changing the business environment and governments are also starting to operate differently.'

Although governance is improving, the 'state take' in Africa's oil and gas industry is also rising. This take reflects the combination of taxes due, royalties, payments and other corporate obligations to governments over the life cycle of projects. In Uganda it is up to 80 per cent of the total pie, for example. But Vela says frontier Africa is typically below international averages, compared to countries such as Venezuela or Russia, where it is 80 per cent to 90 per cent or even Libya under the previous government, where the state take was 98 per cent.

'In Africa it has to be lower because governments need to solicit exploration dollars and ensure the assets remain attractive. In more developed markets, there are fewer issues around governance and therefore the risk is lower.' But, he says, the terms are getting tougher in Africa and, if they prove to be too costly, global oil and gas players might quickly shift their portfolios elsewhere.

The total impact of oil and gas investment tends to be overlooked by governments in their consideration of how much their countries benefit from the industry. Beyond the direct revenues into the national fiscus, countries also gain from balance of payments inflows, direct and indirect employment, technology transfers, value improvements in the supply chain, capital formation, listings, skills inflows and training, and a range of other ancillary spinoffs.

The growth of local content in the sector is another benefit. Already the continent's biggest oil producer, Nigeria, has legislation in place to increase local involvement in the sector. Vela says although there may be insufficient skills available to give substance to such legislation right now, these will develop over time.

'Indigenisation is not unique to Nigeria. It is just called different names in South Africa, Zimbabwe, Botswana, Gabon and other countries. Governments are trying to ensure that people who have a long-term vested interest in exploiting a local resource and in improving its value have a foothold in the sector in their own countries. Local ownership also creates a strong sense of proprietorship at the operational level and encourages innovation and entrepreneurialism as well as indigenous investment in the industry.

'But, although African governments have expressed the desire to broaden ownership of sovereign assets, the difficulties encountered in reconciling equity with corporate governance, coupled with political instability and economic uncertainty, have discouraged local firms from holding financial assets in Africa.'

Nevertheless, the level of African participation in the game is rising. Out of 800 oil and gas companies operating in Africa, more than 100 are African players drawn from 20 different countries. In addition, there are about 35 African state-owned oil companies operating around the continent, some with international investments.

Vela says SacOil's choice to go into what many investors consider to be two of the most difficult markets in Africa was opportunistic. 'We are also looking at other opportunities that are less risky and in different addresses. But they are all in Africa – that is where we are focused.'

THE CORPORATE EVOLUTION

Vela, a chartered accountant and long-time investment banker with Zimbabwean roots, was born and bred in the UK but came to Africa to pursue his interest in private equity and investment banking. He established Lonsa, a private equity vehicle designed to invest institutional capital from London in Southern Africa.

'Through that I got involved with a number of large South African financial services companies, one of which asked if I could find a listed vehicle to bring in funding with the premise of creating a diversified African mineral resources company.' That vehicle was JSE-listed minerals company, Samroc.

'But I have always believed that oil and gas is where the big value is,' says Vela, who shifted the company's focus from mining to the oil industry. Samroc's mining assets were transferred into a separately listed vehicle while

Samroc itself was renamed SacOil in line with its changed operational focus. It retained the JSE listing but moved to the oil and gas sector of the exchange, joining South African giant Sasol and Nigeria's Oando.

SacOil did a secondary listing on the AIM in London in 2011. 'The company needed to do this because there are few oil and gas peers on the JSE. South Africa is more focused on mining in the resources sector and it is difficult for people to really understand what we do, so being listed here doesn't really help us. It is an expensive business and it's not easy to raise money for oil in Africa, particularly if you are a junior company. Although SacOil has had support from South African institutions, it wanted the exposure and profile that being among our international peers would give it. London has typically understood the oil industry better than other jurisdictions.'

Vela maintains that having access to capital from Europe boosts SacOil's other strengths, which are: that it is a well-structured independent African company; it is South African based with a strong management team and board backed by excellent oil and gas industry credentials; it has assets with significant upside potential, and it has an aggressive growth strategy.

The company moved quickly to find oil interests on the continent. It snapped up an interest in Block III in the Albertine Graben basin in the DRC, together with South African company Divine Inspiration Group (DIG). In April 2011, France's Total bought a 60 per cent interest in the block, leaving SacOil and DIG holding a 12.5 per cent stake each, with the remaining 15 per cent held by the state. Vela is upbeat about Total's investment, saying it is tough to get a 'super major' in your corner in the competitive oil and gas environment.

Experts believe the reserves around Lake Albert in the DRC will mirror the huge oil deposits, estimated at more than 1.5 billion barrels, already discovered on the Ugandan side of the lake. In 2012 SacOil was granted the all-important presidential ordinance for Block III by the Congolese government, allowing testing and evaluation to begin in earnest.

SacOil entered the Nigerian market in 2010 and expects to begin production by 2013 in a joint partnership with indigenous operator Energy Equity Resources.

CHALLENGES

Vela identifies the main challenges of operating in Africa as: political risk, establishing a foothold in a highly competitive and international industry, managing volatile markets, getting funding for assets in Africa and overcoming a general lack of oil and gas experience in the industry.

'It is important to always follow due process when entering a market. If you don't, a new government might come along and raise questions about how you got your licence and even overturn it. The last thing your investors want is to find they no longer have title to their investment because of something you have done. We always build international arbitration into our contracts just in case, but so far we have never had to resort to it.'

Despite a high appetite for risk, SacOil views security of tenure as a non-negotiable factor for entering a market. 'This is extremely important because the ownership of oil blocks has to outlast incumbent governments. In Nigeria, so far, no one has ever lost title to an oil asset. The Nigerians respect security of tenure because they understand they have to remain attractive to international investment.'

This has not been the case in the DRC. Before SacOil secured Block III there, Blocks I and II had been awarded to the UK's Tullow Oil, but were later given to politically well-connected South African companies by a government minister who claimed that the original deal had not been given the presidential nod. This sparked long-running legal action that ended up in an international court. A similar problem arose in the DRC's mining industry, involving an international company.

'The DRC is still a young country and very new to oil and gas. Security of tenure has always been a big issue there and one that has been raised regularly. SacOil had a threefold way of dealing with it. The first is to highlight the fact that it was a South African company – our companies seem to have fared better in DRC than foreign companies from elsewhere in terms of tenure. SacOil also has a sovereign investor in the Public Investment Corporation, which is wholly owned by the South African government.

'Lastly, having a "super major" oil producer in the block – Total – is attractive to DRC because it brings many benefits. These include not only foreign direct investment, but validation of DRC's acreage, and it lends credibility to the country's oil assets.

'These factors, together with Total's ability to move acreage up the value curve in a speedy manner, make the arrangement attractive to DRC and should imply a long-term relationship.'

Vela says African companies can have an advantage. 'We are mindful of the risk of operating in Africa but believe that our identity, background and experience enable us to judge the risks involved and to mitigate them. Although the socio-economic disadvantage of being an indigenous player is generally regarded as a risk, there is a distinct advantage to being an African independent. Our DNA is indigenous and this structure is recognised by regional governments and role players alike.

'But even if you are indigenous, you still need to be able to exploit the resources and for that you need capacity, especially financial capacity.'

He adds that being indigenous to Africa does not remove the fact that when you invest outside your home market you are regarded as a foreign investor. 'That is why it is important to establish partnerships with non-political business people who are like minded and who add value. This makes sense as well as being an obvious risk mitigation factor.

'You always need to remember that every address is different. Uganda is very different from Zambia, which is different from Nigeria, and so on. Each market also has its own nuances. You can't take the same approach to the industry in a well-established market such as Nigeria as you would in a new address like DRC. It is important to look at the level of development of an industry in each country when doing business there.'

Vela offers a few tips for doing business in Africa: don't make promises you can't keep; always ensure that any actions taken, if made public, would not embarrass you, your colleagues or your business; put yourself in the shoes of the local partner (who is assigning tremendous potential value) and find a way for them to share in the upside of the investment; retain a sense of community spirit, and ensure you follow due process and have title that is defensible through any changes of government and is acceptable to shareholders.

A VIEW OF THE FUTURE

'The fact that upstream and downstream companies are selling off marginal assets is a major opportunity for indigenous companies. For them, these investments are non-material but, for African companies, it could be life changing to own stakes in these resources. Over time, you are going to have more local companies developing assets, which is good for the continent's oil and energy security.

Vela believes the South African link is important in the oil and gas business. 'This is based on a belief that while South Africa has been endowed with many natural resources, hydrocarbons are not among them. The country has a stated policy of energy security and at some point it is going to have to look elsewhere to secure those sources of energy.

Even though there is a state oil company in PetroSA, the government also needs to tap into private local companies that have acquired acreage in Africa to boost the country's oil imports. A market that accounts for about 30 per cent of the continent's GDP is not one you want to ignore.'

Seed Co Limited, an African multinational headquartered in Zimbabwe and listed on the Zimbabwe Stock Exchange (ZSE), produces and certifies crop seeds in a number of African countries through subsidiaries. Products include hybrid maize, cotton, wheat, soya bean, barley, sorghum and groundnut seeds. It has businesses across Southern Africa and in East Africa. It is looking at expanding into West Africa. Seed Co is a subsidiary of diversified agro-industrial Zimbabwean conglomerate, Aico Africa Limited, which is also listed on the ZSE.

AGRICULTURE

SEED CO

The land reform programme in Zimbabwe brought massive challenges to all aspects of agriculture, not least to the production of seeds, says Morgan Nzwere, Group Chief Executive of Seed Co Limited.

Seed production is an activity well suited to commercial farming as it requires isolation. 'To produce hybrid maize seeds you need to plant crops on reasonably sized tracts of land, far from other maize crops so you don't get contamination of the product,' explains Nzwere. 'We used commercial farmers to do this because they had the land and the experience. After the land was converted into small-scale farms as part of the land reform programme in Zimbabwe, it created a challenge for us in terms not only of the land itself but also the skills.'

As a result, in Zimbabwe seed production dropped from 32,000 metric tonnes per annum in 2000 to 4,500 tonnes in 2008, the year in which Zimbabwe's economic decline reached its lowest point. 'We had to start rebuilding the production base and training the new people that were now on the land. That paid off as we saw production steadily growing to 9,000 tonnes in 2009, doubling in 2010 and reaching 31,000 tonnes in 2011. We've gone full circle in terms of our production base because of these interventions.'

Similarly, yields, which went from four tonnes per hectare in 2000 to 1.9 tonnes a hectare in 2009, rose to 2.8 tonnes a hectare in 2010 and were soon reaching the levels of a decade earlier, he says.

There were many other challenges during Zimbabwe's 'lost decade' – 1998 to 2008 – that resulted from the land seizures, unfavourable policies and growing political intolerance on the one hand, and sanctions by major funding countries and institutions on the other. The challenges included a lack of inputs, serious foreign exchange shortages and a lack of funding.

'Although the economy is normalising and we have regained our production base, supply is still outstripping demand and the gap is taking some time to close. We are selling to the government for its input programmes but it also has major budget challenges and is not buying as much as it used to.'

Governments in Africa, he says, are the biggest purchasers of seed. 'They play a critical role as they are always the biggest customers. Governments are about security. Part of that is food security and food security starts with seed. If you give people seed and they have a good harvest and full granaries your political career is likely to be longer than when tummies are empty.'

Two neighbouring countries – Malawi and Zambia – introduced agricultural subsidy input programmes for small farmers to increase production and yields of staple crops and, although the exercise was costly, it resulted in significant increases in production and productivity, as well as economic growth and poverty reduction. It was also good business for seed companies.

'But the challenge is that subsidies create a dependency mindset. In a year when there is no input scheme, the recipients don't buy seeds, they re-use them and yields immediately fall to what they were before the subsidies were introduced.

The same problem arises where you have donors and NGOs intervening in crises with food relief. 'This tends to build a dependency syndrome, a culture where people get used to getting things for free. While we get good business from NGOs, we get no business in the years that they are not giving away inputs because people sit back and wait for the handouts to come back rather than buying seeds and becoming self-sufficient.'

This has a detrimental effect on free market development in the long run.

Nzwere says NGOs often do not take a long-term view of development. 'They are always looking for quick wins because they have to report to their donors and they are highly mobile. We need a long-term focus so African agriculture can be sustainable. Unfortunately, when short-term interventions end, things tend to go back to what they were and there are no real gains.'

EXPANDING THE FOOTPRINT

Seed Co has been around for more than 70 years, starting as a co-operative to serve local farmers wanting access to improved seeds, and growing into a sizeable company that listed on the ZSE in 1996. 'At that stage, we had 85 per cent market share in Zimbabwe.

'There were many markets in the rest of Africa where we had zero per cent market share or just ten or 15 per cent. It seemed to us that there was a lot more opportunity to grow those markets than to spend our time trying to grow the Zimbabwe business further. It made more sense to aim for even five per cent of a much bigger untapped market than have 100 per cent of one small market.

'We also wanted to diversify our country risk, particularly because our main product – maize – is used across Africa. We also needed to develop regional business to build our foreign currency reserves at a time when this was scarce in Zimbabwe.'

In 1997 the company expanded into neighbouring Zambia and quickly followed with acquisitions in South Africa and Mozambique and new businesses in Botswana, Malawi and Swaziland. In time it moved further afield into Tanzania, Ethiopia and Kenya.

'Zambia is our biggest market after Zimbabwe, but that is also reaching saturation levels. We are looking further afield for new opportunities.'

West Africa is an area of interest. 'Potential demand in the Nigerian market alone is more than in all our other markets together. We see West Africa in general as a huge untapped market because they do consume a lot of maize. We have already done extensive trials there and the results are very exciting.'

Seed Co has had less success in Lusophone markets. It invested in a local company in Mozambique but sold up after a short time and was also unsuccessful in setting up in Angola. 'We found out the hard way that culture and language play a big role in our kind of business and that it is very difficult to do business in countries where you don't share a common background. We did very well in places with a similar Commonwealth heritage and familiar legal frameworks, banking systems and business cultures.'

Seed Co has five research stations – two in Zimbabwe, two in Zambia and one in Kenya – and the company produces mostly maize seed (70 per cent of production, cotton (12 per cent) and soya beans (ten per cent).

'We principally deal in hybrid seeds. These are different from genetically modified (GM) seeds. Ours are conventionally bred through a process of natural selection. You cross pollinate two plants and, if you like the result, you keep cross fertilising the resultant offspring until you come up with a product that has the attributes that you want. With GM you are introgressing a particular trait into a variety that has already been identified as good and the results are achieved a lot faster.

'North of the Limpopo GM crops are still a big no-no,' explains Nzwere. 'It's just a few countries that allow them, such as South Africa, and in some countries they allow non-food GM seeds to be used. It's a fear of the unknown. There is no firm evidence there is anything wrong with them or that they have done any damage and they are a real boon for a resource-poor farmer because they significantly increase yields. I think Africa will eventually adopt them but adoption rates tend to be slower in Africa in general than in other parts of the world.'

Zimbabwe has long had some of the best research facilities in the world. Nzwere says the first hybrid variety seed – SR52 – was released in the country in 1952 and the country was a regional pioneer in the development of early maturing seed varieties for drought areas. Zimbabwe recently developed the world's first 'rust resistant' programme to deal with rust in soya bean crops and it is currently being tested in Brazil.

'We are becoming globalised. Twenty years ago our customers were only in other towns and villages in Zimbabwe. Now when we think of our customers they are people in Lusaka, Nairobi, Arusha, Lilongwe, Accra, Lagos and Addis Ababa and, who knows, in another five years our customers might be people in Rio de Janeiro.'

CHALLENGES

Nzwere says, although the operating environment in Africa is improving, changes are happening slowly. 'For example, even though we have free trade areas in regional trading blocs, there are still many hindrances. Cross border tariffs tend to restrict the movement of goods and there is a lot of paperwork to be done and many protocols to be followed, even within a single bloc.'

A key problem for Seed Co is the lack of harmonisation of registration requirements. Even if a product has been released in one country, another country needs to start the entire testing and registration process from scratch – even if it is in the same region or ecological zone.

'Typically, we spend ten years developing a seed variety and another three years testing it. Each new market in Africa requires the product to be tested for two to three years before the government will approve its release into that country.

'Their logic is that for a new variety to be released it must be better than the existing varieties, so they say we must show them that it is. We believe we can show them this from trials already done across the region with available data, but they don't want to do it that way. It's a big constraint to development.

'Governments tend to be very nationally focused and, because food security is an issue, they want their seed to be produced locally. If they are dependent on another country, and there is a shortage, that country may clamp down and ban the export of seed so they don't run out of their own stocks.'

Another challenge is the lack of infrastructure, something which is a major brake on agricultural development generally in Africa. 'We insist farmers have irrigation so power, water and availability of irrigation equipment are all issues. Transport is also a challenge – seed tends to be bulky so we can't put it on a plane and the state of the roads doesn't make transport as quick as it could be.'

Access to markets has been a long-standing problem for Africa's farmers. Food prices across the world are rising rapidly and yet most of Africa's arable land is unused or under-utilised. Part of the problem is the difficulty of moving small-scale farmers, who dominate the sector, to the next level. There are few incentives for them to grow their output and little official support.

'Demand for seeds is growing, but about 90 per cent of our customers are smallholder farmers who grow just enough to feed their families. The challenge here is the lack of a market. There is no incentive to grow more if there is no market for it. They need warehousing to store their products and effective distribution outlets to sell what they grow.

'Governments need to do more to put in place marketing systems and support mechanisms to guarantee farmers good prices for their excess production – and build export markets and create industries to stimulate agricultural development. There are many end products but very little value addition taking place at the moment.

'But there is also a problem of mindset. As most farmers are in the rural areas, they have difficulty in thinking of a market as being outside of their immediate region or village.'

Nzwere says the lack of a robust financial system in many countries is problematic as the company tries to hedge currency risk by paying local costs in domestic currencies. Land tenure, which constrains agricultural development, because banks do not regard leasehold land as sufficient collateral, is not a big issue for Seed Co customers because most are too small-scale to require bank funding.

Although the company has competition from large players such as Pioneer Hi-Bred and Monsanto from the US and Pannar Seed from South Africa, Nzwere says the biggest competition is from 'retained seed'.

'If farmers don't have resources they just use the seeds from previous crops and replant them. Yield rates are lower and germination percentages are lower but, if someone has no money, they don't have a choice. There is also a growing business in fake seeds. People take grain from their fields, put in seed colouring and put this on the market as legitimate seed. This harms the market because it leads people to think that seeds are a problem and they don't always make the distinction.'

TIPS FOR DOING BUSINESS

Nzwere says it is important to have governments onside when they are an important player in your industry. 'African governments tend to like locally produced goods for their people, rather than depending on goods from elsewhere, and they are a big customer for many things. It is important to become familiar with what the government's programmes are in any country in which you operate.'

He also preaches the virtue of patience. 'In most places things take a long time and you really have to persevere to get results. But, if an investment is not working, it is better to pull out of a market than to think everything will fall into place in time. So your patience needs to be quite strategic. You should set milestones for development, and if you are not achieving any of them early on you should pull out. It will be a lot cheaper to do so sooner rather than later.

'You should not assume that one size fits all – things that work in South Africa don't work in Zimbabwe and what works in Zimbabwe won't necessarily work in Mozambique. To succeed, you really have to understand that culture, region and local issues play a significant role. Their importance can never be underestimated.'

Part of the M&C Saatchi Abel Group in South Africa, M&C Saatchi Africa is an advertising agency network active in East and West Africa. Its international parent company, M&C Saatchi Worldwide, is the world's largest independent marketing communications group with 26 offices in 18 countries globally.

ADVERTISING

M&C SAATCHI AFRICA

The battle of the brands is about to begin in Africa, predicts Rick de Kock, Managing Director of advertising agency M&C Saatchi Africa. As the word spreads about the consumer opportunity in a continent of a billion people with rising incomes and high economic growth levels, global brands from all over the world are rushing in.

'The competition for consumer spend is keen and growing,' he says. 'Some of the world's fastest-growing economies are here and international brands want a piece of the action.'

Interest in the consumer markets of Africa is coming from all over the world, he says. 'We are seeing more brands from India coming down the east coast of Africa and there are a lot of new brands coming from Europe and America such as Walmart and Yum Brands, which is opening KFC outlets across the continent. There are very few coming from China at this stage but that may change in time. And there are also the African brands. Many of the big African brands have traditionally come out of South Africa but that is also changing as African companies spread their wings out of their traditional local markets.

TALKING TO CUSTOMERS

'Consumers are starting to understand that everybody wants to talk to them. With the explosion of new technology, African consumers are more connected to the world than ever before so they have more choice and they know what is good and what isn't. If you try to sell them rubbish, they'll know.'

This rapid penetration of technology into Africa has implications for the way business operates. The landing of numerous submarine cables on African shores since 2009 has given the continent vastly increased access to international fibre bandwidth and the numbers of internet users is rising as the technology becomes more affordable. The number of internet users rose from 4.5 million in 2000 to nearly 140 million by 2012 – with 45 million in Nigeria alone. But internet penetration is still only fifteen per cent of the population, indicating huge potential growth in the future.

Similarly, the GSM Association predicts that the number of mobile phone users in Africa will reach 735 million by the end of 2017.

'We are dealing with a mostly young, dynamic target market that is becoming globally connected through the internet and mobile phones and they understand brands a lot more,' says De Kock. 'The way we communicate with this market will have to change dramatically. Everyone will have to up their game.

'With the massive competition for audiences and consumer spend, advertising messages are starting to fade into each other; they are becoming wallpaper. So advertising has to move from being literal to more conceptual in order to stand out.

'Traditional media such as radio, television and billboard are still key delivery platforms in Africa and they will be for a while. But millions of Africans are now getting their messages from a variety of places. We can't just run a television advert anymore. We have to ask how we can also start tapping into consumers' social networks. The model being used in Africa is changing rapidly.'

De Kock says the biggest spenders in African advertising are, by far, the mobile companies, followed by financial services providers and the producers of alcohol products and fast-moving consumer goods (FMCG). The fastest growing spend is in the alcohol and FMCG industries.

As more and more multinationals arrive in Africa they will challenge local brands, De Kock predicts. 'The challenge for African marketers is to build local brands to the point where they become pan-African and even global brands. There are very few pan-African brands currently that don't come from South Africa.'

The advertising industry in South Africa is far more advanced than it is elsewhere in Africa. 'We have a long tradition of advertising here and this country worked hard to box above its weight in the rest of the world.'

But, he says, the advertising environment in other African countries is changing. 'Over the past few years, advertising in Africa has gathered momentum, the messaging is getting sharper and the production quality is getting a whole lot better. I have seen real strides being made in the industry. Some countries are much more sophisticated than others, for example Kenya where there has been a long tradition of advertising; whereas West Africa is now playing catch up. But it can be difficult to draw skilled people into the industry because it is quite intangible. It's not like becoming a lawyer or a doctor,' notes De Kock.

THINKING LOCALLY

'You are not dealing with homogenous societies within regions, or even within countries. Foreigners have tended to regard Africa as one country rather than acknowledging the many differences in nationalities, cultures, religion and languages. The worst thing you can do when you are trying to sell something to people is to offend them by being culturally insensitive.'

The advertising industry reflects, in part, the society in which it operates. 'This means you can't adopt a one-size-fits-all approach,' says De Kock. 'If you want to be relevant, you have to spend money making adverts that are particular to a market and that means you cannot re-use material that has been made for other markets. You have to invest in understanding your consumers to know what drives them and what visual language would appeal to them.

'You need to pay attention to the cultural differences between North,

East, West and Southern Africa. There are also local differences that need to be taken into account, even within countries, when developing advertising campaigns. Nigeria, for example, has more than 250 ethnic groups while in East Africa, where Swahili is widely spoken, there are variations of the language between countries such as Kenya and Tanzania.

'You can speak to people in official languages such as English but if you really want to resonate with markets you should try to build in the local languages and regional peculiarities. Humour is something that needs to be handled carefully – what is funny in one market may not be funny in another.

'Religious sensitivities also have to be taken into account. In many countries we would think nothing of showing men and women in bathing costumes on a beach together. But this would be a real problem in countries in North Africa for example. And even within countries you need to consider these issues because of religious diversity.'

De Kock says such factors make it crucial that multinationals operating in Africa truly understand the markets they are trying to reach. In the past, market information has been difficult to find. However, recently market research firms have proliferated, servicing companies that are competing for advantage in a crowded marketplace. 'But, at the end of the day, it really helps to have a presence on the ground. No one knows a market better than someone who lives in it.'

Although he believes South African companies have a big role to play on the continent, 'people from the rest of Africa have a lot to teach us about entrepreneurship. If you drive through African cities late at night, you will see many entrepreneurs hard at work, with their workplaces lit only by candles or torchlight. The sense of energy across the continent is massive, particularly in East and West Africa. Nobody stands still. They are always finding ways to make money.

'There is no doubt things are moving and, with the developed world in trouble, investors no longer regard Africa as being so risky. There is almost a sense that if you can lose your shirt on Wall Street, Africa seems quite tame. In fact, if you're not doing business in Africa already, you've possibly missed the boat.'

Founded in 1949, United Bank for Africa has its headquarters in Nigeria and is listed on the Nigeria Stock Exchange (NSE). During the banking consolidation in Nigeria that began in 2005, sparked by a sharp increase in capitalisation requirements, UBA merged with Standard Trust Bank, bringing its assets to $19 billion in 2011. It is one of the top three banks in Nigeria in terms of market capitalisation and size of customer base. In addition to its 19 African operations, it has offices in Paris, London and New York.

FINANCIAL SERVICES

UNITED BANK FOR AFRICA

'If you can succeed in business in Nigeria, you can succeed anywhere in Africa. The similarity of the Nigerian market to other African markets makes it easier for us to effectively navigate the risks and leverage cultural peculiarities,' says Phillips Oduoza, Group Managing Director/CEO of the UBA Group, one of Nigeria's biggest banks.

Using its experience in the Nigerian market, UBA grew one of the largest banking footprints on the African continent in less than a decade. In 2005 it had a single non-Nigerian operation – in nearby Ghana. By 2012 it was trading in 19 countries.

AFRICAN OPERATIONS AND EXPANSION

Ghana was a natural choice for the group's initial expansion given its proximity to Nigeria, the fact that the two countries share a common language – English – in the midst of a mostly Francophone region and that they share a similar business culture.

UBA was the first of many Nigerian banks to be granted a licence in Ghana. In spite of high levels of competition, not only from Nigerian financial institutions, but also from international and local banks, Ghana has been a big success for UBA. 'It is our best performing market outside of Nigeria. GDP growth there is heading for double digits and not only has oil production started but the country is one of the most stable and secure on the continent. There is also a lot of foreign investment and we are making good profits there,' notes Oduoza.

In 2007, from its towering headquarters building in Marina at the heart of Lagos's central business district, UBA decided to explore a broader Africa strategy, starting with West Africa and then moving further afield to markets that had never heard of Nigerian banks.

Within four years it was established in Liberia, Burkina Faso, Benin, Cameroon, Sierra Leone, Guinea, Côte d'Ivoire and Senegal in West Africa, as well as in Gabon, Chad, Kenya, Mozambique, Zambia, Uganda, the DRC, Republic of Congo and Tanzania in Central and Southern Africa.

Together with Nigeria and Ghana, this brought the country operations to 19. The group favoured greenfield undertakings, making acquisitions in only two markets – Republic of Benin and Burkina Faso.

'We acted quickly once we made the decision to expand beyond Nigeria's borders. The window of opportunity in Africa is not going to be open forever and, as it narrows, entry barriers are going to get tougher.'

The first priority was getting licences quickly and then consolidating. 'Our initial focus was building businesses in the regions nearest to Nigeria, leveraging on our superior knowledge of the business terrain in these locations, before venturing into other key economies in the rest of Africa.'

All markets it has gone into are smaller than its home base. Nigeria's huge population of about 150 million people means the bank is used to having one Nigerian branch catering to as many customers as an entire operation elsewhere. 'We are used to dealing with large volumes here so we had to adjust to smaller numbers.'

While competition in the consolidated banking sector in Nigeria is fierce, with banks continually having to innovate in the fight for market share, UBA has encountered surprisingly little competition in its expansionary exploits, with more risk-averse rivals tending to avoid the small, challenging markets that now make up part of the group's footprint.

'There are very few banks that have the same profile and structure as us. Most of those that do are international banks such as Standard Chartered, Citibank and Barclays. Having said that, our biggest competitor is in fact another African banking group – Ecobank, headquartered in Togo – which is in many of the same places as us.

'The potential in countries such as Chad and Guinea is huge even though many consider them to be difficult markets. Guinea is the largest exporter of bauxite in the world and that alone represents a very big opportunity in a market with little banking competition. In fact, our Guinea office broke even after just two months of operation. We see a lot of foreign direct investment going into Guinea and the banks have a big role to play in developing the country. The same applies to other places. They may be small now but they have large growth potential, especially those with natural resources,' says Oduoza.

The selection of target countries in the expansion programme was based on three key guiding principles: the size of the financial services opportunity, the growth potential within the sector and the inherent risk to investible capital. The bank devised indices to determine how each candidate country matched up against each principle. Twenty countries were selected. Two of the initial selection in which the bank is yet to operate are Mali and Angola.

DRIVERS OF EXPANSION

Oduoza says expansion was informed by statistics on African growth during this century. 'With abundant natural resources, a young and growing population and a large potential market, we believe that Africa is the last global frontier after the emerging powers of China, India and Brazil. Banking penetration in Africa is still below 30 per cent, which presents a large opportunity for innovative financial services within the continent.

'There are also vast infrastructure financing opportunities across the continent, with an estimated funding shortfall of $55 billion between available and required funding. With a rate of return on donor-funded infrastructure projects averaging between 30 per cent and 40 per cent, these investments can be highly profitable.

'Trade in Africa is set to grow significantly in response to increasing economic openness and the promulgation of favourable policies. The growth of the middle class also represents a viable market for global businesses to tap into.'

Despite this optimistic outlook, there are African countries that do not suit UBA's business objectives. 'These countries either present very little opportunity in financial services or present significant risks – more risks than the group is prepared to tackle right now. For example, the political situation in Somalia and Sudan make them unattractive at this time. Some other countries have relatively small economies that, today, present no justification for setting up operations, such as Djibouti and São Tomé. But future developments may improve their attractiveness.'

UBA has not set its sights on the South African market in the near term because of the very high levels of competition from local banks and the relative sophistication of the economy compared to UBA's other markets. 'As trade between South Africa and other African countries evolves, we will definitely look at doing something there in the future.' UBA already has an agreement with one of South Africa's biggest insurance companies, Metropolitan Life, to deliver insurance services to its market in Nigeria.

CHALLENGES

Managing 750 branches and more than seven million customers across some of sub-Saharan Africa's most challenging markets is tough. 'We have had to deal with regulatory issues, cultural differences, skills acquisition challenges, weak business support, poor market information and so on,' says Oduoza.

One of the biggest issues has been logistics. 'Intra-African flight schedules have been a significant bottleneck in terms of getting things done. If you have appointments at short notice, it is difficult to move around. For instance, when our head office team travelled to Mozambique to facilitate the start-up strategic plan for the country operation, bad weather caused a slight delay in the arrival of the flight from Nigeria to Kenya. This led to the team missing the connecting flight to Mozambique. They waited for three days before an alternative connecting flight could be arranged.'

Government bureaucracy is a further stumbling block. 'The public sector has been the major driver of economic activities in many states, including Nigeria, resulting in large costs to economies in terms of bureaucracy and economic mismanagement. We have got used to dealing with this, but it doesn't make life easy.'

Political volatility continues to be a risk despite improvements across the continent. 'For example, we had to suspend our operations in Côte d'Ivoire for a few months during the political impasse in that country. But we resumed operations once peace was restored.'

Sovereignty issues can also be problematic. UBA has tried to reduce costs and improve efficiencies across its multiple markets by developing a shared services platform out of Nigeria. However, several regulators have demanded that the bank locate its IT resources in the host country, which has pushed up costs. The same attitude prevails regarding hiring foreigners in certain places, with governments insisting that managers have to be locals.

Staffing has seen its own challenges. 'Access to skills to operate our continental network has put pressure on the flagship operation in Nigeria. We have had to move some of our people from their operational base at home to provide leadership in fledgling African operations. We would have preferred to run all our operations with CEOs from Nigeria to ensure standardisation and uniformity of brand and operation; the CEO sets the pace. But we didn't have a big enough pool of talent so had to develop a set of managers from other African countries – and it has worked very well.'

Policy instability is a continuing challenge. 'In several places in which we operate, minimum capitalisation requirements for banks have been raised and we have had to comply with this.' Monetary policies can change frequently as governments respond to problems such as rising inflation. 'We are held hostage to the objectives that governments are pursuing at any time and we have to live with that and adapt.'

But there are also benefits for banks in this area as African governments start to set priorities and lend at preferential rates to enable banks to provide affordable funding to priority sectors.

'I must point out that in all of these challenging areas, the continent has recorded significant progress in recent times and things can only get better.'

GROWING OPPORTUNITIES

The size of the opportunity in Africa right now is a big drawcard for investors, observes Oduoza. 'We are increasingly being asked by people from outside the continent about what they should invest in. Despite the capital flight in 2008, in the wake of the global crisis, money is starting to flow back to Africa because assets are very cheap.'

The growing awareness of opportunity in Africa is also helping to unlock funding for long-term lending. UBA has had two successful bond issues to strengthen its capital base and is finding it easier to set up credit lines with development finance institutions.

China, he says, is an obvious funding opportunity. The bank has already exploited the emerging market giant's interest in Africa – in 2007 it entered into a partnership with the state-owned Industrial and Commercial Bank of China to leverage infrastructure financing opportunities in West Africa. 'There is a lot of potential for these types of partnerships now.

'There are also big opportunities for leapfrogging in the African business environment. An example of this is the rapid and unprecedented adoption of mobile banking. This has shown the massive potential for innovative financial services to reach new and under served financial services markets.'

What has UBA learned from its expansion programme? Oduoza replies: 'UBA's venture into Africa has yielded valuable lessons for the group and revealed the key success factors for building a financial services business in Africa. Firstly, a rigorous strategic approach to expansion is crucial, and so is continuous re-evaluation.

'There must also be strong capital management structures to achieve capital retention, especially in the early stages of the business. Keeping dialogue open with the regulator and other key stakeholders is very important. We have focused on building relationships across the board. In Africa, possibly more than in any other region, building the right local partnerships and trusted networks is critical because each country has its unique ways of executing transactions.'

Innovation is crucial to staying ahead of the game. UBA has designed the likes of trade and remittance payments products specifically for African markets. 'It is important to have unique products for specific environments. Products developed elsewhere in the world may not succeed in Africa because of the particular needs of and problems in our markets, in the areas of electricity supply and infrastructure, for example. There also needs to be a supportive framework for the effective transfer of innovations and successes to ensure all group entities can benefit from these.

'And lastly, standardisation, governance, risk management and control must be institutionalised and continuously monitored if you want to succeed in Africa.'

UBA's African expansion has been good not just for the banking group but also for raising the profile of Africa and Nigeria in particular. 'Our country doesn't have the best image. Many negative impressions are based on ignorance about Nigeria and this is changing as people see the quality of what we are doing,' says Oduoza.

The Africa Legal Network (ALN) is an independent alliance of leading law firms in Africa. It is the only grouping of its kind in Africa, with close working relationships between its members and an established network of Best Friends across the continent. ALN provides common knowledge sharing platforms and enhances the capacity and capability of its members to service a growing volume of high-value domestic and international corporate and commercial advisory work across Africa. ALN also coordinates cross-border groups focused around industry sectors.

ALN's member firms share common values and are located in three major regional economic groupings – East African Community, Southern African Development Community and COMESA, which have a combined population of 325 million people.

Anjarwalla & Khanna is one of the largest law firms in Kenya with 50 corporate lawyers and offices in Nairobi and Mombasa. It has the country's biggest team of corporate, commercial and M & A specialists and its client base includes banking and financial institutions, private equity funds, venture capital and institutional equity investors, real estate developers, project developers and financiers, multilateral lenders, industrial and commercial companies, professional firms as well as government and public organizations both locally and internationally.

LEGAL SERVICES

AFRICAN LEGAL NETWORK

'This is really a very exciting time to be a lawyer in Africa, given the potential for economic growth across the continent and the skills that will be required to help that development,' says Roddy McKean, of leading East African corporate law firm Anjarwalla & Khanna. Anjarwalla & Khanna is the founding member of Africa Legal Network, which is an alliance of leading law firms in over 12 countries.

'We're going to see some dramatic changes in the practice of law in Africa over the coming years. African law firms have been increasing their reach and experience on the continent to the extent that many are now able to take on major transactions for international companies that previously only used firms based in Europe or the US. Global investors are recognising that firms based on the continent have capabilities we didn't have a decade or even five years ago,' says McKean, a partner in the firm, which is based in Nairobi. He was previously Head of the Africa Practice at Webber Wentzel based in South Africa where he was responsible for developing its practice in the rest of Africa.

'Historically, if there was a project in Africa, such as an M&A transaction, an infrastructure project or a privatisation, companies would default to London or Paris for advice. The view was that there was no capability in Africa to advise on the transaction. Much of the work in Francophone Africa was run out of Paris by large independent French firms or the Paris offices of international law firms. Over the last few years, as law firms in Africa have developed their cross-border capability, that expertise is increasingly becoming accessible here. And the added benefits are that we are based on the continent, we travel regularly on the continent and are probably a more cost-effective alternative to those international firms.

'This is a kind of beneficiation within the legal industry. And this makes sense because we have more expertise on the ground than the international firms with whom we are competing. It is also a clear indication that lawyers based in Africa are driving change in the way in which their clients' businesses and transactional activity can be supported by their legal advisers.'

He says the shift to African-based expertise will extend to resolution of large contractual disputes as international arbitration expertise develops within African firms. Much of this work, amounting to billions of dollars of fees every year, leaves the continent. Such cases often involve actions against governments for failure to respect contracts, or to address changes unilaterally made to licences or concessions to private sector companies, particularly with regard to natural resources.

'We would prefer that these African problems are dealt with in Africa so that the benefit accrues to the local economy. As a standard provision, international arbitration is a preferred method of resolving disputes in African countries – as it is in other emerging markets – given concerns about the inefficiencies, uncertainties and delays of taking action through the local courts. Some countries have developed their own arbitration centres but they have not been very effective, so that is an area where we need to develop greater expertise.'

THE BUSINESS CASE FOR AFRICA

During the global economic crisis, much of Africa, outside of South Africa, remained relatively unscathed and GDP figures for many economies on the continent remained remarkably robust. Sub-Saharan Africa is now viewed as one of the world's last investment frontier markets.

McKean says the amount of work the firm has undertaken in Africa has 'exploded' in recent years. 'For many years Africa was at the bottom of the investors' list of emerging market destinations. They were deterred by the perception of Africa being a high-risk place in which to operate. And that is not surprising given that media reports about Africa tend to focus on the negative aspects such as disease, famine, war and poverty. But the reality is that those knowledgeable companies that have been investing in Africa over the years have often found the returns here to be the highest of any emerging market.

'Having spent five years working in a different emerging market region, in Asia, I know those markets and the challenges in those countries are actually quite similar to what you find in Africa. In some ways it is easier to do business in Africa,' says McKean.

'The high level of activity by the original BRIC countries (Brazil, Russia, India and China) in Africa is to some extent driven by a desire to acquire natural resources, but they also understand that the risk issues are similar to the risks in their home regions and so have a level of comfort which perhaps companies from more developed markets do not have. Africa perhaps has an advantage for investors in that, when you are investing in a business in China or India, you are likely to have a large number of competitors in that space whereas in Africa there is often little competition – all those negative perceptions have kept out a lot of competitors.'

But that situation is rapidly changing, particularly in the wake of the economic slowdown in developed country markets. 'Our own client base is becoming much more global,' notes McKean. 'We have retained our North American and European clients but are now seeing much more activity from large companies from China, India and Brazil, as well as the Middle East.'

Much global investor interest has been piqued by the amount of activity in natural resources industries. 'But the perception that Africa is purely a natural resources play is changing. A growing consumer market is rising, fuelled by economic growth, and we are seeing this in cities such as Lagos, Lusaka, Nairobi, Accra and even Kigali. Investors are looking at a wide range of associated sectors such as financial services, telecoms, healthcare, fast moving consumer goods, retail and real estate, to name a few.

'Africa can also benefit from what is termed "the demographic dividend", where its percentage of working population versus total population will continue to increase well beyond 2050 – whereas the relevant figures for developed economies are declining and even China and India will reach a peak within the next 20 to 30 years.

'The agriculture story is also very interesting because although Africa has 25 per cent of the world's arable land, less than ten per cent of it is currently being utilised. That is a huge opportunity and we are already seeing more deals coming through in this sector. Africa could become a significant food generator for the world if it handles this correctly. There are big opportunities in introducing large mechanised farming as opposed to the general small-scale subsistence farming which happens at the moment. Similarly, local beneficiation in food processing will benefit local economies. However, there needs to be more co-operation between African governments to develop the sector and, as with the broader natural resources debate, they need to make sure that all the benefits don't go to foreign companies and governments which are searching for land to provide food security for their people. We have already seen a number of foreign governments buying land here for this purpose.'

McKean says, because South Africa is the most developed market in Africa, it has a different business approach to other African countries, where certain types of transactions have not been done before.

However, there are some fundamental 'must haves' when considering any investment. Choosing the right local partner is key in Africa. 'Extensive due diligence on the industry, the market and your partner is vital, particularly background checks on individuals and their position and reputation in the local business community. If one is investing in natural resources or infrastructure projects, it is also important to fully assess country and political risk and to evaluate the impact of regime change on your project,' explains McKean.

Much private equity investment on the continent involves taking a strategic, but not necessarily a controlling, stake in a business. This has an impact on the legal structuring and documentation of any investment, to ensure that the private equity investor retains effective influence on the portfolio company. Monitoring the investment on an ongoing basis requires active involvement and presence in a country. Given the size of the continent and the lack of direct flights between countries, this presents its own practical challenges.

Finding good management can be a major challenge. Thus far, the predicted return of many well-educated and trained executives from the

Diaspora has not yet lived up to expectations.

There has been a large increase in multi-jurisdictional mergers and acquisition transactions in Africa.

'The deals we are doing in African countries are often pioneering deals, of types that have not been done before in certain countries. For instance, the regulatory framework may not cater for a particular deal structure and we need to invest time talking to local regulators to explain why certain structures are being proposed, to demonstrate the benefits to the local investee companies and economy and to allay fears that international investors are trying to bend the rules for their own benefit.'

'Although South Africa has historically seen itself as a gateway into Africa for both South African and international companies, McKean questions the view that South Africa will always be the gateway to Africa in any broad sense. As the most developed economy on the continent at the moment, it has a natural advantage. However, as other economies develop, that position is already under threat. 'For the future, the continent is just too large for there to be only one gateway. So if South Africa wishes to retain an influential position on the continent, it must decide what role it wants to play and which of its cities it will promote. It needs to be more proactive about promoting that role and creating the environment which will attract international companies,' observes McKean. 'At the moment there is a certain amount of apathy and a lack of vision from South Africa while countries like Nigeria, Kenya, Mauritius and even Rwanda are positioning themselves as gateways in various industry sectors and also to capture investment inflows from specific regions outside the continent.'

'The gateway concept is a constantly evolving thing as regions develop. There is now a clear regionalisation developing on the continent with cities such as Nairobi and Lagos now being seen as regional hubs for East and West Africa respectively. Let's not forget that at one time Hong Kong was the gateway to the whole of Asia. But when Singapore developed itself as a gateway in Asia, Hong Kong had to reinvent itself as an international financial centre for China. You can't stand still; you have to constantly evolve to remain competitive.'

THE LEGAL LANDSCAPE

McKean explains that in the late 2000s, a few of the large South African firms such as Webber Wentzel recognised that they needed to develop a strategy for Africa as some of their clients were becoming more active on the continent. 'I was asked to drive that process at that firm then. At the time, we needed to build up our capacity to serve our clients in the rest of Africa wherever they were operating and to do this we needed to add skills and develop a broader offering. We had to develop an English law capability as well as specialist language and other skills to enable us to support our clients in Francophone Africa. Firms needed to demonstrate industry knowledge and expertise across a range of industry sectors.

More recently, as the international investment spotlight has turned to Africa, many of the international law firms are looking to either establish their own offices or develop more substantive relationships with firms in Africa. We have seen that specifically in South Africa, firms such as Norton Rose have entered the market through a merger with Denys Reitz while Linklaters have forged an alliance with Webber Wentzel. The raison d'etre for such alliances goes beyond South Africa's borders and the international firms see these arrangements as a springboard into the rest of Africa.

'Whether or not one is based in Africa, a key part of any law firm's ability to operate across the continent is to develop a strong network of leading law firms in every country. It is important to spend time and energy doing due diligence on firms across the continent so that you can feel comfortable directing clients to the best firm in each particular situation. You need to work in collaboration with many firms in many countries and develop very close relationships with them.

ALN was one of the first African based groupings to offer a multi-jurisdictional approach. It was founded in 2003 by Anjarwalla & Khanna, initially as an East African group but it has expanded to include Botswana, Burundi, Ethiopia, Malawi, Mauritius, Mozambique, Rwanda, Sudan, Tanzania, Uganda and Zambia. 'One of the attractions of ALN is that all the firms within the ALN group shared a common vision with other members of creating something new and different to anything else in the market, with the ultimate goal of creating a pan-African law firm.

'ALN was also a response to the fact that the market was becoming more sophisticated and clients wanted something more than an informal network. ALN is much more than that. We have integrated facilities such as a central management team, common branding and international marketing and we have cross border practice groups that meet regularly to share know-how, particularly in key industry sectors. In short, it creates a pan-African platform for members to work together on multi-jurisdictional projects. It is our shared vision that we will expand ALN to all the key jurisdictions in Africa.'

The African legal fraternity is sizeable but very fragmented, says McKean. In South Africa a large firm has 350–400 lawyers, but in other large African countries the largest law firms have a maximum of 50 to 60 lawyers. There is a huge skills shortage although many firms are taking active steps to address this. For instance, through training and know-how, initiatives being driven by ALN (together with its associated firm in South Africa, Webber Wentzel, and some of its international firm relationships), ALN is able to participate in a skills transfer to law firms in Africa and provide them with resources in the form of knowledge, precedents and skills development. 'These initiatives will go towards helping Africa to develop its own locally based sophisticated legal expertise.

We are seeing a growing interest in the Francophone region from international investors, particularly in the natural resources space.'

An innovation that aims to make it easier for investors to operate in that region is The Organisation for the Harmonisation of Business Law in Africa (OHADA), a system of business laws and implementing institutions adopted by 17 Francophone countries in West and Central Africa and introduced in 1993. 'The idea is to make it easier to do business across borders by harmonising the laws across the OHADA countries. The initial interest by investors in this was limited but with the natural resources boom, there is increased activity across the region.'

McKean points out an interesting development in the Francophone region: the Anglicisation of Rwanda under President Paul Kagame. This includes changing the legal system from the French civil law system, which applies in the rest of Francophone Africa, to the English language common law system. Whilst this may be driven by a political agenda, it has created some issues for the legal fraternity in the country.

KEY TRENDS

McKean says there have been a number of trends developing over the last few years that have an impact on the way international investment is negotiated.

Local content and resource nationalism

Regulators and governments are taking a more sophisticated approach to foreign investment. 'In the past there have been concerns about a new "Scramble for Africa", where foreign governments or international companies have been accused of stealing the crown jewels by acquiring preferential concessions on major mineral rights in exchange for preferential funding or the provision of infrastructure projects. Clearly the principal concern is that such investors are taking over local assets, thereby prejudicing the local population in terms of not providing jobs or benefiting the local economy.

'This suspicion of foreign investment informs the resources nationalism debate that is gaining ground. Some governments have introduced retrospective legislation for resources deals that attempt to benefit the local economy. Economic resource nationalism is the most prominent form at the moment and can be seen in governments revising tax and royalty policies, concession agreements and ownership requirements to maximise revenue streams. For example, the governments of Angola, Burkina Faso, DRC, Guinea, Ghana, Liberia, Mozambique, Tanzania and Zambia have announced or enacted adjustments to their mining and tax regimes in recent years. Many governments now require a free carry interest in projects. The changes in the tax regimes take many forms from windfall taxes to increased import and export duties.

Local content is an issue gaining ground which is not just related to natural resources and it is applied in different countries in many different ways. As countries either discover new resources, such as oil and gas in the case of Uganda, Ghana, Tanzania and Mozambique, or become more sophisticated in their dealings with international investors, different approaches are taken and often on an industry by industry basis.

'In South Africa, there is black economic empowerment, which has a specific historical background and context, and provides a highly complex regulatory environment which many investors find difficult to get to grips with. In other African countries it is more about providing greater local participation in ownership of assets, deriving economic benifit from projects and providing long-term sustainability of projects. This is expressed in many different forms - such as indigenisation in Zimbabwe, for example, where the government has promulgated legislation providing that control of all foreign-owned companies invested in the country must pass to local Zimbabweans. Botswana also has local content regulations, which are devised in terms of policy rather than mandatory rules, as do many other countries. In some cases, countries have introduced controls on quotas for expatriate workers exercised through the issuing of work permits.

In Angola the number of permits is tied to the size of the investment. Zambia has introduced legislation which provides effectively for all domestic commercial transactions to be carried out in kwacha which has caused some concerns for international investors funding projects in US dollars as indexation is not currently permitted. There are an increasing number of countries looking at this issue and taking different approaches as to how to benefit and perhaps protect their own economies.

In some countries, foreign companies carrying out initial public offerings on local stock exchanges have to reserve a certain percentage for local citizens. Another trend is for investment agreements to include obligations for multinational investors to assist with the building of infrastructure in Africa, alongside institutional and public-private initiatives.

These changes are all just part of the new investment landscape in Africa and one which any investor must understand clearly before entering into any individual country.

Environmental, social and governance (ESG) principles

'ESG principles are going to be an increasingly important issue for foreign investors and they cover a broad range of areas,' says McKean. These principles had their roots in the need for guidelines for companies and institutions investing in developing markets to better align their practices with the broader objectives of society. This has been driven by the development finance institutions such as the International Finance Corporation and others who, given their developmental mandates, were keen to develop best practice standards for investee companies in emerging markets and to guide corporate behaviour.

The principles cover a number of areas. Firstly, more emphasis has been placed on environmental issues, offering guidelines for companies to pursue their investment in ways that do least harm to the areas in which they operate.

The social principles try to ensure companies enhance the sustainable development of local economies and communities on a long-term basis. The last of the ESG principles relates to corporate governance and includes the requirement to run a business transparently, making appropriate disclosure and complying with international anti-corruption initiatives such as the FCPA in the US and the UK's Bribery Act, as well as any national legislation in this regard.

This type of legislation is far reaching, says McKean. 'For example, you don't need to be a UK-headquartered company to fall under the UK bribery regime; simply having a subsidiary there could have an impact. Equally, a Chinese or Brazilian company with a New York listing would come within the remit of the FCPA. Chinese multinational companies are starting to take these initiatives more seriously, so you are likely to get a more level playing field for companies operating in Africa from all parts of the world.

'These principles are starting to change the way multinationals do business and the way they relate to governments. Companies cannot afford to fall foul of them so they are finding ways to ensure they are able to comply with them even in countries known to be corrupt.' He cites the example of a large international shipping company, which not only has in-house anti-corruption guidelines, but ensures that in ports it has a lawyer on hand to stop containers being impounded by corrupt officials when bribes are not paid. 'There is a lot of pressure on companies to comply with an increasing amount of international legislation. Some of their strategies are preventative – they make sure they are not falling foul of laws and have complete transparency about what they are doing.

'We encourage clients to talk to African governments at the highest level about corruption. It is not in anyone's interest over the long term for this to carry on. Investment can be lost to countries because companies are so constrained by this raft of legislation and they cannot afford to operate in countries where they may not be able to operate without being forced into what might be deemed corrupt practices in international legislation.'

Competition policy

Competition policy is growing rapidly at a national and regional level. Almost every African country now has some form of competition policy in place, though they were at different levels of development and implementation, and the regional economic communities were putting in place their own competition policy frameworks, overarching states' national policies.

'Countries are all at different levels of development in terms of competition policy across the region. There is little experience of how policy should work. A good example of how things are developing in this area is the introduction in early 2013 of a competition regime for the COMESA region which covers 19 African countries in East and Southern Africa. It introduces a supra-national framework of merger control and business conduct rules which will affect all companies operating in the region and will be enforced by a new COMESA Competition Commission.

This will have major implications for any business considering an acquisition/disposal or investment/exit within the region but also extends to general business activities. The regulations provide that transactions above prescribed thresholds of combined annual turnover or assets must be notified. However, currently the thresholds are set at zero. In addition, the regulations raise many new issues which require clarification and which will need to be considered and indeed tested over the coming years. A failure to comply with the rules opens companies up to substantial fines and penalties. There is no doubt that new investors in African countries will be faced with new challenges as competition policies develop over the coming years.'

TAX ISSUES

A key element in any deal structuring is tax. Solutions developed elsewhere to optimise tax efficiencies do not necessarily work well in an African context. Because foreign investment is relatively new to many African countries and tax systems in Africa tend to be unsophisticated in global terms, certainty on tax treatment can be difficult to attain.

Issues such as whether carried interest and proceeds on the disposal of investments should be taxed at capital gains rates or normal income tax rates (in countries where a distinction exists) are likely to arise. Answers usually need to be found through the application of general principles, in the absence of specific relevant legislation or case law. African countries tend to impose high levels of withholding tax on cross-border cash flows, including dividends, interest and management or advisory fees. Minimising these taxes through the use of appropriate tax treaties can present challenges because, with a few notable exceptions, most African countries have very few tax treaties. As with the legal systems generally, the influence of the colonial past can often be discerned in the choice of treaty partners and many of the treaties are very old, says McKean.

Mauritius has sought to build an attractive treaty network with African countries and has been largely successful, though some treaties with robust economies such as Nigeria are not yet in force.

CONCLUSION

Echoing many an Africa hand, McKean says new investors must realise that Africa is not a single country. It is the second largest continent in the world, with 54 countries, all with their own political, cultural, lingual, legal and regulatory frameworks and business cultures. 'People often generalise about Africa as a homogenous region and are unaware of its sheer size. The whole of continental Western Europe can fit within the borders of one African country, the Democratic Republic of Congo.

'Some investors might consider Nigeria and Ghana as being very similar because they are both Anglophone countries in West Africa but the reality is that they are quite different in terms of the way you do business, the legal and regulatory framework and the business culture. It is so important to do due diligence on a country-by-country basis to understand the risks, know who you are dealing with and who you need to talk to.'

Wilderness Holdings Limited specialises in ecotourism and conservation, is dedicated to responsible tourism and has almost 70 luxury camps in wilderness areas in Botswana, The Republic of Congo, Kenya, Namibia, Malawi, South Africa, Zambia, Zimbabwe and the Seychelles. It is the holding company for many of Africa's premier ecotourism brands such as Wilderness Safaris (Premier), Wilderness Safaris (Classic), Wilderness Air, Wilderness Adventures, Wilderness Explorations and the Wilderness Collection. Wilderness Holdings listed on the Botswana Stock Exchange (BSE) and the Africa board of the JSE in 2010.

TOURISM AND ENVIRONMENT

WILDERNESS HOLDINGS

'I believe that you can do well out of doing good,' says Andy Payne, former CEO of Wilderness Holdings Limited, and adds that this philosophy is rather different from that of corporate social investment, which suggests you can do well *and* do good.

Payne, interviewed in early 2012 before he left the group in the first quarter of 2013, cites the example of North Island in the Seychelles where Wilderness built a luxury lodge from natural materials and returned natural wildlife and fauna to the area in a $15 million project. The island was later bought for $70 million by a foreign investor. Wilderness made a commitment to managing the island from an environmental point of view and has increased the size of its environmental team to monitor the wildlife and engage in improving the sustainability of management systems.

'The Wilderness business model is to build sustainable conservation economies and balance financial, social and environmental equity,' says Payne. 'It has a good proposition, but it is a hard sell. I have tried to convince investors that bottom drawer investing is not a bad thing. You are backing a good team with a good plan and the resources to implement it.

'I have spent a lot of time talking to fund managers and investors. A lot of people see the light but they cannot connect to it. The main reservation is whether this is a model that makes money because so much of the investment is in creating sustainability. But investment in conservation is becoming increasingly important.

'The company has also provided development and employment in remote areas where people have no other opportunities. Some investors recognise the value proposition and once they come on board they become disciples of this way of doing business.

'The "Made in Africa" brand is really growing and will be much bigger in ten years' time than other places that are hot right now, like China. This will open an interesting window of opportunity for tourism.

'A sustainability platform is critical in Africa because it's going to become more and more important,' asserts Payne. 'The voice on the ground is louder than it's ever been on these issues and it makes business sense. Environmental equity is also critical. Africa is known for its natural resource base and we have a niche that no one can copy. To spoil it is sinful. The wilderness is a great legacy for our children.'

Despite its value proposition, the tourism business is exposed to political and economic forces and perception issues that it cannot control in its source markets, which are mostly in developed countries. 'When the financial crisis unfolded in October 2008, Wilderness had 12 per cent more bed nights booked in our camps than the previous year but then we faced a US election, late Thanksgiving holidays and the onset of the recession. It was like hitting a stationary bus.

'The initial response was one of caution. Clients were saying they would rather not pay for a safari in Africa because they were not sure if they would have the money for it or whether we would even be in business. Within three months we were 25 per cent down over the previous year. The situation stabilised and people started buying again. When the financial results came out a year later, in February 2010, the company had clawed back from minus 25 per cent to minus eight per cent and it has gone back to pre-recession levels.

'But the crisis fundamentally changed the way our industry works. People are now looking for greater value; they are shopping around more and our time to close a travel file is three to four times longer than it used to be. So the company has had to work harder to get the same numbers. We have had to realign our business for lower numbers.

'A big challenge for us is that a lot of our economic indicators are being driven by the East but our source markets are in the West and, because they are weak, these are challenging times.'

'The company's guests are mostly international – about 50 per cent from the United States with the rest mainly from Europe and the UK and, to a lesser extent, South-East Asia. There is a small domestic underpin – we get a lot of business via South Africa but there are not many South African clients.'

There are also risks within destination markets. For example, Zimbabwe, once Wilderness's biggest operation, was affected by the country's decade-long economic decline up to 2009. 'We had some challenges in Zimbabwe, where we have five camps and nine sites, but we are getting good growth there now – we had a 31 per cent increase in bed nights in the 2010/11 financial year. There is still a huge opportunity for tourism. I believe there will be a great deal of emotional support for the country when things really turn around and hopefully we will benefit from that.'

THE CORPORATE EVOLUTION

Wilderness Holdings grew from Wilderness Safaris, which was established in Botswana in 1983. The company started out with luxury camps, providing journeys and experiences for globally discerning travellers, and kept this brand until the mid-2000s.

'The change in focus came after we hosted guests on North Island in the Seychelles, which we bought to rehabilitate and re-introduce endangered wildlife and local bird species. One guest offered us funding to accelerate the 30-year programme but later withdrew the offer because he felt our commercial business, rather than the island, was going to be the beneficiary.

'We digested the message and realised that it was the other way around – our tourism operation had been funding the conservation business on the island for the past ten years. So, instead of being a beneficiary of funding, tourism was the major contributor to the rehabilitation programme. Realising this, we changed our business model. Up to that point we had believed we were in the business of providing journeys and experiences to globally discerning travellers. But we realised we were actually in the business of building sustainable conservation economies.'

The business remains exclusive and aimed at the high end of the market with rates from $500 per person per night to $3,000, depending on the camp and the brand.

Wilderness has more than three million hectares of Africa 'under influence' and about 70 safari camps and lodges across nine countries, with a few new markets in the pipeline. The biggest lodge is the 40 bed Pafuri Camp in South Africa's Kruger National Park and the smallest, with between six and 12 beds, includes Zarafa and Little Mombo in Botswana.

'The company employs about 2,800 people across operations, drawn from 30 ethnic groups and most of them from the informal sector. We know from our own research that every employee can have up to eight dependents so, although we are a small business, we have a large multiplier effect.'

An important project for the company is Children in the Wilderness in which children in the areas where the company operates are taught to appreciate and look after the environment. The programme aims to develop environment leaders who will care for their natural heritage. 'This has exceeded our expectations – we have had 2,500 children to date through the five-day programme.'

Given the remoteness of its operations, the company builds its own infrastructure and has put in place a vertically integrated model that includes an air operation to fly guests and staff to the camps. 'It is not a schedule service but a feeder airline. We work out of hubs – Maun in the Okavango Delta in Botswana, Livingstone and Lusaka in Zambia, Windhoek in Namibia and Victoria Falls in Zimbabwe.'

African travel specialists located in 48 countries build Wilderness products into tourist itineraries. 'They are our trade partners. The Wilderness brand is attached to strategically aligned properties such as the Cape Grace Hotel in Cape Town or Victoria Falls Hotel in Zimbabwe and our customers can build these into their experience.'

TOURISM AND LOCAL COMMUNITIES

Community-based tourism has become a powerful product, says Payne, citing the example of Damaraland in Namibia. 'In 1974, a people called the Riemvasmaakers – of Nama, Damara and Herero descent – who had settled north of the Augrabies Falls National Park in South Africa, were "relocated" some 100km north to southern Damaraland in what was then South West Africa. Life was not easy for this resettled community, and drought in the 1980s saw Damaraland with badly reduced wildlife resources and an unemployment figure of more than 70 per cent.

'The concept of community conservancies had begun in Namibia but in 1998 we brought in private enterprise in the form of a joint venture with the community around a camp on their land, centred on the desert-adapted wildlife experience and staffed almost entirely by community members.' The deal involved the leasing of land and equity for the community that, today, runs the camp and has been able to build community centres and other infrastructure with its equity.

'Since then, about 50 more community-based conservancies have sprung up in Namibia using this model, which is now recognised internationally. The country is viewed as a leader in this type of conservation and there is more land in Namibia under community-based conservation than there is in the national parks – demonstrating the impact a good model can have.

'About 85 per cent of the people in our camps are employed from surrounding communities and have never had a job before. The moment of truth in our business is when staff and guests meet on the ground. These aren't sophisticated university graduates but they host some of the richest and most influential people in the world – and they do it well.

'So there's a huge level of authenticity in the offering. This is their land and they are advocates of what we are trying to do and they tend to deliver beyond expectations, particularly as they also benefit from our success.

'This improves the guest experience from a human point of view as well as a conservation perspective. And this makes the product better and the commercial benefit is greater as a result,' says Payne.

CHALLENGES

The biggest challenge tourist companies face is negative market conditions, which is something it cannot control. Part of this challenge is South Africa's exchange rate against source market currencies. The weak performance of product in South Africa and Namibia is a reflection of these products being too expensive in world terms because of the exchange rate.

'Any country that wants to promote local tourism must be price competitive in a world where people are looking for greater value for money,' says Payne. 'When an exchange rate (the rand) moves 27 per cent in two years it is difficult to perform optimally. Although we charge in dollars, many of the destinations have costs linked to the rand so we do feel the negative impact of events in South Africa.

He says visas can be a tricky issue. Although he can see the revenue raising rationale from a government point of view, an insistence on visas and the attendant bureaucratic process is not good for business. Another problematic area in the political domain is state-ownership of national airlines. 'The issue is how important it is to have the national flag on the tail of an aircraft versus the huge benefits from increased tourism. The people who control the air, control the ground. If you have a blockage from an air point of view, no matter what you do on the ground you can't deliver. All of these things have an impact.'

Personal sentiment plays a major role in tourism. People stopped visiting Zimbabwe because of the political situation rather than because of any problems with the tourism product, he says. And they may return for a related reason – a desire to help economic growth in a reformed Zimbabwe, in much the same way as people did in Rwanda after the genocide.

'Unfortunately politicians don't realise the impact their statements can have on sentiment towards their country. If high-powered people are controversial, it creates negative sentiment and that is a problem for tourism because it is one thing people can say no to. They can quickly turn off the tap and wait awhile before looking at a market again, if they ever do.

'Governments are responsive to tourism but generally I'm not sure they understand its full potential. If I just take Botswana, about 55 per cent of GDP comes from extraction and less than ten per cent from tourism. In mining, the focus is on capital but in tourism it is on people and that is a big generator of employment, especially in the informal sector.

'You can train completely unskilled people to work in camps within just a few months. This is very important for rural development. Even in cities, the impact is dynamic and ranges from supporting airlines, hotels and restaurants to creating new opportunities in terms of tour operators, real estate and specific attractions like wine farms, in the case of Cape Town.

'The company has been fortunate because tourism is on the front page of the countries in which it operates. Wilderness is also working with governments and sharing information – it is part of a commitment to operating transparently and the company sees it as part of its responsibility. For example, in Botswana we shared our insights about our source markets with the tourism authority, for them to use in their own marketing strategies. Things are more about a partnership today than they have ever been.

'But this could be a challenge in markets that have no tourism experience and infrastructure such as Central Africa and places like Nigeria, which is viewed purely as a business destination. But in these regions, in time, you are going to get some tourism stars performing and, once they do, others will follow. For example, I believe Ghana will drive cultural tourism in West Africa, and Gabon from a wildlife point of view.'

Another important issue is marketing the brand. 'You have to create demand for our extraordinary natural resources, so the ability to market those around the world is critical, as is ensuring easy and more affordable access and value for money. Tourism ministries in African countries are not that good at keeping the brand and special destinations connected to the customer. Once you've got the demand, you can do anything.'

Payne says the supply chain is a major factor in his business. 'Because we operate so remotely, our airline is important. Apart from flying people in, we also fly in fresh goods and our dry goods are transported by road. Some of our turnaround trips are two to three days.'

The camps are self-sustaining in many ways. 'The company has had to build its own roads and provide its own water from boreholes and harvesting rainwater. We process our sewage. We use natural materials for building wherever possible and generate our own power. Some camps are 100 per cent solar powered – all our new camps are built in this way and we are retrofitting older camps too.' The company takes climate change seriously and continuously monitors its carbon emissions.

Land tenure is mostly by way of long leases with governments in national parks.

GOING FORWARD

'Over the next few years Wilderness is going to focus on three core areas – Zimbabwe, Botswana and Tanzania – and it is expanding in East Africa. This region is highly competitive and that is one of the risks it is going to face moving into that market. The company is not first out of the starting blocks there.

Wilderness Safaris opened two new camps in the Republic of Congo in 2012 and a luxury camp in Kenya, in partnership with other investors, and further tourism opportunities are emerging in unlikely places. 'Gabon is committed to tourism and it is quite a sophisticated country. There is even a Michelin star restaurant in Libreville.

'There is the re-emergence of companies in the mould of the old Lonrho group that own assets across a wide range of sectors such as mining, tourism and logging and governments are taking a stake in these businesses. We hope to increase the sustainability message in the operations by our involvement with these companies.

'In West and Central Africa, the tourism challenge is bigger because the region has so much oil. But we are interested in developing a tourism model that can contribute to saving the African rain forest. Currently the only thing that probably contributes to its survival economically is carbon credits and I'm not sure that is totally sustainable.'

INDEX

2010 Fifa World Cup 168, 178
2010 World Economic Forum Gender Report 71
53 Extra 167
Aba 157
Abacha, Sani 181
Absa 71
Abuja 157
Abuja Declaration 9
Accor 112
Accra 1, 9, 90, 202, 223
Actis 85–90, 92
Addis Ababa 112, 202
Afghanistan 181, 184, 186
Africa: Crude Continent: The Struggle for Africa's Oil Prize 16
'Africa Rising' 53
Africa: The bottom billion becomes the fastest billion 25
African Business magazine 22
'African Century' 17
African Development Bank (AfDB) xvi, xx, xxiii 25
African Economic Outlook 2011 25
African Futures 2050 23
African Leadership Academy 28
African Leadership Network 28
Africa Legal Network (ALN) 220, 226–7
African Magic 168
African National Congress (ANC) 174
African Renaissance xiii, 153
African Sun 112
African Union (AU) 65
African Women's Decade 74
'Africapitalism' 61
Africa's Future: Darkness to Destiny 16, 18
Africa's Third Liberation: The Search for Growth and Jobs 52
Aico Africa Limited 198
Airtel see Celtel 183
Alatovik, Tarik 38
Albertine Graben basin 194

Algeria 32, 37, 133, 135
Alternative Investment Market (AIM) 190, 194
American 43, 71, 122–3, 133, 223–4
ANC Youth League 174
Angbazo, Lazarus 131–6, 138
Anglicisation 227
Anglo American 71
AngloGold Ashanti 94–5, 97–100, 102–3
Anglophone 158, 232
Angola 3–4, 32, 41, 44, 46, 48, 131, 133–4, 136, 141–2, 144–5, 147, 153, 163, 168, 171, 175, 201, 215, 229
Anjarwalla & Khanna 226
Apapa port 156
Arab Spring 36
ArcelorMittal 71
Argentina 43
Arusha 202
Asia 10, 12, 29, 37, 40, 42, 49–50, 57, 84, 86, 134, 153, 170, 173, 223, 225, 237
Asiko, William 117–121
Atkins, Charles 38
Atlantic 41, 45
Audi 78
Australasia 76
Australia 43, 78, 97, 104, 170, 173, 178

Banco do Brasil 48
Bank Group, The xvi
Barclays 214
Beira 144–5, 147
Beit Bridge 146
Bekker, Koos 162
Belgium 112
Benguela railway line 144
Benin 214
Berlusconi, Silvio 79
Bharti Airtel 47
BHP Billiton 46
Bidco 63

Bidvest Group 63
Big Brother Africa 168
Big Brother Amplified 167
Bill Gates Foundation, The 178
Binedell, Nick xiv
Blair, Tony 55
Block I 195
Block II 195
Block III 190, 194–5
BMW 78
BNDES 48
Boston Consulting Group 29
Botswana 71, 124, 145, 154, 162–3, 173, 176, 192, 201, 226, 229, 234, 237–8, 240–2
Botswana Stock Exchange (BSE) 234
Bouazizi, Mohamad 36
'Brand Africa' 77
'Brand Germany' 78
'Brand South Africa' 82
Branson, Richard 78
Brazil 34, 41–4, 47–50, 88–9, 98, 138, 144, 202, 215, 223, 230
Brenthurst Foundation 52
Bretton Woods Institutions ix
Bribery Act 229
BRICS 34, 42–3, 48, 223
Bright Star Contol System 137
British 2, 43, 45, 55
Brozin, Robbie 171–2, 174–9
Bukedde 167
Bunia 101
Burkina Faso 214
Burundi 226

Cabinda 134
Cairo 10, 84
Camara, Moussa Dadis (Captain) 102
Cameroon 181, 183, 214
Camtel Mobile 183
Cape 10, 18, 154
Cape Grace Hotel 238
Cape Town 108, 118, 154, 238, 240
Cape Verde 124
Carlson Companies 111
Carlson Rezidor Hotel Group 106–7, 111
Carrefour 35

Carroll, Cynthia 71
CDC 84
Celtel 63, 183
Central Africa 62, 131, 214, 227, 241–2
Central Bank Governor 81
Centre for Dynamic Markets (CDM) 40
Chad 214
Chaka Chaka, Yvonne 82
Changes 167
Channel O 168
Chianti 78
Chicken Inn 172
Chickenland 170, 172
Children in the Wilderness 238
China 3, 12, 24, 32, 34–6, 41–3, 46–50, 58, 88–9, 128, 138, 144, 158, 207, 215, 218, 223, 225, 230, 236
China Development Bank (CDB) 42
China National Offshore Oil Corp (CNOOC) 46
China Steel 46
Chironga, Mutsa 28–9, 38
Chirundi 146
CIC Holdings 140
Citibank 58, 214
Citilodge 113
City Lodge 113
Clarke, Duncan (Dr) 16–17
Club Carlson 106
CNBC Africa 16
Coca-Cola Africa 117
Coca-Cola Africa Foundation 117
Coca-Cola Company, The 116–121, 133
Colbro Transport 140
Cold War 21, 54
Colombia University 98
Comedy Club 167
Commercial International Bank 86
Common Market for Eastern and Southern Africa (Comesa) 10
Commonwealth 84, 201
Conakry 114
Congo-Brazzaville 183
Continental Africa 95
Copenhagen 110–1
Copperbelt 146
Country Inns & Suites By Carlson 106
Côte d'Ivoire 7, 59, 214, 217

Crowne Plaza 112
Cyprus 184

Da Silva, Luis Inacio ('Lula') 48
Dabengwa, Sifiso 181–2, 184–5, 187–8
Dakar 110
Damara 239
Damaraland 239–40
Dangote Industries 63
Dar es Salaam 1, 136, 144–5
De Beer, George 141–8
De Beers 78
De Kock, Rick 207–10
De Villiers, Doug 76–7
Democratic Republic of Congo 46, 55, 94–5, 97, 103, 114, 144, 157, 194, 214, 232
DESTINY 68, 74
Destiny Man 68
DestinyConnect 68
Developing Health Globally 134
Dhlomo, Khanyi 68–9
Diageo 5
Diaspora 63, 93, 136, 224
Discovery Health 81
Divine Inspiration Group (DIG) 194
Djibouti 46, 216
Doing Business Index 6
Dorr, Norbert 38
Dow Jones Industrial Index 130
Drifta 167–8
DStv 160, 163, 167–8
DStv Mobile 160
DStv Online 160
Duarte, Fernando 172
Dubai 174, 184,
Duffy, Richard 95–9, 103
DuPont 122–7
Durban 9, 114, 118, 144–5, 148
DVB-T2 168

Earth Institute 98
East Africa 46, 49, 78, 111–2, 127, 167–8, 198, 210, 242
East African Community (EAC) 10
Eastgate 150

Ecobank 214
Economist, The 53
Egypt 7, 22, 32, 36–7, 70, 86, 118, 133
Elumelu, Tony O 60–1, 64
Emerging Markets Payment Holdings 86
Energy Equity Resources 190, 194
English 210, 213, 220, 226–7
Enugu 157
Equatorial Guinea 134
Ernst & Young 29, 47
Eskom 132
Essar 47
Ethiopia 3, 37, 112, 121, 124, 134, 153, 164, 201, 226
Etisalat 183
Etosha Transport 140
Euromonitor 173
Europe 2, 9, 12, 37, 43, 49–50, 53, 76, 78–9, 85, 91–3, 108, 111, 113, 127, 140, 143, 164, 194, 207, 221, 223, 225, 232, 236
Export–Import Bank (EXIM) 42, 46
Express Cartage 140
Extractive Industries Transparency Initiative (EITI) 100
Exxon Mobil 171

Far East 143
Ferrari 79
Financial Times 40, 53
Fitch Ratings 42
Forbes 68
Ford 35
Foreign Corrupt Practices Act 100, 229
Fortune 500 35
Fortune magazine 71
France 32, 43, 79, 112
France Telecoms 183
Francophone 6–7, 43, 112, 158, 213, 220–1, 226–7
Freedom House 55
Freetown 114
French 43, 45, 112, 221, 227

Gabon 46, 114, 192, 214, 241–2
Gabreselassie, Haile 78

Gaddafi, Muammar 174
Games, Dianna xi, xvii
GE Capital 130
GE Energy 134
GE Energy Management-Switchgear Manufacturing and Assembly 134
GE Oil & Gas 134
GE Oil & Gas Repair, Training & Global Service Sales Centre 134
GE South Africa Technologies 137
Geita 96, 99, 101
General Electric (GE) 35, 130–8
General Motors 133
Germany 78, 140
Ghana xiv, 1, xix, 32, 36, 47, 94–5, 99–101, 121, 126, 132, 134, 154, 157, 163–4, 168, 176, 184, 213–4, 228, 232, 241
Ghana Power Sector Reform Programme 132
Gleneagles G8 55
Glo Naija Sings 167
Global Fund to Fight AIDS, Tuberculosis and Malaria (GFATM) 101
Global Impact Investing Rating System 64
Global Pacific & Partners 16
Global Reporting Initiative 100
Gordian knot 18
Gordon Institute of Business Science (GIBS) xiv, 40
Gore, Adrian 81
GOtv 167
Grameen Bank 72
Great Barrier Reef 78
Greenpeace International 82
GSM Association 182, 208
Guinea 7, 46, 94, 98–102, 104, 114, 136, 184, 214–5, 228
Guinea Bissau 4, 184

Harare 145
Harford, Simon 85–93
Harvard 78
Harvard Business Review 30
Hausa 168
Heirs Holdings 60, 64

Herbst, Jeffrey 52
Herero 239
Hilton 111
HIV/AIDS 1, 8, 178
Holgate, Kingsley 178
Hong Kong 225
Hotel Missoni 106, 109
Huawei 46, 49
Human Rights Watch 103

i-Pad 167
Ibis 112
IBM 133
Ibrahim Index of African Governance 124
Iduapriem 99
IJ Snyman Transport 140
Ikeja City Mall 86
Imperial Group 140, 143
Imperial Logistics 140–1, 143
Imperial Logistics International 143
India 3, 24, 32–6, 42–3, 46–7, 49–50, 58, 85, 88–9, 128, 143, 207, 215, 223
Indian Ocean Islands 107, 114
Industrial and Commercial Bank of China (ICBC) 46, 218
Innscor 171, 173, 175
Insensato Corazao 41
Institute for Security Studies (ISS) 22–3
Intellidex 69
Interbrand Sampson 76–9
Interchain Logistics 140
Intercontinental Hotel 111–2
International Finance Corporation 229
International Monetary Fund 36
Investcom 11, 180, 184
Investec Bank 190
Iran 181–3, 186
Italy 79
It's Time for Africa 47

Jacobsen, Arne 111
Jacob's Cross 167
Jara 167
Johannesburg ix, x, xi, 9–10, 16, 40, 52, 84, 94, 102, 110, 118, 134, 150, 154, 170, 172, 225,

Johannesburg Stock Exchange (JSE) 170, 181, 190, 193–4, 234

Kagame, Paul 227
Kampala 9, 167
Kapiri Mposhi 144
Kasembulesa 146
Katanga province 143, 146
Kenya 5, 32, 47, 65, 85, 114–5, 118, 120–1, 126–7, 130, 132–4, 145, 154, 157, 163, 167–8, 171, 179, 201–2, 209–10, 214, 216, 225, 231, 234, 242
KFC 173, 179, 207
Khumalo, Collins 161–2, 164, 169
Kibali 99
Kigali 115, 223
King Code on Corporate Governance Principles 184
Kinshasa 1, 99
Kiswahili 168
Korean 138
Kruger National Park 238

Lagos xxv, 1, 28, 84, 110, 134, 156–7, 167, 185, 202, 214, 223
Lake Albert 194
Lansana 102
Lascaris, Hunt 209
Latin America 37, 40, 42, 49, 57, 84, 86, 121, 134
Le Roux, Eugene 178
Lebanese 184
Legacy Group 112
Leke, Acha 28–9, 38
Lesotho 71
Levy Centre 152
LG 35
Liberia 46, 164, 184, 214
Liberty Africa 152
Liberty Holdings Group 150
Liberty Prominade 154
Liberty Properties 150–1, 153
Libreville 114, 242
Libya 7, 22, 32, 36, 46, 174, 192
Lilongwe 145, 202
Limpopo 202

Lin, Justin 22
Lions on the Move 28–30, 34, 36–8
Little Mombo 238
Live Positively 120
Livingstone 238
Lobito 136, 144–5
London x, 94, 110, 173, 184, 190, 193–4, 212, 221, 225
Lonrho group 242
Lonsa 193
Luanda 41, 44, 134, 142
Lubumbashi 145
Lund, Susan 38
Lusaka 1, 152, 202, 223, 238
Lusophone 46, 201

M&C Saatchi Africa 206-7
M-Net 160, 162–3, 167
Machu Picchu 78
Maddison, Angus 18, 22–23,
'Made in Africa' 236
Maghreb 86
Magic Swahili 167
Malabo 134
Malawi 134, 142, 145, 164, 200–1, 226, 234
Malaysia 43, 173, 176
Malema, Julius 174
Mali 4, 94, 99–101, 134, 215
Malthusian 18
Mandela, Nelson 78, 82,
Maputo 1, 145, 176,
Marina 214
Marriot 112
Marriott 111
Mashariki Mix 167
Massmart 224–5, 228
MasterCard Worldwide 25
Maun 238
Mauritius 78, 109, 124, 164, 180, 225–6, 231
McKean, Roddy 221–7, 229–31
McKinsey & Company 28–9
McKinsey Global Institute 38
McKinsey Quarterly 38
McLachlan, Andrew 107, 109–111, 113, 115
Mercedes 78

Metropolitan Asset Managers 190
Metropolitan Life 216
Mexico 121
Meyer, Nico 161, 164, 167–8
Michelin star 242
Micro Distribution Centre (MDC) 120
Middle East 29, 32, 42, 49, 111, 113, 127, 170, 173, 180, 182, 184, 223
Millennium Promise 98
Mills, Greg (Dr) 52–3
Mitchell's Plain 154
Moatize 46, 144
Mobile Telephone Networks (MTN) 11, 49, 63, 81, 180–4, 186–7, 226
Mombasa 145
Mongbwalu 99
Monitor 29
Monsanto 204
Moody 25
Moon, Michael xi
Morila 99
Morocco 32, 109, 118
Mount Kilimanjaro 78
Moyo, Carlman 123–9
Mozambique 3, 32, 46–7, 48–9, 114, 121, 134, 136, 144–6, 153, 164, 171–2, 178, 201, 205, 214, 216, 226
MPLA 44
Mr Price 157
Mtanga Farms Limited 64
MTN 11, 49, 63, 81, 180–4, 186–7, 226
MTN Group 180
MTN International 180
MTN Mauritius 180
MTN Rwanda 183
Mugabe, Robert 55, 173–4
MultiChoice 160–3, 165, 167
MultiChoice Africa 161–2
MultiChoice Nigeria 162
Murray & Roberts 49
MWEB 160

Naidoo, Kumi 82
Nairobi 9, 84, 90, 130, 202, 223
Nama 239
Namibia 94, 99, 100–1, 145, 163–4, 178, 228, 231, 234, 238–9

Namibië Multi Loads 140
Nando's 81, 170–9
Naspers 160, 162
National Pension Scheme Authority of Zambia 150, 152
Navachab 99
Ncube, Mthuli (Professor) xvi
Ndalo Media 68, 72, 74
Nelson Mandela Square 150
Nestlé 5
New York x, 94, 212, 230
Nhleko, Phutuma 184
Nigeria xix, xx, xxi, 1, 5, 25, 28, 31–3, 36, 47, 54, 60, 63–5, 70–1, 81, 85–6, 112, 118, 121, 126–7, 131–5, 137, 152, 154, 156–7, 162–8, 171–3, 176, 178–9, 181–6, 190, 192, 194–6, 201, 208, 210, 212–4, 216–7, 219, 225, 231–2, 241
Nigeria Stock Exchange (NSE) 212
Nollywood 63, 167–8
North Africa 5, 18, 22, 24–5, 114, 133, 210
North America 32, 85, 223
North Island (Seychelles) 235, 237
North Kivu 99
Novotel 112
Nyembezi-Heita, Nonkuleleko 71
Nzwere, Morgan 199–200, 202, 204

Oando 194
Obama, Michelle 110
Obasanjo, Olusegun 182
Obuasi 99, 101–2
Odebrecht 44, 46, 49
Oduoza, Phillips 213–9
Ogbu, Samuel 151–7
Okavango Delta 238
Okonjo-Iweala, Ngozi 71
Olympic 82
Omnicon Group 206
ONGC-Mittal Energy 47
Onitsha 185
Onne 134
Orascom see Etisalat 183
Organisation for the Harmonisation of Business Law in Africa (OHADA) 6, 220, 227
Organisation of African Unity (OAU) 65

Oscar 82
Outside Edge expedition 178

Pafuri Camp 238
Pan-African ix, 9, 63, 65, 85–6, 90, 162, 209, 226
Panamax vessels 144
Pannar Seed 204
Paris x, 68, 94, 112, 212, 221,
Park Inn by Radisson 106, 108–9, 112, 114
Park Plaza 106
Passione 41
Payne, Andy 235–6, 238–241
Pep Stores 157
Petrobras 45
Petrologistics 140
PetroSA 197
Pick n Pay 153
Pioneer Hi-Bred 127, 204
Pizza Inn 172
Player, Gary 82
Port Harcourt 134, 157
Portugal 3, 41, 170, 172
Presley, Elvis 78
Pretoria 23
Pretoria University 40
PricewaterhouseCoopers 163
Proctor & Gamble 35
Profile Books 16, 18
Protea Hotel Group 107
Protea Hotels 112
Public Investment Corporation 85, 190, 195
Pullman 112

Radisson Blu 106, 108, 110–2, 115
Radisson Blu Hotel Sandton 110
Radisson Blu Royal Hotel 111
Radisson SAS 111
Ramos, Maria 71
Rand Refinery 102
Randgold Resources 99
Renaissance Capital 25
Republic of the Congo 114, 214, 234, 242
Responsible Jewellery Council 100

Ressano Garcia 146
Rezidor 107–8, 110–4
Riemvasmaakers 239
Rio de Janeiro 202
Rio Tinto 136
Rome 18
Rooster of Barcelos 172
Rosettenville 172
Roxburgh, Charles 38
Russia 34, 111, 192, 223
Rwanda 65, 115, 134, 181, 183, 225–7, 240

SA Tourism 68
SABMiller 81
Sadiola 99, 101
Samroc 193
Sandton 110, 154
Sandton City 150
Sanusi, Lamido 81
SAS Airlines Group 111
SAS Catering and Hotels 111
Sasol 194
Saudi Arabia 174, 182
São Tomé 216
Scandinavian Airlines (SAS) 111
Schoeman, Roland 82
Seed Co Limited 198–9, 201, 203–4
Sena line 144
Senegal 37, 134, 214
Senova 112
Serena 112
Seychelles 109, 124, 234–5, 237
Sheraton 111
Shoprite 63
Siemens 35
Sierra Leone 114, 164, 214
Siguiri 99, 101–2
'Silicon Savanah' 65
Sofitel 111–2
Somalia 216
Sony 78
South Africa Congo Oil Company (SacOil) 190–1, 193–6
South African x, 2, 9, 47–9, 69, 71, 81–2, 86, 89–90, 110, 113, 143, 152–5, 157, 162–4, 174, 178–80, 185, 187, 190,

193–5, 197, 206–7, 210, 216, 220–1, 224–8, 231, 237
South African Entertainment and Media Outlook 2011–2015 163
South Korea 43
South West Africa 239
Southeast Asia 134, 173, 237
Southern African Development Community (SADC) 10
Southern Hemisphere 45
Southern Sun 112
Southern Tanzanian Highlands 64
Spain 57
Standard Bank 3–4, 43, 46, 49, 63, 81, 150, 154
Standard Bank Group 150, 154
Standard Chartered Bank 5, 214
Standard Trust Bank 212
Stanlib 154
Stefanutti Stocks 49
Stockholm Stock Exchange 111
sub-Saharan Africa 5, 25, 28, 42, 55, 57, 70, 91, 107, 123, 126–7, 137, 160, 163–4, 206, 222
Sudan 70
SuperSport 160, 167–8
SuperSport 9 East 167
Swahili 210
Swaziland 150
Syria 181

Table Mountain 78
Tanzania 3, 36, 64, 94–6, 99–102, 114, 118, 121, 134, 136–7, 143–6, 154, 157, 163–4, 179, 201, 210, 214, 226, 242
Tanzania-Zambia Railway (Tanzam) 136, 144
Tanzania-Zambia Railway Authority 137
Tata 47
Tazi-Riffi, Amine 38
Terfous, Nadia 38
'The Hopeless Continent' 53
The Palms 86
The World's Women 2010 71
Theron, Charlize 82
Three Cities 112
Tinsel 167

Togo 214
Tony Elumelu Foundation 60, 64
Total 190, 194–5, 197
Tracker 86
Transnet 137
Transport Holdings 140
Truckafrica Group 140
True Love magazine 68
Tullow Oil 195
Tunisia 7, 22, 32, 36–7
Turkey 43
Tusker 78
Tutu, Desmond 82

UBA Group 213
Uganda 3, 47, 114, 121, 134, 154, 157, 163–4, 167–8, 179, 181, 183, 192, 196, 214, 226, 228
UN Global Compact 100
Unilever 5
United Against Malaria 178–9
United Arab Emirates 43
United Bank For Africa (UBA) 60, 63, 212–3
United Kingdom 28, 53
United Nations (UN) 71, 100–1
United Nations Development Programme (UNDP) 98
United States (US) xv, 1, 12, 18, 23, 35, 37, 43, 45, 49–50, 53–54, 65–6, 78, 81–3, 87, 91, 98, 100, 104, 108, 110, 117, 122–3, 130, 143, 156, 170, 173, 178, 204, 221, 228–9, 236
United States Embassy 124
University of Denver 23

Vale 41, 45–6, 50, 98, 136, 144
Van Wamelen, Arend 38
Vela, Robin 191–7
Venezuela 192
Victoria Falls 238
Victoria Falls Hotel 238
Vlisco 86
Vodafone 35
Walka 167–8
Wall Street 211

Walmart 207, 224, 228, 230
Walvis Bay 145, 147
Warri 157
Washington DC 28
Webber Wentzel 49, 220–1, 226
West Africa 63, 91, 98, 121, 127, 131, 140, 150, 165, 179, 191, 198, 201, 209–10, 214, 218, 232, 238, 241
West/Western 2, 11, 36, 41, 43–5, 49, 62–3, 87, 138, 143, 153, 236
Western Cape province 154
Western Europe 232
White, Lyal (Dr) 40–1
'Why Africa is leaving Europe behind' 53
Why Africa is Poor: And What Africans Can Do About It 52
Wilderness Adventures 234
Wilderness Air 234
Wilderness Collection, The 234
Wilderness Explorations 234
Wilderness Holdings Limited 234–5, 237–9, 242
Wilderness Safaris 234, 237
Windhoek 238
Woolworths 157
World Bank 6, 22, 24–5, 28, 42, 91, 119, 123
World Cup 81, 168, 178
World Economic Forum 70
World Economic Outlook 36
World Gold Council 100
World Health Organisation 9

WP Transport 140

Y-AGE 74
Yatela 99
Yemen 181
Yoruba 168
Young Power Women in Africa 68
YouTube 169
Yum Brands 207
Yunus, Muhammad 72

Zain 47
Zambezi River 144, 156
Zambia 3, 36, 46–7, 59, 136–7, 142, 144–7, 150, 152, 154, 163–4, 167–8, 173, 183, 196, 200–1, 214, 226, 231, 234, 238
Zarafa 238
Zeino-Mahmalat, Till 38
Zimbabwe ix, xx, 1, 55, 58, 111, 142, 146–147, 156–157, 164, 171, 173–176, 192–193, 198–199, 201–202, 205, 229, 234, 237–238, 240, 242
Zimbabwe Stock Exchange (ZSE) 198, 201,
Zimbabwean 171, 173–4, 193, 198
Zimbulk Tankers 140